Culturally and Linguistically Responsive Education

Culturally and Linguistically Responsive Education

DESIGNING NETWORKS THAT TRANSFORM SCHOOLS

EDITED BY

MARTIN SCANLAN
CRISTINA HUNTER
ELIZABETH R. HOWARD

HARVARD EDUCATION PRESS
Cambridge, Massachusetts

Paperback ISBN 978-1-68253-399-4
Library Edition ISBN ISBN 978-1-68253-400-7

Library of Congress Cataloging-in-Publication Data is on file.

Published by Harvard Education Press,
an imprint of the Harvard Education Publishing Group

Harvard Education Press
8 Story Street
Cambridge, MA 02138

Cover Design: Endpaper Studio
Cover Image: Saint John Paul II Catholic Academy mural by the students of Saint John Paul II Catholic Academy, Lower Mills Campus, Dorchester, Massachusetts. Photo by Christopher Soldt.

The typefaces used in this book are Anko, Roboto, and Ziggurat.

CONTENTS

PART THREE

IMPLICATIONS

PREFACE

SCHOOLS THROUGHOUT the United States are becoming more diverse across multiple dimensions. Shifts in immigration patterns—from a century ago, when the vast majority of immigrants were European, to now, when half are from Latin America and three in ten are from Asia—have led to increased variation in race, ethnicity, culture, and language.[1] This trend is likely to continue, as the immigrant population in the United States is expected to rise from 36 million people in 2005 to 81 million in 2050.[2] Thus, students who speak languages other than English or in addition to English at home are the new mainstream in US schools.[3]

Sometimes leaders of schools with a growing population of students from diverse backgrounds are portrayed as facing daunting challenges, needing to help their communities overcome divisive hurdles that inevitably accompany demographic shifts. This book is written from a different perspective, whereby educating this new mainstream presents tremendous opportunities. Visionary leaders at all levels—from department chairs to building principals to district superintendents to regional and state policy makers—are embracing the new mainstream by *transforming* their classrooms, schools, and school systems to be culturally and linguistically responsive. At the classroom level, innovative teachers are developing the knowledge, skills, and dispositions to adapt their teaching and learning to simultaneously advance both content knowledge and language development. At the school level, imaginative principals are creating service delivery models that foster multilingualism and authentic cross-cultural appreciation in manners unimaginable in monocultural, monolingual environments. At the district level, creative leaders are replacing structures focused solely on building English language and literacy with ones that value and promote the use of home languages and possibly even foster bilingualism and biliteracy for all. At the state level, bold policy makers are advancing structures that affirm multilingualism by supporting two-way immersion schools and the Seal of Biliteracy.[4]

Culturally and Linguistically Responsive Education was written to help educational leaders, including school principals, teacher-leaders, and others, to better educate the new mainstream. Specifically, it illustrates how to harness the synergy of collaborative learning—within and across schools—to dramatically advance educators' knowledge, skills, and dispositions toward culturally and linguistically responsive schooling. It does this by presenting the story of how a unique group of two dozen preK–8 schools from across the United States, the Two-Way Immersion Network of Catholic Schools (TWIN-CS), have worked together since 2012 to radically change how they educate students from diverse cultural and linguistic communities.

These elementary schools began as monolingual English environments, providing strikingly few support services for students who spoke languages other than or in addition to English at home. Simply put, they were in most ways culturally and linguistically *non-responsive*. School leaders were painfully aware that their schools needed to make significant changes in order to more equitably provide quality education for all students—particularly those from families whose mother tongues were not English. By forging a unique alliance comprising colleagues in similar school settings around the country, local experts to serve as mentors, and a coordinating team of faculty, staff, and students from Boston College, these schools transformed in dramatic fashion. Through the adoption of a two-way immersion (TWI) model, this partnership assisted the schools in fostering bilingualism and biliteracy for *all* students, while increasing achievement levels as well as enrollment.

Although these are Catholic schools, they all faced changes similar to those many public and charter schools face in the current era of shifting demographics, falling enrollments, budget constraints, and high-stakes accountability pressures to increase achievement for all students. And although they chose a specific service delivery model (TWI), there are other pathways for schools to become more culturally and linguistically responsive.[5] Thus, we argue in this book that leaders across contexts—from traditional public to charter to private, from secular to religious, from elementary to secondary—can design networks to transform their schools. This volume seeks to capture lessons from this group of schools, illustrating how cultivating communities of practice through a networking approach both within and among schools can empower educators to create culturally and linguistically responsive schools.

DO I REALLY NEED ANOTHER BOOK?!

As professional educators, you are subjected to what can seem like a cacophony of voices competing for attention, trying to persuade you to rethink your practices. From webinars and blog posts to journal articles to books, a wide and ever-growing array of resources are available to guide your work. Some describe the importance of culturally and linguistically responsive schooling more broadly, or describe specific models of such schools.[6] *Culturally and Linguistically Responsive Education* is distinct in that it draws from the experience of various schools in the process of transforming to become more culturally and linguistically responsive. Additionally, these schools were all part of the same network that advanced this process using strategic and scaffolded networking within and across schools, as well as with families and community members, to facilitate learning. This volume focuses on this process and unpacks specific practices that the educators have engaged in, highlighting both what is working and what is problematic. Hence, if you are an educational leader, eager to embrace cultural and linguistic diversity as an asset and to foster innovative collaboration within and across schools to advance culturally and linguistically responsive practices, read on! This is a key resource for you.

Culturally and Linguistically Responsive Education is organized into three sections. In part I, chapter 1 lays the foundation for the book, defining what we mean by culturally and linguistically responsive schooling and providing the context of the story of transformation reported here. Chapter 2 presents the theory of action, the origins, and the design of TWIN-CS. Part II comprises six chapters that dig into the details of the change process. Each of these chapters presents a practice of schools engaged in this network and is authored by university faculty and/or other bilingual experts who served as mentors and worked directly with these schools as part of the network design. These chapters describe how the schools transformed to be culturally and linguistically responsive, how networking advanced the organizational learning in this practice, and how educational leaders can apply this practice within other models and contexts of culturally and linguistically responsive schooling.

Part III comprises two final chapters. In chapter 9 we step back to look at the big picture, showing how organizational learning within and across schools in this network has emerged over time and benefitted the schools, emphasizing how this learning was recursive and overlapping across the structures and practices. In chapter 10, we draw conclusions and describe implications for educational leaders in schools and school systems.

Thus, the purpose of *Culturally and Linguistically Responsive Education* is to help educational leaders—from teacher-leaders to building principals to district superintendents to state-level policy makers—learn to leverage networking to foster organizational learning that advances culturally and linguistically responsive schooling. This volume is intended to provide lessons for educational leaders striving to improve service delivery models to educate students from diverse linguistic backgrounds. More broadly, it provides lessons that can help educational leaders strategize and leverage networking to advance organizational learning to address other pressing educational priorities as well.

PART ONE

CONTEXT

Embracing the New Mainstream Through Culturally and Linguistically Responsive Schooling

MARTIN SCANLAN, CRISTINA HUNTER, AND ELIZABETH R. HOWARD

INCREASING CULTURAL and linguistic diversity is affecting schools across all sectors and geographical settings. You are likely witnessing a growth in this diversity in your setting, whether you work in a traditional public school enrolling students from the immediate neighborhood or a charter school drawing students from across town, whether you are in a religious school or a secular school, whether you work in early childhood education or with adolescents on the cusp of independence, and whether your school is in a highly populated urban neighborhood or a small rural town. More students are navigating two (or more) languages within and across their homes, schools, and communities. As a result of this shift, schools are called upon to ensure that their teachers have the professional knowledge, skills, and dispositions to effectively teach students whose primary home language is not English.[1] At the minimum this entails reforming curriculum and pedagogy; however, ideally it further involves adapting a comprehensive service delivery model so that it is *culturally and linguistically responsive*.[2]

Culturally and linguistically responsive schools do three things: first, they promote all students' sociocultural competence;[3] second, they respect and cultivate proficiency in home and community languages in addition to English;[4] and third, they provide strong curriculum and instruction to promote high-level academic achievement. Culturally and linguistically responsive schools can take a variety of approaches to pursuing these goals. Across the United States, schools employ a range of service delivery models to support students designated as English Learners (ELs)[5]—and some are more culturally and linguistically responsive than others. One way to categorize these models is into three types: *dual language education*, or programs where the goal is bilingualism and biliteracy in English and a partner language; *transitional bilingual education*, whereby language-minoritized students' home language is used as a foundation to English; and *English-only instruction*, where the focus is on English-language development with no use of students' home languages (see table 1.1).[6]

Across these three types, all models seek to further students' academic achievement and develop English proficiency. However, they differ in their placement of language-minoritized students, their language goals, and the integration of students' home language in the process of teaching English and academic content.[7] While transitional bilingual and English-only models seek to develop students' English as quickly as possible, dual language education strives to develop bilingualism and biliteracy—both in English and in students' home languages. Another difference across models is their emphasis on sociocultural competence. Beyond developing an understanding of what culture consists of and how cultures vary, sociocultural competence involves developing an understanding of yourself and others, thus developing a strong sense of self and identity. It means that the teaching and learning environment must "include multiple opportunities for students to develop positive attitudes about themselves and others, and to develop cultural knowledge and a sense of their and others' identities—ethnic, linguistic, and cultural— in a non-stereotyped fashion."[8] Developing sociocultural competence helps

TABLE 1.1

Spectrum of service delivery models to educate students designated as ELs

	DUAL LANGUAGE EDUCATION		TRANSITIONAL BILINGUAL		ENGLISH ONLY
	A	B	C	D	E
Model	developmental (or maintenance) bilingual education	two-way immersion	transitional bilingual education	English as a second language	structured English immersion
Language of instruction	bilingual	bilingual	bilingual	English	English
Language goal	proficiency in two languages	proficiency in two languages	proficiency in English	proficiency in English	proficiency in English
Language-minoritized student placement	separated (usually whole-day)	integrated	separated (part-time or whole-day)	separated (usually part-time)	integrated

Source: Adapted from Martin Scanlan and Francesca López, *Leadership for Culturally and Linguistically Responsive Schools* (New York: Routledge/Taylor and Francis Group, 2014), figure 4.1; Julie Sugarman, *Beyond Teaching English: Supporting High School Completion by Immigrant and Refugee Students* (Washington, DC: Migration Policy Institute, 2017).

ensure that students develop a strong sense of self and an understanding of how to navigate situations with others who are different.[9] Sociocultural competence is an explicit component of dual language education models but less directly emphasized in transitional bilingual and English-only.

In this book, the model of culturally and linguistically responsive schools that the educational leaders build is one example of a dual language education model: two-way immersion (TWI), also commonly referred to as dual immersion. The strategic and scaffolded networking we describe can work across other models as well, however. As educational leaders at the school and district level analyze their current approaches and discern which service delivery model is best for their contexts, they can ground their approach by seeking to implement one that promotes culturally and linguistically responsive schools.

AN ILLUSTRATION OF SCHOOL SYSTEM TRANSFORMATION

As an illustration of how a school system transforms to become culturally and linguistically responsive, consider what has happened in the Madison Metropolitan School District during the first two decades of the twenty-first century.[10] In 2000, this public school district in Wisconsin was taking a pedestrian approach to meeting the needs of students who had limited proficiency in English. Its schools were implementing a type of English-only model. The theory was that this model would support students designated as ELs by initially clustering them into separate classrooms in which they would receive additional English-language supports, and then over time transition them back into general-education classrooms. However, as this approach was implemented, the schools realized it was not working well. Students were not developing adequate English skills to effectively keep up with their native English-speaking peers. On top of this, these students were not receiving access to the same curriculum and instruction in other subject areas, leading to gaps in learning outcomes, engagement, and high school achievement. With few signs of significant improvement, dissatisfaction with the service delivery model spread, and school leaders realized a change was needed.

This dissatisfaction resulted in the launching of the Nuestro Mundo Community School,[11] a TWI public charter school. TWI blends equal numbers of students who are native in English and who are native in a second, target language. The goal of TWI schools is to achieve bilingualism and biliteracy for all students in that target language (which at Nuestro would be Spanish). Nuestro Mundo Community School was developed by an organizing committee of diverse stakeholders, including public school teachers, parents, and community members. Frustrated with stagnant outcomes for students designated as ELs, the majority of whom were Latinx, the committee began negotiating with the Madison Metropolitan School District to explore alternative approaches to educating students whose home language was not English. The organizing committee argued that the model the district was using was not effective—especially for the growing population of Latinx students. These students, isolated from peers, had little academic success. They were both losing their mother tongue and also not making great gains

6

in English. The committee argued that the TWI model provided an attractive alternative approach and moreover would prove attractive to many native English-speaking families eager to foster bilingualism and biliteracy for their children. It pointed to the strong empirical base which demonstrated that TWI schools, when designed well and implemented with fidelity, help all students develop bilingualism, biliteracy, and sociocultural competence, as well as attain strong academic outcomes.[12]

Although the district administration strongly resisted the proposal to start Nuestro Mundo Community School as a pilot TWI school, the organizing committee convinced the school board to allow it to move ahead. What has resulted is phenomenal on two counts. First, Nuestro Mundo Community School itself has become an established school with enrollment that has increased in both numbers and diversity with some evidence of academic success. Initially starting with 49 kindergarten students in 2004, Nuestro Mundo Community School has grown to over 300 students in grades K–5 in the 2017–18 school year. Over 60 percent of the students are Latinx (compared with the district average of 20 percent), and over half the students in Nuestro Mundo Community School qualify for free or reduced-price lunch (compared with the district average of 42 percent). Importantly, students have steadily improved academic performance on state standardized tests in recent years. More specifically, three-quarters of fourth graders scored proficient or advanced in English math and reading at the fourth-grade level.[13]

Second, in addition to establishing some solid roots as an independent school, Nuestro Mundo Community School has served as an incubator for change throughout the school district. Madison Metropolitan School District now provides dual language education throughout the district, offering both developmental bilingual education and TWI, which are dual language models that differ only with regard to the population that they serve (developmental programs serve only students designated as ELs, while TWI programs combine students designated as ELs and native English speakers). The district has also taken a position of embracing languages, as evidenced in their renaming the office serving students designated as ELs "Multilingual and Global Education."

On its own, this vignette about Madison Metropolitan School District can serve as an interesting and inspiring anecdote, suggesting that a district *can* move from a model of service delivery that treats linguistic diversity as a deficit—something to "transition from"—to one that treats it as the asset that it is. However, an anecdote like this does not provide school leaders with a guide for how to initiate and sustain such change, and questions remain. How do school principals spread culturally and linguistically responsive practices throughout their building? How do district leaders catalyze the positive results from one pioneering school into system-wide change? The chapters that follow respond to these questions by providing a detailed look at how a network of schools, formed with the explicit purpose of becoming more culturally and linguistically responsive, was structured and operated to meet this goal.

A WORD ABOUT CONTEXT

We recognize that this story of transformation emerges from a special niche. The Two-Way Immersion Network of Catholic Schools (TWIN-CS) comprises two dozen Catholic elementary schools located across the United States. These schools are all creating culturally and linguistically responsive schooling by working to shift their historically monolingual English programs to TWI programs. They are all pursuing this as private, faith-based institutions. As we show throughout this book, however, schools across sectors and contexts can learn from what is happening in TWIN-CS schools, particularly how they are using networking within and across their schools to dramatically advance culturally and linguistically responsive schooling.

To learn from TWIN-CS, it is essential to consider the multiple stories that compose schools. In her renowned TED Talk "The Danger of a Single Story," Chimamanda Ngozi Adichie describes how inherently complex human beings are, with each of our individual lives comprising a vast library of narratives.[14] Just as we should not reduce people to individual stories, nor should we do so for schools. Catholic schools tell many stories. As faith-based institutions, they tell stories of conversion, religious belief, and ritual. As small, independent schools, they tell stories of site-based management and independence. As private, tuition-driven institutions, they tell stories of inclusion and exclusion. In this book we focus on a different story, as a subset of these schools' journey from monolingualism to bilingualism and multiculturalism.

To hear this story, it is important to remember that these schools share a preponderance of features with neighborhood, magnet, and charter schools serving diverse populations of students. A majority of students attending TWIN-CS schools live in poverty, and the schools themselves are often underresourced, thus creating very real challenges in attaining appropriate materials for curriculum, instruction, and assessment. Likewise, many of these schools struggle to recruit, train, and retain qualified teachers, particularly those who are bilingual and biliterate. Finally, TWIN-CS schools work in an ongoing way to overcome societal barriers such as xenophobia and discrimination. In short, we argue throughout this volume that educational leaders across school sectors—religious to secular, private to public—experience challenges similar to those of TWIN-CS school leaders and can therefore learn from these schools' experiences.

THE IMPORTANCE OF TERMINOLOGY

Nationally, migration patterns have resulted in increased diversity across multiple dimensions, including home language, national origin, and immigration status. Correspondingly, students have multilayered identities, for which there are various terms that highlight different features. Leadership for culturally and linguistically responsive schools demands using terms thoughtfully and in critically reflective manners.

One key dimension to consider is students' linguistic identity.[15] Schools frequently refer to students whose mother tongues are not English as English Learners, or ELs. This term has affordances and constraints. One affordance is that it unambiguously expresses these students' formal designation, which under federal, state, and district policy allows them to access certain resources to assist them in developing their English-language skills. Hence, this label calls attention to the important duties that schools have in creating opportunities to learn for these students. A constraint of this term is that since it foregrounds the English learning, it obscures the valuable asset that these students bring: their mother tongue. While not as offensive as some terms (such as "limited English proficient"), the label is nevertheless problematic. To avoid this deficit implication, some use *emergent bilingual* as a more asset-oriented term. In many ways this term is more productive, and we

9

encourage school leaders to consider using it if appropriate in their contexts. However, since this book tells the story of a network of TWI programs, all of which are promoting the bilingualism and biliteracy of all students, the use of the term emergent bilingual is itself confusing. All students in TWI settings are emergent bilinguals, and the term does not enable us to distinguish students based on home language profiles or policy classifications. Hence, when discussing student populations in TWI settings, we refer to *students designated as ELs* for students who have been given that classification, and we use the more general term *bilingual learners* to describe any student in a given program.

Other dimensions of identity include culture, ethnicity, and national origin. For instance, many students designated as ELs in the United States have roots in Central or South America. Some may identify as Latino, others as Latino/a, others as Latin@ or Latinx. People may choose to identify with a country of origin, such as Mexican-American or Chicano.[16] In this book we choose to use the term *Latinx*. Again, we recognize this term's affordances (while the term Latino/a is more balanced in referencing males and females, it still reflects a gender binary, which the label Latinx overcomes) and constraints (such as its incongruence with the conventions of Spanish, a gendered language).

In our attempts to illustrate critical reflection in our use of terminology, we also use the term *linguistically minoritized* to call attention to the way that many students designated as ELs and native bilinguals are subjected to inequitable power relationships by forces of hegemonic Whiteness.[17] Many students can be considered "minoritized," which Khalifa, Gooden, and Davis describe as "racially oppressed communities that have been marginalized—both legally and discursively—because of their non-dominant race, ethnicity, religion, language, or citizenship."[18] Of course, students have many other layers of identity beyond these—such as gender identity, immigration status, and religious beliefs, just to name a few. This discussion of multiple dimensions of identity frames the rationale for culturally and linguistically responsive schools and informs the following chapters that describe the work of the TWIN-CS Network.

A Theory of Action

MARTIN SCANLAN, KRISTIN BARSTOW MELLEY,
CRISTINA HUNTER, AND ELIZABETH R. HOWARD

A THEORY OF ACTION is a mental map illustrating our understandings about how the world works and how to enact change.[1] It acts like a Global Positioning System—a map and compass combined—to guide one's practical, daily decisions. Theories of action are often articulated as statements spelling out what to do and why. Our theory of action is that strategic and scaffolded networking that is grounded in an asset-based orientation advances culturally and linguistically responsive schooling. At its core, *networking* is the building of professional relationships. We focus on networking that connects educators to one another, both inside their schools and with colleagues in other schools, as well as that which connects them to families and community members. By *strategic* networking, we mean fostering relationships that will advance the organizational learning of the schools. By *scaffolded* networking, we mean differentiating these relationships based on the particular needs of educators in various contexts. By *asset-based orientation,* we mean viewing the knowledge and experience of students, families, and communities as strengths. Thus, this theory of action emphasizes that all networking is not equally valuable, and that only networks with these essential characteristics are likely to advance culturally and linguistically responsive schooling.

In this chapter, we first describe two bodies of literature that undergird this theory of action: culturally and linguistically responsive schooling and organizational learning. We then explain how the design of the Two-Way Immersion Network for Catholic Schools (TWIN-CS) reflects this theory of action.

CULTURALLY AND LINGUISTICALLY RESPONSIVE SCHOOLING

One key strand of literature undergirding our theory of action describes leadership for culturally and linguistically responsive schooling. As discussed in chapter 1, while culturally and linguistically responsive schools take on many forms, all share three dimensions: building students' sociocultural competence; respecting and cultivating proficiency in home and community languages in addition to English; and promoting all students' academic achievement. These three components are well supported by a wide range of scholars.[2] They mirror what Brisk has identified as "three essential goals" that schools must have for emergent bilinguals: ensuring that they experience sociocultural integration[3] with both their school community and the broader society, building their "language proficiency to academic grade level," and providing them access to the same curriculum and instruction that all students receive.[4]

Two-way immersion (TWI) is one approach to culturally and linguistically responsive schooling. Bringing together students with home language profiles ranging from English monolingualism to varying levels of bilingualism in English and another language, TWI programs cultivate bilingualism and biliteracy, strong academic outcomes, and sociocultural competence.[5]

The components of culturally responsive and linguistically responsive teaching intersect. Culturally responsive teaching is demonstrated by exhibiting critical consciousness, asset orientations toward diversity, and support of students' construction of knowledge with respect for their lived experiences. It reflects what is sometimes called asset-based pedagogy, exhibited by teachers (a) being critically aware of the social and cultural dimensions that contribute to student marginalization, (b) demonstrating knowledge of students' cultural identities, and (c) validating and integrating these identities into their curriculum and instruction.[6] Culturally responsive school leadership is characterized by critical self-awareness, directly confronting barriers of racism at both individual and institutional levels, ensuring that teachers and school environments are culturally responsive and inclusive, and engaging students and parents in authentic partnerships.[7] Recent scholarship is pushing culturally responsive school leadership to also be *culturally sustaining*. This emphasizes the need to continually evolve to embrace an ever-expansive understanding of literacies and cultural identities, and to work to affirm, sustain, and develop those attributes in all students, particularly those from linguistically and culturally minoritized communities.[8]

Linguistically responsive teaching reflects an awareness of sociolinguistics, seeing the interconnection and interdependence of language and culture as well as an asset orientation toward linguistic diversity.[9] It reflects an awareness of the intersections of race and class with societal choices about which languages and which varieties of a language are valued and which are not. Students designated as English Learners (ELs) are linguistically minoritized students whose needs have traditionally not been met by US schools.[10] In terms of a repertoire of knowledge and skills, linguistically responsive teaching involves developing an appreciation of the particular strengths and experiences of all students, and scaffolding the teaching and learning environment for students who are becoming bilingual. Such scaffolding includes analyzing the language demands embedded in classroom tasks and expectations, fostering frequent and meaningful opportunities for these students to interact with students who are fluent in English, and affirming home languages by incorporating practices and approaches such as translanguaging. Translanguaging is a pedagogical approach that values the languages and language varieties spoken by students and community members, and promotes their use in addition to academic English for carrying out academic tasks.[11]

An abundance of literature provides recommendations for classroom teachers about implementing culturally and linguistically responsive practices in their classrooms.[12] This literature focuses on honoring the knowledge and skills students bring to the classroom and building on these, through practical pedagogical strategies that scaffold students' learning as they develop their content knowledge. This means teachers "are responsive to the diversity of their students."[13] Fundamentally, culturally and linguistically responsive teaching practices have a positive effect on student learning outcomes.[14]

There is growing evidence that language-minoritized students in well-executed dual language education models—such as TWI—have stronger educational outcomes than their counterparts in other models.[15] Importantly, culturally and linguistically responsive schooling can not only serve to expand individual opportunities to learn and strengthen school-community relationships,[16] but also promote more equitable learning environments for students who have traditionally been marginalized.[17] This focus on equity is central to the history of bilingual education in the United States, as it gained traction in conjunction with the civil rights movement as a means of pursuing educational equity for Spanish-speaking Latinx students.[18]

However, language-minoritized students continue to be marginalized, even with efforts that might appear to affirm cultural and linguistic diversity. For instance, efforts to formally acknowledge and reward individual students' advanced proficiency in bilingualism and biliteracy, such as a Seal of Biliteracy, are at times critiqued as being enacted primarily to benefit White, native English-speaking students, not students of color coming from homes of linguistically minoritized students. Even whole-school models that cultivate bilingualism and biliteracy, like TWI, are not silver bullets. They have been critiqued as promoting elite bilingualism and not meeting the needs of students of color. While additive bilingual education approaches are often conceptualized and promoted as models to serve language-minoritized students, if not enacted with care these approaches can still fall short of their ostensible goals of remediating educational inequities.[19]

ORGANIZATIONAL LEARNING, NETWORKS, AND COMMUNITIES OF PRACTICE

Alongside literature on culturally and linguistically responsive schooling, the literature on organizational learning undergirds our theory of action. Organizational learning, a strand within the broader body of scholarship on organizational theory,[20] examines how schools "incorporate external and internal information . . . for short- and long-term decisions about organizational and classroom improvement."[21] From a sociocultural perspective, organizational learning is a collective endeavor, not an individual one.[22]

Organizational learning in schools often occurs via educators experimenting and adapting innovations to their current contexts.[23] This requires a requisite level of teacher autonomy and empowerment. Marks and Louis describe organizational learning and empowerment as rooted in relationships: "School staff provide each other with support, exchange ideas and reach consensus, and treat each other in professional and egalitarian ways."[24] This literature emphasizes the importance of establishing cultures that empower teachers to shape and reform their teaching and learning environment, fostering relational trust among educators and promoting boundary spanning and assistance relationships.[25]

The nature of relational networks within a school affects these practices. The isolation of classroom teachers can be a barrier to productive collaboration, experimentation, and innovation.[26] Conversely, teaching and learning practices are strengthened when educators collectively question routines, jointly pursue creative ways of teaching and learning, and support each other's professional growth.[27] Social networks are important in generating trust among educators in schools.[28] Policies that support ongoing, substantive interactions among educators "provide opportunities for teachers to learn the social location of expertise, which can alter teachers' strategies for reaching out to others and the social networks that result."[29] Ainscow asserts that "strengthening collaboration within schools, between schools and beyond schools" fosters the flow of latent expertise in productive manners.[30] This sharing of expertise can build professional capital, which refers to the combination of knowledge and skills (human capital), relationships (social capital), and judgments (decisional capital) that ground educators' professionalism.[31]

The sociocultural learning theory of communities of practice provides a lens for understanding how networking advances organizational learning. Communities of practice are groups of individuals who engage with each other to learn new practices and processes. This theory holds that we learn through experiencing the world and engaging with it, and that learning that is personally transformative involves membership in communities of practice.[32] Trends in research on organizational learning apply this notion of communities of practice. One example of this is the formation of networked improvement communities (NICs).[33] NICs are narrowly tailored communities of practice that provide a structure for practitioners to systematically identify and confront problems of practice. NIC participants articulate a working theory of improvement: a series of tightly crafted hypotheses to drive their improvement efforts. This working theory of improvement addresses three questions: What specifically are we trying to accomplish? What change might we introduce and why? How will we know that a change is actually an improvement? Typically this working theory of improvement is developed and tested through cycles of disciplined inquiry. These are rapid, iterative processes of initiating small innovations, prototyping, failing, reporting, and adjusting based on the failures.

Other applications of communities of practice include research-practice partnerships and design-based research.[34] Both of these critique the limits of research that is conducted solely from a university or scholarship orientation, and point toward the value of engaging practitioners in conceptualizing and implementing research. When teachers and administrators influence the direction of researchers' inquiry, they are able to increase the likelihood that the studies address problems of practice that are pressing. These trends in research on organizational learning—from NICs to research-practice partnerships to design-based research—all explicitly build communities of practice among educators in preK–12 schools and colleagues from other contexts, such as universities. In sum, networking is a potentially valuable lever for fostering organizational learning within schools. Many waves of education reform that are currently guiding systemic approaches to innovation within and across schools—such as efforts to create networked improvement communities and research-practice partnerships—are grounded in the notion of fostering learning via communities of practice.

THE STORY OF TWIN-CS

This book bridges these bodies of literature on culturally and linguistically responsive schooling and organizational learning to show how strategic and scaffolded networking that is grounded in an asset-based orientation advances culturally and linguistically responsive schooling. We illustrate this through the story of TWIN-CS.

The story of TWIN-CS emerges in the context of the complicated history of Catholic schooling in the United States. Though as early as the seventeenth century Catholic schools existed in the nation, the history of these schools is generally traced from the late eighteenth century. From 1783, when the first parochial school was formed in Philadelphia, enrollment in US Catholic schools grew steadily for nearly two hundred years, peaking in the 1960s. These schools ranged in structure, including parochial schools connected to parishes and schools run by religious orders. From their inception up through the 1960s, the schools were religiously homogenous, rarely enrolling non-Catholics, especially at the elementary level. Across other dimensions, however, they were considerably diverse. These schools largely took all comers, charging little or no tuition. As a consequence, the schools included many immigrants and students living in poverty. Since the middle of the twentieth century Catholic elementary schools have in many ways grown more selective. For instance, facing increasing costs and declining subsidies from parishes or religious orders, most have become increasingly dependent on raising funds via tuition. Consequently, they have enrolled more and more students from wealthier homes and fewer students living in poverty. At the same time, they have become more diverse across multiple dimensions, including race, language, and, perhaps most surprisingly, religion.

Importantly, throughout this history US Catholic schools have been recognized as effective at raising achievement levels of students who have been traditionally marginalized.[35] In a predominantly Protestant nation, many European immigrants to the United States were ridiculed for their faith in Protestant-oriented "common schools."[36] Thus, particularly in many urban centers, Catholic schools provided a space in which home culture and language were welcome—in contrast to public schools.[37] Historically, ethnic Catholic schools offered what Sanders called an "enticing alternative" to assimilationist-oriented public schools.[38] In contrast to the public schools, in which the curriculum and instruction emphasized English monolingualism, Catholic schools were at times much more embracing of the culture and language of immigrant communities. Some Catholic schools provided bilingual education. For example, at the turn of the twentieth century in Chicago, immigrant populations that were numerous—such as the Polish, Lithuanian, and Czech and Slovakian—formed parish schools that conducted some classes in English and devoted the rest of the academic day (as well as many extracurricular activities after school) to the home languages of students. Non-English-speaking immigrants—such as Germans—were more eager for schools to get built before churches because they had a language to preserve.[39] Even when the Chicago Catholic school systems sought to unify its diverse schools with a standardized curriculum in 1917, provisions were granted for schools to teach catechism and reading in any language.[40] However, in recent decades Catholic schools have largely underserved English learners, particularly by providing minimal support to meet their linguistic, academic, and sociocultural needs.[41]

Three Key Aspects of Catholic Schooling: Mission, Governance, and Resourcing

Three aspects of this history of Catholic schooling are important for unpacking the story of TWIN-CS: mission, governance, and resourcing. First, a hallmark feature of Catholic schools is being rooted in and guided by a mission. Modeled on the person and teachings of Jesus Christ, all Catholic schools' missions share certain features: to educate students to be fully alive by learning who they are, how to live in communion with others, and how to serve the common good of society.[42] The National Standards and Benchmarks for Effective Catholic Schools (NSBECS) ground and guide a school's mission.[43] The NSBECS were created to articulate the qualities of an effective Catholic school. The NSBECS help schools actualize their mission by guiding schools through processes of ongoing improvement based on Catholic principles, such as inclusion, faith formation, academic excellence, and more.[44]

Catholic schools vary in how they articulate and fulfill their missions. For instance, some Catholic parish schools are rooted in the traditions of the parish community, which often have a rich ethnic and cultural history. Others have missions focused on the charisms of a specific religious order. Still other Catholic schools are affiliated with networks that have their own specific missions.[45] Thus, while always reflecting a broader philosophy of Catholic education, the character of each school's mission is lived out uniquely in the particular context of the community.

A second feature of Catholic schooling that is important for unpacking the story of TWIN-CS is governance. Governance is the process determining the expectations, systems, and management of an organization. The vast majority of Catholic elementary schools operate as semi-autonomous organizations, with decision-making authority vested at the local school level. Most commonly, these are parish schools, with the priest of the parish, referred to as the pastor, designated as the governing authority. While a parish council or school board may serve to advise the pastor, ultimate authority on key organizational decisions (e.g., hiring and firing, setting budget) resides with the pastor. Alternatively (and less commonly), some elementary schools are governed by boards of limited jurisdiction. These boards typically comprise a range of stakeholders who collectively serve as the governing authority. In addition, most Catholic schools—whether board-governed or parish-governed—coexist in a region known as a diocese or archdiocese. These are frequently loosely coupled, with largely decentralized policies and practices structuring teaching and learning.[46]

In practice, this local control of governance results in the school administrators—specifically principals—operating with considerable levels of autonomy. They need to negotiate with their pastor or board, but often can make decisions without consulting a centralized authority, such as a diocesan school office. While many educators may find this appealing, it can also have its drawbacks. The school's ability to grow and change is, in many ways, determined by the (limited) knowledge of its leaders. When schools operate autonomously, they often have less interaction with emerging scholarship and educational insights that challenge and improve schooling. Innovation becomes rare as the same teaching and learning goals are sought year after year. Importantly, new models of Catholic school governance are emerging that complicate this autonomy. For instance, some schools have formed networks based on shared approaches to curriculum and instruction and mission, both at the national level (such as Cristo Rey high schools) and regionally (such as Seton Catholic Schools in Milwaukee, Wisconsin). Such networks can facilitate collaboration across a range of areas, including professional development, curriculum design, and fundraising.[47]

A third feature of Catholic schooling that helps ground the story of TWIN-CS is resources. Most Catholic elementary schools tend to rely heavily on tuition as a primary source of funding, and this tuition has grown significantly higher over the last five decades.[48] The cause of this tuition increase is commonly understood as the result of changes in the teacher workforce—the cost of replacing nonsalaried religiously vowed women and men with salaried lay teachers.[49] While practices of tuition assistance and scholarship are widespread, in general Catholic elementary schools tend to serve fewer families of middle and low income than in the past.[50] There are exceptions to this, however—including both schools with strong philanthropic bases and schools that receive public funding—that are able to serve significant numbers of students living in poverty.[51] In addition to reducing the accessibility of Catholic schools to families with more limited income, the increased reliance on tuition has also resulted in modest salaries that are typically lower than public school teaching salaries. Educators with specialized skills—such as bilingualism—are in high demand across public and private school sectors, placing an additional challenge to Catholic schools seeking to attract them.

Of course, these three elements—mission, governance, and resources—are not unique to Catholic schools. Schools across sectors—from traditional public schools serving students in a particular geographic region, to charter schools serving students across a district, to private secular schools—must articulate mission, operate within a governance structure, and attain resources.

We highlight these elements here because of the important role they play in the evolution of TWIN-CS. While member schools of TWIN-CS share some features of mission, governance, and resources with other schools in this sector, the process of radical change has also reshaped each of these dimensions. The strategic and scaffolded networking with an asset-based orientation has allowed these schools as organizations to collaboratively learn to envision and enact missions to more effectively serve emergent bilinguals, thus addressing a key struggle of schools in this sector. It has also helped them reform structures of governance, distributing decision making in manners that allow schools to innovate. Finally, it has helped them attain new resources needed to grow into culturally and linguistically responsive institutions.

The Evolution of TWIN-CS

TWIN-CS is an initiative of the Roche Center for Catholic Education in the Lynch School of Education and Human Development at Boston College. The goal of the initiative is to sustain a robust network of schools committed to

20

expanding opportunities to learn for students designated as ELs, since these students have been overlooked, particularly in Catholic schools. The purpose of TWIN-CS is to contribute to remediating this injustice in this sector of schools.

TWIN-CS was conceptualized as a long-term partnership to scaffold member schools' evolution from English-only models to TWI bilingual models of service delivery.[52] A design team, consisting of faculty from multiple universities with staff and graduate students at Boston College, as well as other institutes of higher education, was established to lead the innovation. In fall 2012, the design team created an application process open to Catholic elementary schools across the United States. Schools applying to be member schools were asked to document critical factors driving their need for transformation. One of these factors was changes in student demographics. These data helped identify the schools experiencing dramatic growth in the number of EL students. This included both students currently enrolled and children living in the schools' neighborhood or attending the parish who were potential enrollees. Across schools, the vast majority of potential enrollees had students who spoke Spanish as their home language.

A second factor was the schools' commitment to improving the educational opportunities for students designated as ELs. Applicants recognized that they were not effectively serving these students academically, and that their schools' learning environments, including their curricular resources, did not reflect the cultural and linguistic diversity of the student body. Applicants were motivated by a desire to operate schools where home language was part of a student's educational identity. They wanted to renew the school's mission and legacy by providing an expansive, global education, grounded in their students' many gifts. The design team selected twelve initial member schools that demonstrated a clear vision for transformation, support across their community, and fiscal sustainability for the long road ahead.

During spring 2013, the design team began its work with the twelve member schools. Webinars were designed to introduce educators in these schools to one another, address common concerns, and review leading research on dual language models. These online meetings were useful, though limited. They provided support to schools; however, participants were not accustomed to this format of learning and collaborating. Many remained uncomfortably quiet, unwilling to take risks to engage in this nascent "community of practice." During this period, each member school formed implementation teams of selected individuals (faculty, administrators, and, on occasion, parents) to lead the transformation to TWI. With design team guidance and financial support, each implementation team hired a local professional with experience and expertise in bilingual schooling to serve as a mentor. The mentor, who was frequently a faculty member at a local university or an administrator in a local public school or district, joined the implementation team to provide expertise and coaching in TWI. The mentor also helped the implementation team gather data on student learning outcomes, particularly language assessments. With some initial donor support, Boston College financed the entire TWIN-CS initiative, including funding the mentors and staffing the design team.

To conceptualize TWIN-CS as a network, it is helpful to visualize the relationship of these different units (see figure 2.1). Mentors are embedded in implementation teams within member schools. The design team serves as the hub and connective cord. It provides technical support to implementation teams, assisting in areas of mission and identity (e.g., integrating the goals of bilingualism and biliteracy into the schools' missions), governance and leadership (e.g., distributing authority for decision-making regarding the TWI model across an implementation team), academic excellence (e.g., providing professional development on designing and implementing curriculum across two languages), and operational vitality (e.g., developing plans for communication, marketing, enrollment management, and development to better serve linguistically minoritized students).[53]

The inaugural summer academy in 2013 was a pivotal moment for TWIN-CS. Eighty educators from the implementation teams of the twelve member schools traveled to Boston for five full days of learning, sharing, planning, and retooling their TWI programs. Presenters included leading scholars in the field of bilingual education, teachers from the country's first Catholic bilingual school, and partner organizations. School implementation teams took stock of assets and gaps in their school resources, engaged in cultural competency training, rewrote their mission statements, and engaged in spiritual and prayerful activities. The academy provided a platform for implementation teams to develop new knowledge and strategies to navigate the

FIGURE 2.1

Key organizational units engaged in mutualism in TWIN-CS

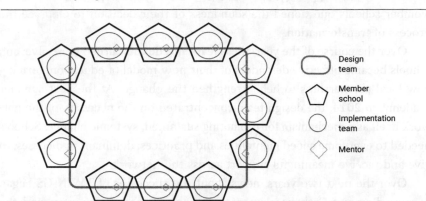

⬭	Design team
⬠	Member school
○	Implementation team
◇	Mentor

changes of the coming year. It also created new connections for participants, helping to form professional bonds beyond buildings and dioceses. By the close of the first summer academy, it became clear that this annual gathering would serve as the keystone event of the network.

Growing TWIN-CS

The relationships that began at the academy were strengthened through the year-round efforts of the design team. Fall 2013 began the first academic year for member schools participating in TWIN-CS. Of the twelve member schools, six were launching dual language programs, two were extending and strengthening programs that they had already started, and four were engaged in an additional planning year in order to buttress resources and structures before initiating the new instructional model. Member schools took careful, measured steps toward beginning (or continuing) their process of moving their schools from monolingual service delivery to TWI.

While progress during this first year was steady, it was not without setbacks. Some schools faced insurmountable challenges, resulting in their withdrawal from TWIN-CS, and in one case eventual closure. Despite their potential to become excellent TWI schools, some schools lacked the resources and time to overcome urgent fiscal matters. These setbacks affected TWIN-CS as a whole, triggering fear and doubt among some participants. Some member schools questioned the soundness of their decision to embrace the process of transformation.

Over the course of the year, these fears and doubts turned to resolve, and schools became effective defenders of their new model of education, forming new local partnerships to help strengthen the change. At the next summer academy, in 2014, the design team concentrated on the necessity of the network itself as a mechanism for promoting sustained, systemic change. Schools needed to overcome siloed mentalities and practices, dominant in dioceses, to give and receive meaningful support across the network.

Over the next two years, news about the successes of TWIN-CS began to spread among Catholic elementary schools across the country, and the network grew in many ways. Year after year, more schools became part of the network, and each school was expanding their TWI model to include more grade levels. Mentors, principals, and teachers were increasing their learning and problem-solving capacity by accessing the expertise of the expanding network.

By the fall of 2016, signs of positive change were abundant. Schools began to see their enrollments not only stabilize but in some cases increase dramatically. The cultures of the schools were palpably different. Mission statements were printed on school walls in two or more languages. School celebrations were becoming rich multicultural events. Volunteer parent leadership groups began to resemble the ethnic diversity of the school community. Some schools reported that students were acquiring both program languages more quickly than many teachers had anticipated. Parents driving carpools could not believe their ears as their young passengers chatted away in Spanish and English and Mandarin.

However, the process of transforming these TWIN-CS member schools also involved disruptions. For example, sudden changes in the administration made a number of schools even more vulnerable. In 2015, TWIN-CS consisted of seventeen schools. Of these, nine had already faced leadership changes since becoming dual language schools. Three of the nine eventually withdrew from TWIN-CS as the new leaders (pastors and principals) chose to return the school to monolingual instruction.

Entering the 2018–19 school year, TWIN-CS was in a period of maturation and stability, featuring twenty Catholic schools, eight of them among the original twelve. The knowledge and expertise in culturally responsive schooling formed within the original member schools has changed their status in the network from learner to leader. This is perhaps most visible in their increasing role of assisting new member schools. Further, these advancing member schools, requiring less support from the design team, have shifted away from the supportive center of TWIN-CS to make way for new member schools. Schools who have been members of TWIN-CS for three or more years have self-reported positive growth in many areas, including student performance on standardized tests, school enrollment, faculty professional development, fiscal vitality, and cultural inclusivity.[54] With this basic history of TWIN-CS in mind, we now turn to look more closely at how networking advances organizational learning for this geographically disparate group of schools striving to grow culturally and linguistically responsive.

A THEORY OF ACTION: NETWORKED LEARNING IN TWIN-CS

The three key structural dimensions of networking that advance organizational learning in TWIN-CS are reiterated in figure 2.2. Each member school has an implementation team (represented by a rectangle) consisting minimally of the principal and lead teachers who spearhead the TWI model. Each school also has a mentor (represented as a triangle) who serves the implementation team by providing coaching. Mentors are typically university faculty whose expertise is bilingualism and bilingual education. The design team (represented as an octagon) bridges mentors and implementation teams across all TWIN-CS member schools. The design team is composed of faculty, staff, and graduate students at Boston College who coordinate and direct the whole of TWIN-CS.[55]

The *practices* of the theory of action—the strategic and scaffolded networking—are captured in the arrows. Four main practices of professional development and technical assistance are in-person and/or virtual direct consultations, internet-based support (shared online resources including Google Docs and a website), bimonthly webinars (focused professional development

FIGURE 2.2

Networking within one TWIN-CS member school

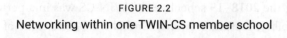
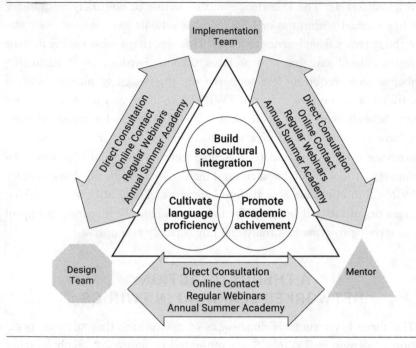

for particular subgroups, such as teachers, principals, or mentors), and the annual summer academy (a five-day working conference for teams from each member school). Finally, the *content* of the network, represented in the internal circles, always involves three important dimensions of culturally and linguistically responsive schools: sociocultural integration, language proficiency, and academic achievement. The circles show that these three dimensions are mutually reinforcing.

While figure 2.2 shows the actors, practices, and content within one school, figure 2.3 illustrates the networking across three member schools. For illustration purposes, only three TWIN-CS member schools are depicted here. This shows how the design team serves as a hub connecting member schools, and also how networking occurs among the schools directly, such as

FIGURE 2.3

Networking across TWIN-CS

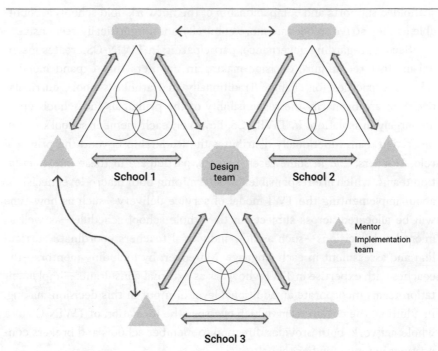

from mentor to mentor (triangles) or implementation team to implementation team (rectangles).

These structures are allowing the TWIN-CS member schools to collaboratively and innovatively advance culturally and linguistically responsive schooling via the three key features discussed earlier: mission, governance, and resources. First, regarding mission, participating in TWIN-CS provides member schools with a critical space to reflect, evaluate, and respond to discrepancies between the aspirations of their mission and the realities of their operation. Discerning mission effectiveness with other network members, educators gain new understandings of the purpose of Catholic education and identify new approaches to fulfill their school missions. Participating in the summer academies and in the webinars, implementation teams have engaged in processes of reconceptualizing and rewriting their mission statements to reflect an inclusive and holistic commitment to educate all students. The scaffolded supports and companionship of the network hold schools accountable as they strive to become more culturally and linguistically responsive.

Second, regarding governance, participating in TWIN-CS creates mechanisms that reconfigure decision-making in manners that expand member schools' capacities for change. Traditionally in Catholic schools, curricular decisions are primarily the responsibility of the principal, and schools operate largely in isolation. In TWIN-CS, however, each member school's implementation team functionally distributes the leadership beyond the principal role. Teachers, and in some cases, parents, participate in these implementation teams, which are responsible for determining both macro-level decisions about implementing the TWI model of service delivery—such as how time will be allocated across subjects in the whole-school schedule—as well as micro-level decisions—such as how individual teachers coordinate curriculum and assessment in each language. Moreover, by including mentors—the coaches with expertise in TWI who work as external consultants—implementation teams incorporate an additional level of input in this decision-making. In addition, the design team, which oversees the formation of TWIN-CS as a whole network, both provides direction to member schools and brokers connections among member schools.

Third, regarding resources, TWIN-CS supports member schools in identifying and accessing resources to successfully conduct their whole-school change. Importantly, as member schools initiated the process of replacing their monolingual English approach to curriculum and instruction with the TWI model, many discovered another form of isolation: identity. Nearly all are the only bilingual Catholic school in their diocese, and in most cases in the state. The networking structures of TWIN-CS have started to reduce this isolation. For instance, through a resource bank within a password-protected website, regular webinars, and direct consultation, structures have evolved in TWIN-CS to foster knowledge sharing and facilitate the exchange of resources among member schools. These resources range widely, from details about internal fiscal operations to classroom curricular materials. Implementation teams access information and resources from their mentor, implementation teams in other member schools, or the design team. Material resources, which were the first to be exchanged, are cataloged in an online "warehouse" and made accessible to all TWIN-CS educators. Over time, conceptual resources have become more abundantly shared, passed from school to school through conversation and storytelling. These highlight the schools' triumphs and failures to help others navigate avoidable mistakes and hard-fought battles. Educators gripped by uncertainty and confusion readily find those with experience and recommendations. These many forms of resources support all actors of radical change.

In conclusion, TWIN-CS provides a provocative example of strategic and scaffolded networking grounded in an asset-based orientation that is advancing culturally and linguistically responsive schooling. From this overview of the story of TWIN-CS, we now turn to part II, where mentors across TWIN-CS reflect on six different practices that were central to becoming more culturally and linguistically responsive.

PART TWO

PRACTICES

Engaging in Critical Conversations

COREY MASLOWSKI

MOVING FROM A SCHOOL CULTURE in which the home-languages cultures of language-minoritized students are treated as liabilities to one that treats them as assets is a major shift for all stakeholders, including teachers, students, and families. Rather than being imposed from external forces, this shift needs to be internally cocreated via engagement in deep and critical conversations. Here, *critical conversations* are those that help stakeholders understand and embrace the purpose and benefits of engaging in this productive, bold change.

I begin this chapter by defining critical conversations, describing their role in managing organizational change in the process of becoming a culturally responsive school. I then share how these critical conversations helped Two-Way Immersion Network for Catholic Schools (TWIN-CS) member schools evolve into culturally and linguistically responsive communities. I conclude by discussing how this practice extends to other contexts.

USING CRITICAL CONVERSATIONS
TO MANAGE CHANGE

Imagine the following scenario: An elementary school in a metropolitan area is changing its curricular model to meet the changing needs of its community. In the last decade, the racial demographics of the students in the school have shifted from an equal representation of Black and White students to a largely Latinx population, 60 percent of whom speak languages other than or in addition to English at home. Stakeholders from the school have decided to start a two-way immersion (TWI) program in kindergarten with the goal of extending it through eighth grade. Students will now be taught content in both Spanish and English using culturally responsive instructional materials that are reflective of the community and honor the school's represented cultures. The school's goals have now changed to making sure all of their 300 students become bilingual and biliterate, a goal that not all stakeholders value or appreciate because the previous programming was comfortable—and was "working" for them as teachers, and as parents. Advice from experienced consultants has been sought. Site visits to other successful programs have occurred. Board members have created a direction for a new and innovative program that will help students learn and families become a community. Excitement is palpable as the planning—which has been in process for over a year—is finally coming to fruition. The first day of school is a celebration: music is playing, balloons are flying, and the local media is there. Spirits are high. It is the start of the school year and anything seems possible.

As the school year progresses, the reality of day-to-day operations begins to temper this initial enthusiasm. Unforeseen and unexpected challenges occur when the new literacy curriculum is confusing to students, parents, and teachers. Some monolingual English staff members are frustrated by new timelines because their work needs to be translated to help all families stay informed. Additionally, tensions are developing across the teams of English and Spanish teachers. Some English teachers feel excluded and perceive that most of the support and attention is going toward the Spanish teachers, while some Spanish teachers feel frustrated by the relative lack of instructional materials and professional development opportunities for Spanish instruction, and the resulting need for them to translate so many materials and ideas to make them workable. A range of emotions—confusion, frustration, hope, fear, excitement, and exhaustion—are sensed everywhere. For some in the school community, the stress of change becomes overwhelming: two teachers resign in November; twenty students transfer to other schools in December; and some community members begin to question the validity of the new program before New Year's Day. Clearly, some critical conversations are needed to help the program flourish!

At the start of a transformative initiative, such as shifting to a culturally and linguistically responsive approach to education, it is incumbent upon leaders to predict and help manage conflict. Although we will likely be unable to forecast all of the reactions of our many staff members, we must equip ourselves with the necessary tools to navigate potential problems. The practice of engaging in critical conversations is a key leadership tool.

Defining Critical Conversations

Schools are amazingly complicated organizations, employing and serving many stakeholders. On any given day, the process of making decisions at a school can quickly become stressful and complicated, as those decisions often require the input of countless individuals with diverse perspectives. Balancing individual perspectives with the needs of the broader community contributes to organizational complexity. Bolman and Deal describe organizations as "populated by people whose behavior is notoriously hard to understand and predict. Interactions among diverse individuals and groups make organizations even more complicated."[1] Because of these complexities, as leaders guide big decisions they need to help people understand the larger picture. Often, however, we find ourselves enmeshed in thinking about difficulties and hurdles rather than focusing on the larger picture. This is when critical conversations are so important to managing change.

For the purpose of this chapter, I define critical conversations as purposeful dialogues that address conflicts associated with major organizational changes. Thus, I am distinguishing critical conversations from day-in, day-out conflict resolution. Multiple issues arise in the normal course of affairs in schools, and efforts to resolve them range widely, from helping children navigate a conflict on the playground, to urging a teacher to change an instructional practice, to responding to a parent upset about their child's schedule.

In contrast, critical conversations are structured dialogues that address broader issues that are controversial and difficult and are emerging from a larger organizational change.

Distinguishing Technical Problems from Adaptive Challenges

Effectively engaging in critical conversations first requires understanding the nature of the conflict itself. One way to understand conflicts is by distinguishing *technical problems* from *adaptive challenges* (see table 3.1). Both are important, and both emerge during organizational changes. However, technical problems tend to be more concrete and logistical, and their resolution is often relatively straightforward. Adaptive challenges, on the other hand, are typically more abstract, systemic, and embedded with cultural values. Thus, technical problems, though vexing, are much easier to address than adaptive challenges, which can be exceedingly complex to resolve. In the metropolitan school example, some technical problems that emerged were related to the confusion that arose around implementing the new curriculum and program model. The adaptive challenges, however, related to shifting beliefs about the value of providing instruction through two languages to ensure bilingualism and biliteracy for all. Compared with solving technical problems, addressing such adaptive challenges takes more time, requiring ongoing professional development and sustained effort.

Educational leaders must distinguish technical problems from adaptive challenges. Consider, for example, a teacher who notices that a group of his students are not finishing their homework. In response, he ensures that these students write down their assignments and that they place the homework in their backpacks. When that doesn't work, the following week the teacher decides to ask for a parent signature in the folder. The week after that, he is dismayed to find that many parents are not signing the homework notebook, and these students still are not coming with their homework. Next, he tries punitive measures in the hope of changing the outcome. But still, the problem persists. At this point, the teacher has adopted several strategies, with little time in between, to try to change behaviors. He has been treating this as a technical problem. Upon talking with a few students, he learns that what he perceived to be a mere technical problem is, in fact, an adaptive challenge. One of the students who is not completing the homework must

TABLE 3.1

Technical problems versus adaptive challenges

TECHNICAL PROBLEMS	ADAPTIVE CHALLENGES
Easy to identify	Difficult to identify
Often lend themselves to quick and easy solutions	Require changes in values, beliefs, roles, relationships, and approaches to work
Often can be solved by an authority or an expert	Must be solved by the people with the problem
Require change in just one or a few places, often contained within the organization	Require change in numerous places, usually across organizational boundaries
People are generally receptive to technical solutions	People often resist acknowledging adaptive challenges
Solutions can often be implemented quickly, even by edict	Solutions require experiments and new discoveries and can take a long time to implement

Source: Adapted from Ronald Heifetz and Donald L. Laurie, "The Work of Leadership," *Harvard Business Review* 75, no. 1 (1997): 124–134; and Ronald A. Heifetz and Marty Linsky, *Leadership on the Line: Staying Alive Through the Dangers of Leading* (Boston, MA: Harvard Business School Press, 2002). © 2009, Eric Svaren, Groupsmith, Inc.

babysit younger siblings until ten o'clock at night. Another one is currently homeless. A third student is bored with the homework because he mastered the content the first time it was introduced in class. As this anecdote illustrates, it can be tempting and seem logical to implement strategies to address technical problems without recognizing the larger adaptive challenges that are at play.

However, helping people manage change and navigate the tensions of adaptive and technical challenges is no small feat. Many school leaders may shy away from the task and treat adaptive challenges as technical ones, fearful of the amount of work required or the level of resistance expected in addressing adaptive challenges directly. Heifetz and Linsky describe how leading people through adaptive challenges requires navigating ambiguity and uncertainty: "[W]hen you lead people through difficult change, you challenge what people hold dear—their daily habits, tools, loyalties, and ways of thinking—with nothing more to offer perhaps than a possibility."[2] These possibilities are the bedrock of helping us accomplish something great, such as transforming a school to be culturally and linguistically responsive. As might be expected, in the midst of change it can be easy for stakeholders to revert to previous mental models for "how schools work."[3] In correctly distinguishing between technical and adaptive challenges, and choosing how to address them, critical conversations are a vital tool.

Understanding that managing change can present an adaptive challenge leads educational leaders to create space for critical conversations about change and conflict. This space promotes understanding multiple perspectives from stakeholders, and allows school leaders to coach staff members, families, and students to move together more effectively. Simultaneously, it allows them to recognize their own limitations (and the limitations of those around us) related to change.

To distinguish between technical problems and adaptive challenges, it is useful to understand what Heifetz and colleagues call the "productive zone of disequilibrium." This refers to the space where your level of discomfort rises enough to motivate trying something different, but has not grown to the level that it becomes overwhelming and paralyzing. Difficulties and conflicts raise our level of disequilibrium.[4] Technical problems tend to both surface and resolve themselves more quickly. They disrupt our equilibrium, but since we are able to adapt practices to address them, they subside relatively quickly. In contrast, adaptive challenges surface more slowly and take longer to address. It takes patience and persistence to work through adaptive challenges.

While a moderate level of disequilibrium is healthy in motivating change, when people move too quickly or are pushed too hard, they tend to avoid work or resist change. Heifetz and colleagues describe balancing the level of urgency to motivate people to engage in adaptive work: "If the level is too low, people will be inclined to complacently maintain their current way of working, but if it is too high, people are likely to be overwhelmed and may start to panic or engage in severe forms of work avoidance."[5] One form of work avoidance, scapegoating, can take the form of blaming families or not assuming positive intentions—which relates to prejudice and bias, to which we now turn.

Addressing Prejudices and Biases

As part of an adaptive challenge, engaging in critical conversations around culturally and linguistically responsive schooling involves addressing prejudices and biases. Prejudices and biases are ubiquitous, and when they remain unaddressed they present formidable barriers to moving through change in a productive manner. Critical conversations create space for surfacing and processing these. While prejudices and biases affect our responses across multiple dimensions of diversity, such as ethnicity, language prestige, exceptionalities, and belief systems, some of the most difficult responses are around race and racism.[6] Critical conversations are a key tool that allows educators to analyze their personal and systemic beliefs related to race and racism. In doing so, they help themselves and others understand their own biases and prejudices, as Singleton explains:

> Examining the impact of race in our own lives serves as a precursor to examining the impact of race in the larger context of school. As we become personally aware of our own racialized existence, we can more deeply understand the racial experiences of others. Without doing this, we will continue to assess the racial experiences of others through our own distorted lens.[7]

Fostering culturally and linguistically responsive schools entails bringing together students, parents, and educators from many different cultural and linguistic backgrounds in the community. While ideally these differences are embraced and celebrated, they also can surface prejudices and biases, including a deficit mind-set. Managing change in this context therefore requires directly addressing these difficult and often undiscussed issues, including racism, power imbalances, and privilege.

Without addressing prejudice and bias directly, a purportedly culturally and linguistically responsive school—such as a bilingual school—can paradoxically perpetuate the same social inequities as its monolingual precursor.[8] First, leaders need to be intentional in helping stakeholders examine the structures of power in the school. These include formal authority, as well as informal power. Who are the formal teacher-leaders? Who on staff are highly regarded by their colleagues? Who are the vocal parents within the parent-teacher organization? Who is on the advisory board? Do the demographics of these entities mirror the population of the students of the school? If not, why is this the case, and what modifications can we make as a school community to ensure that our school structures itself as truly responsive to the community? Importantly, leaders need to help others see racial, cultural, and linguistic differences through an asset-based orientation. This can be a big adaptive challenge requiring a dramatic shift in thinking. Without intentional outreach, planning, and work, the technical can overtake the adaptive, and similar, common patterns can perpetuate themselves, taking us away from being a culturally and linguistically responsive school.

In summary, managing large changes in schools is inherently complicated, and critical conversations can help stakeholders navigate this process, allowing people to articulate their beliefs. To help transition to more culturally and linguistically responsive schools, educational leaders need to foster opportunities for all educators in the community to engage in critical conversations about managing change. Key factors that influence the success of these critical conversations include recognizing the difference between technical problems and adaptive challenges, stakeholders' own reactions and tolerance toward the changes, and stakeholders' previous experiences, including cultural, linguistic, and racial differences, which may be different from their own. It is essential for stakeholders to reflect on these experiences before beginning to address the larger school community. I now turn to describe my experiences with critical conversations and how these have helped TWIN-CS member schools manage change to become culturally and linguistically responsive.

CRITICAL CONVERSATIONS IN TWIN-CS

The organizational change in TWIN-CS has been dramatic, moving from monolingual models of instruction to TWI models fostering bilingualism and biliteracy. Several structures within TWIN-CS have helped foster critical conversations to allow these schools both to distinguish technical problems from adaptive challenges and to address biases and prejudices in managing the change process. Each member school starts out at a different stage in this change process, but implementation teams are still able to learn collaboratively. There has not been a simple formula for how or when to engage in these critical conversations. Rather, member schools have engaged in them in a variety of manners, in order to be responsive to the diversity of their communities. In my experience, four important aspects of these critical conversations are mentorship, school climate, mission articulation, and mission implementation.

Mentorship

One key aspect of fostering critical conversations in TWIN-CS is the role of mentors as critical friends. To guide the planning and implementation of the move from a monolingual to the TWI model of schooling, TWIN-CS has encouraged and supported mentors to facilitate critical conversations both within schools and throughout the network. Having served as a TWIN-CS mentor while simultaneously working as a principal of a public Spanish-immersion school, I have been in a unique position to appreciate the reciprocal role of mentorship by having been on both the giving and the receiving end of shared learning.

In my professional role as an elementary school principal in a public Spanish-immersion school, as well as a receiver of guidance, I recognize the value of working with external consultants as "critical friends." When looking at systems and processes, we often do what we do because we know the history. We know what has "worked" and what has not, because we have created and modified our systems to help us at a particular moment in time. As months and years pass, stakeholders in the organization can become resistant to seeing new opportunities. As a principal, I have found that external consultants can shake this up, bringing outside knowledge, support, and perspectives. They offer differing narratives and examples of successes, sharing new perspectives as well as rationales for considering them. External consultants can ask probing questions with a level of autonomy, since they are not directly tied to results. In all of these ways, they help scaffold critical conversations for communities engaging in bold changes. For example, in the school where I serve as principal, we are currently working with consultants who have encouraged our professional development leadership team to think and speak as a community about our expectations related to the use of English and Spanish in the building. This came up after confusion arose around our new social-emotional curriculum. As we began implementing this, we were immersed in the process, failing to realize our own blind spots. In this case, this new curriculum was taught exclusively by English-speaking staff.

41

This had created unintended negative consequences at our school. The critical friend's perspective opened up a conversation that allowed us to see this problem and adjust. We now intentionally deliver this important curriculum in Spanish as well as English.

While as a public school principal I have been on the receiving end of such consultation, as a mentor within TWIN-CS I now also serve as the consultant, working with Risen Christ Catholic School (RCCS) in Minneapolis. RCCS was founded in 1993 when five local parish schools combined to create a new identity to continue to offer a high-quality Catholic education. Approximately 98 percent of the students qualify for free or reduced-price lunch, and 91 percent of students are designated as English Learners (ELs). Since the fall of 2014, RCCS has been transitioning from a monolingual English-speaking school to a 50/50 TWI program, where 50 percent of the students' instruction is in Spanish and 50 percent is in English.

As the mentor, an important part of my role is acting as a critical friend. This involves creating space to both anticipate and unpack problems and issues that arise. To strategically plan, I organized regular phone calls with RCCS principal Liz Ramsey to talk about current successes, struggles, and opportunities. Through regular communication, I was able to assist her in developing frameworks and navigating critical conversations regarding structures, schedules, beliefs, and curriculum. For example, when determining a new language arts curriculum, teachers held differing beliefs about which series would be better. While choosing resources seems technical, it can also be adaptive, as individuals are forced to self-reflect and express their individual beliefs and consider how those beliefs are influencing their perceptions of the curriculum. The team had been working toward resolution, but some additional questions that I posed as a mentor made the final decision easier.

While mentors across TWIN-CS engage in similar work, they do so in manners specific to their particular contexts, and coming from their particular experiences. For instance, my colleague Bridget Yaden has served as a mentor for Holy Rosary Bilingual Academy in Tacoma, Washington. She comes to this role from a different perspective than I do. While I am a principal in a public TWI school, she works as a university professor and is also a parent leader at the school. She shared the importance of having time and space to reflect with others to enact change. As a mentor, she has helped process change with the principal: "We regularly meet on Tuesdays and do 'walk and talks.' Having a regular time and space to talk has really helped us build our relationship." Collectively, the mentor and principal have been able to process the changes that have been occurring and plan accordingly with professional development. Within schools, we all have our own contexts, our own history, and we are at different places in our journey. Different perspectives allow us to think differently about our work, both technically and adaptively.

Though mentors approach their role as critical friends differently, the design team of TWIN-CS takes steps to provide some coherence across the entire network in how they do so. For instance, the assistant director for the TWIN-CS network, Mary Burns, hosts monthly conversations with mentors and principals to discuss current work. As a mentor, I have found these conversations helpful for focusing, supporting, and encouraging my work as a critical friend. I have benefited from dialogue with fellow TWIN-CS mentors who have helped provide guidance as we have encouraged each other and offered multiple perspectives for the work with each of our member schools.

School Climate

Another specific way critical conversations are important is in fostering a positive and cohesive school climate. Recognizing that colleagues bring multiple perspectives and hold their own "truths," educational leaders need to continually monitor and clarify expectations when changing systems within their schools. Internal communications, tied to mission, are essential to keep team members moving forward in a cohesive manner. Lacking this, community members may end up making up their own narratives. In my experiences in TWIN-CS—both in RCCS and communicating with fellow mentors in other schools—I have seen a range of concerns and questions surface as the member schools engaged in conversation about managing the change from monolingual to TWI schools. This process pushed some beyond their "productive zone of disequilibrium."

In my role as mentor, I used critical conversations to help articulate and normalize behaviors to foster positive school climate. During the beginning of the change process, some members of the RCCS community had anxiety about moving to the TWI model. This was a barrier to a positive and cohesive climate. I worked with a team of teachers and the principal to help them facilitate a process by which small groups of teachers shared their goals for the year and described the behaviors that would need to be institutionalized in order for them to realize those goals. Then, those behaviors were shared with a larger group, and they were categorized and restated. As a next step, representatives from those groups met to draft a set of adult norms for the building. Staff members gave input, and they collectively ratified those norms. Participants reported that this process helped alleviate concerns and build cohesion among the staff.

Another example of how critical conversations helped foster a cohesive and positive school climate in the midst of managing change occurred at the annual summer academy in 2018. There I worked with RCCS implementation team members and a TWIN-CS design team member to review the previous school year and plan for the next one. We discussed several actionable items, such as revisiting our staff norms to include voices of non-teaching staff. Their lack of inclusion was inhibiting our school community and leaving out very important voices. While these actions were seemingly technical, they helped the team dig deeper into the adaptive changes that the school community was experiencing. The group was excited about the progress and was able to articulate a plan for the following year. This spurred ongoing conversations that have helped empower faculty and staff members to see their leadership in action in the larger organization.

Just as I learned from my own interactions as a mentor to the RCCS team, other colleagues across TWIN-CS have shared with me how intentional critical conversations contributed to fostering a positive and cohesive school climate in their contexts. For instance, Principal Carrie Fuller of All Souls World Language Catholic School in Alhambra, California, described using critical conversations to manage people's expectations, when things work and when they don't: "It's important to be clear with people about expectations and what we want. You can tout all the research, but [TWI] is not a silver bullet . . . we have to help people manage when things don't go as well as wanted." From her perspective, leaders are not expected to have all the answers, and it is fine to tell people that: "If I don't know the answer, I will tell them that, [do the] research, and then ensure that I circle back to them." This is the adaptive part of leading—being fine with not being the expert on everything. A critical part of being in a leadership role is to ask questions to help guide next steps.

As another example, Principal Michael Guerra of St. Matthew Catholic School in Phoenix, Arizona, described carefully considering the environment for the staff members: "So many times we get lost thinking about culture . . . what type of culture will we cultivate for our students, for our families, for each other? We have to make critical decisions that impact people, and we need to talk to others to see how to do that. It's important that our staff know what we are about." When making decisions, Guerra feels it is important to stay true to yourself—and to share those beliefs with others. He spoke about the importance of ensuring that his students' families were integrated and supported by the school. "We want parents to be engaged. It just looks different than some schools. They know that we are there for them. They know they can trust us, and that has helped build our reputation for other families, too." By modeling this, he has seen other team members be adaptive and try new approaches to how they interact with families.

While it is important to take risks within the zone of disequilibrium, as Principal Guerra has demonstrated and encouraged of others, his goal is to maintain positive school climate. He also talked about how crucial it is to model strong relationships with other leaders in the school, including the priest, parish administrator, assistant principal, TWI coordinator, teacher-leaders, and parents. When stakeholders know the "why" behind the direction of the school, this encourages them to also be adaptive.

The examples show how TWIN-CS member schools have used critical conversations to assess their current realities and worked adaptively to move closer to their missions as they serve their communities. Their work is guiding their schools to be more culturally and linguistically responsive to their communities and creating more cohesive and positive school climates.

Mission Articulation

A third way that critical conversations help manage change is in articulating the school mission. Change processes are times of ambiguity. In the absence of certainty, such as when we are working to solve adaptive challenges, people can create their own narratives, sometimes assuming that their beliefs accurately reflect the direction of the organization. However, individual "truth" is not universal Truth. Engaging in critical conversations is important in order to forge a common understanding within the community.

In the context of TWIN-CS, some schools had begun to adopt TWI, while others were new to the model. Regardless, all were going through a transformational journey moving into a new reality. An important focus for critical conversations has been crafting the school mission and vision. As a collective of bilingual Catholic schools, the design team stressed the importance of aligning the mission to both the *Guiding Principles for Dual Language Education* and the *National Standards and Benchmarks for Effective Catholic Elementary and Secondary Schools.*[9] At the TWIN-CS summer academy, implementation teams met to discuss the importance of the mission, and why it is essential to get input from stakeholders when articulating and revising it.

Because of the complexities involved in balancing the multiple perspectives of stakeholders, creating and revising a mission can be challenging. For that reason, it is important to have critical conversations; to gather feedback from students, parents, faculty, staff members, and community members to help understand their current reality, in an effort to recognize potential biases; and to create broad buy-in to shape the future of the school. Once completed, the mission serves as a map and compass for the direction of the school and symbolizes who the community is and why the school exists. As new initiatives present themselves, the community can use the mission as a barometer to determine congruency. Does the initiative align with the mission? If not, it shouldn't be a focus for the school. The mission helps insulate the school from potential political, financial, and personal external forces. As leaders, parents, staff members, and students change, the mission should help guide all decisions, including the strategic plan.

At RCCS, an array of stakeholders, from implementation team members to the school president and board, crafted the following mission: "Risen Christ Catholic School is a K–8, bilingual, multicultural and financially accessible school of excellence, educating children in mind, body, and spirit to live and lead in the example of Jesus Christ." Decisions to incorporate specific language such as "bilingual," "multicultural," and "financially accessible" emerged from critical conversations about the school's direction. Revising the mission provided the school community a cohesive focus for strategic planning. As president of RCCS Michael Rogers explained, "There are many great opportunities out there, but we can't be everything to everyone. We need to be clear about our mission to ensure that we're looking out for our students."

Reconsidering mission is particularly difficult in schools with long histories. When RCCS made the transition to TWI, it had been in existence for over twenty years, and many staff members and community members had strong commitments to an established mission for the students and families they were serving. The implementation team needed to address these concerns when managing the change process. RCCS principal Liz Ramsey described how important it was for current staff to understand and support the new TWI model and to be invested, if they wanted to continue to be employed in the school. As the years progressed, some staff members chose different career paths.

Across TWIN-CS, other member schools were managing this change process from their own starting places. Different school contexts require different strategies for critical conversations to foster mission. Whereas RCCS, in the example above, was an existing monolingual school in the process of adopting the TWI model, All Souls was opening its doors as a brand-new TWI school. Thus, instead of shifting their mission, they needed to articulate a foundational one from the outset. In this context, creating core values, which articulated who they wanted to be, was a precursor to establishing the mission. Principal Fuller described the excitement and complexities of creating a unified path: "Everyone had a vision for what they wanted the school to be, but as a community, we hadn't yet decided what it should be." There were many involved stakeholders, and Fuller saw the opportunity to have people work together to create something great for their community. "Everyone was dreaming up what they wanted it to be," she recalled, but "nobody had clearly stated what we wanted." Together, the board, teachers, staff members, and parents established the school name to accurately reflect the vision. To create alignment, they also worked with a parent who specialized in marketing to create focus groups to develop core values. The core values they landed upon include honoring Catholic tradition, embracing excellence, believing in joy-filled learning, and building language fluency. Similar to RCCS, All Souls was able to harness critical conversations in order to engage others, gather multiple perspectives, and create a unified and shared vision upon which programmatic structures can be built.

Mission Implementation

Just as critical conversations can help a community reconsider its mission, they can also assist in implementing the mission. Implementation cannot occur without involving countless stakeholders. During the planning process for implementing change to a culturally and linguistically responsive school, stakeholders must choose a program model. In the case of TWIN-CS, this means choosing the model of TWI schooling: Should it be a 90/10 model? Should it be 50/50?[10] Once the program model is selected, additional decisions need to be made. One of the most challenging decisions involves creating a schedule to accommodate this model. While seemingly straightforward, this in fact poses a complex challenge. When assigning time allocations to classes, faculty are assigning importance or priority. By doing that, staff members, administrators, and parents can have their own beliefs about what should be taught, when, and for how long. Where are the commonalities? Where are the differences? Because these decisions can challenge people's beliefs, as well as their positions, they can be very difficult. However, with a clear and unified mission in place that focuses on the goal of student learning, stakeholders can more easily work together in the process of implementing that mission.

As a mentor at RCCS, some of the difficult critical conversations I helped lead were about scheduling. Moving to conceptualize and put into place a new schedule might seem like a technical problem—but the complexities can make the experience more of an adaptive challenge. Critical conversations can be essential to helping participants stay within a productive zone of disequilibrium as they move to resolve the issues. Previously at RCCS, two kindergarten teachers had each taught one group of students in English. However, in the first year of the TWI implementation, the teachers were going to share responsibility for both groups of students: one would teach in English and the other in Spanish. When I began working with the school, the initial schedule these teachers had built took the content that had been previously taught in kindergarten and simply added a Spanish language arts block. This was leading to problems in getting students enough time to learn other subjects in Spanish. Knowing that adding hours to the school day was not feasible, these teachers had to find ways to revise the schedule to work smarter within the given time frame. After the first year, it became evident to the teachers and principal that additional scheduling changes were needed to optimize student learning. For instance, there was more time in social studies and science than in math, but students were not demonstrating mastery of math content. Therefore, we added more time for math instruction (and decreased minutes for social studies and science) the following year. While this strengthened the program, after the second year we met as a team and created yet another version of the schedule, which allowed more time for literacy and math in both languages, further reducing the time for social studies and science, with the idea that more content would be delivered through language arts. We continued to be adaptive and make modifications to the students' schedule as we learned more about what the students needed and changed past practices. Critical conversations such as those around scheduling are essential to determine how to implement the mission.[11]

Another area where critical conversations helped us in implementing the mission was professional development. Unequivocally, the greatest resource any school has is its personnel. When planning for and implementing culturally and linguistically responsive schools, educational leaders must recognize the central role that the staff members play in fostering language, culture, and climate. Critical conversations are essential in developing great employees.

In a TWI school, the language is a piece of the intricate puzzle, but it is not the whole of the puzzle. Teachers are tasked with teaching more than Spanish and English in traditional ways. Teachers must differentiate the many needs that their students have, and this can create dissonance among them. It is an adaptive challenge, not a technical problem. In my experience, I have found it important to facilitate dialogue to help educators with a variety of linguistic profiles, and to appreciate the importance of one another's work in this context. Several TWIN-CS leaders referenced helping support and mentor teachers from other countries as they adapted to teaching in dual language contexts within the United States. For teachers who did not grow up in the United States, it can be important to have critical conversations and reflect on their roles in the US context as educators to students who (and whose parents) may or may not have been born in the United States.

Critical conversations about implementing mission can engage teachers in their commitment to the school community. Principal Ramsey recognized that the human resources of RCCS—especially the classroom teachers—were the key to implementing the school mission. She also knew that these teachers filled a unique niche, and as highly qualified bilingual instructors, they were in demand. In this context, she often engaged them in conversations about vocation, directly addressing the opportunity that dual language schools provide for the Catholic church to fulfill its social justice mission: "Teaching is a calling and, in our school, teachers can live their faith." As an educator, she felt moving to the TWI model was different from other initiatives in the past. They were truly aligning actions to their mission, serving an important community that has not always been served in Catholic schools in the United States.

As RCCS (and other member schools in TWIN-CS) moved to the TWI model, and the mission (and subsequent strategic plans) were implemented, some English-speaking teachers feared losing their jobs. For some, this meant reevaluating their roles, beliefs, and expectations. As staffing changed, some teachers who stayed watched their friends and colleagues leave because of the TWI program. This required critical conversations to navigate. Initially, some school principals within TWIN-CS hoped that current monolingual English teachers might be able to learn Spanish in a few years to be able to teach in Spanish. One said, "I have a couple of years; I can figure out how to speak Spanish." They discussed strategies—such as taking night classes, reading books in Spanish, or learning through computer programs. The school leaders needed to help the teachers realize that while their desire and willingness to learn Spanish was laudable, becoming functionally bilingual is a long process. Coming to grips with the reality that the long-term direction of the school would require someone with different knowledge and skills than they had was a hard reality for these teachers. Navigating these critical conversations took these principals demonstrating sensitivity, thoughtfulness, and courage.

Principal Fuller has worked with her team at All Saints World Language School to institutionalize school programming. Owing to a variety of factors, including the local public schools paying substantially more, teachers left and with them, so did their institutional knowledge. Because of the adaptive challenge of teacher turnover, Fuller and the team talked about how to systematize. They currently invest time and resources to document curriculum for current and future teachers so that they do not need to continue "reinventing the wheel." In this case, critical conversations have allowed the team to face challenges they know they will continue to face, and change their system to help meet those challenges.

RCCS faced a similar adaptive challenge, and many new teachers joined a veteran staff within a few short years. Implementing the new model required considerable professional development for new and more experienced teachers alike. Two RCCS teachers, Claire Jordan and Megan Wright, shared that ongoing critical conversations with colleagues helped others understand that student language production in English will initially be lower than what they may have seen in monolingual educational contexts, but will be on par or beyond peer norms by the upper elementary grades. Both shared that it was beneficial to participate in professional development through the TWIN-CS network. Wright said, "Being a part of TWIN has helped me have conversations with others and realize that everyone is having similar problems . . . nobody has all the answers." Jordan agreed, stating, "Sometimes, we feel isolated because we are the only school in the Archdiocese doing what we are doing."

For the teachers in TWIN-CS schools, there is great value in attending workshops, pursuing professional development opportunities, reading, and visiting other schools. Being that TWI schools are relatively new concepts in education in the United States, much can be gained by connecting with people that are doing or have previously done the work. For leaders, it is important to recognize these challenges and to hire great people, support them, develop them professionally, and work to retain them.

Intentional critical conversations within the network related to mentoring, building climate, creating or recreating a mission, and implementing that mission have helped create a guide to success within the TWIN-CS network. However, challenges exist in all organizations, and critical conversations can be helpful in other contexts as new schools, programs, or initiatives are designed.

APPLYING LEARNINGS FROM
THE TWIN-CS NETWORK

As discussed at the outset, critical conversations are key for managing change. In particular, they can help leaders distinguish adaptive challenges from technical problems, and directly help them confront bias and prejudice. As I have shared, critical conversations within the network of TWIN-CS have been essential in managing change, particularly regarding mentoring, school climate, mission articulation, and mission implementation. There are several ways these experiences have lessons for other contexts.

First, leaders across contexts can incorporate critical friends to both initiate and scaffold critical conversations. Leaders do this by seeking multiple perspectives to inform and evaluate current programming. Because each stakeholder offers important yet limited perspectives on the overall organization, it is important to ensure that different possibilities are explored. Having consultants provide feedback, support, and ideas has been invaluable to me as a leader, as well as to TWIN-CS schools. I have spent most of my career as a professional educator in public institutions and have seen how critical friends can help identify and process challenges in an array of educational contexts. I have also come to realize that my diverse experiences have provided me with a different lens, enabling me to ask questions and share my own experiences. Having this collaborative experience and deep conversations with other colleagues has been beneficial and helped me to reflect on my own beliefs. We have grown together. I would encourage other educators to explore experiences that allow them to gain different perspectives. As the years have passed, working with TWIN-CS to enact technical and adaptive change has helped me become a better mentor, a more well-versed educator, and a better educational leader.

Second, whether moving toward a culturally and linguistically responsive school, such as a TWI school, or implementing another initiative, it is essential to remember that full implementation takes time because of the adaptive nature of the work. Because of this uncertainty, nurturing a positive climate during times of change is essential. It is important to have critical conversations to help set up systems and to understand the nuances of planning and implementation, continually involving stakeholders throughout the process. Of equal importance is anticipating that humans tend to be creatures of habit. Leaders need to anticipate and prepare for adverse reactions that can be ignited by people's fear of change. Understanding where the adaptive challenges are, as well as identifying the productive zone of disequilibrium, can help leaders plan and intentionally address these challenges.

Finally, as I have shared, critical conversations in TWIN-CS have helped school communities both articulate and implement their mission. Leaders across contexts can learn from this by intentionally gathering widespread input to help their organizations articulate their current reality. By striving for broad-based feedback from stakeholders, leaders can identify potential biases. Creating or revising the mission helps others see the identified path for moving forward. In doing so, individuals can see how their participation aligns (or does not align) with the vision and direction of the larger community. For those in formal leadership positions, the mission helps direct what work needs to be prioritized and which could potentially move us farther from our stated end goal.

Throughout the journey with TWIN-CS, it has become apparent that improvement is guided by intentional structures related to mentoring, being mindful of building climate, and crafting and implementing the mission. Because success is not always linear, it is important to honor and reflect on the voices that affect the important collective work. By having regular, ongoing, and intentional critical conversations to guide planning and implementation, the TWIN-CS network schools continue to grow and strengthen, and the journey of transformation is becoming smoother for all involved.

4

Assuring Model Fidelity

MARÍA CRISTINA LADAS

AS SCHOOL AND DISTRICT LEADERS strive to better educate culturally and linguistically minoritized populations, a fundamental decision involves the selection and implementation of an appropriate model to achieve those aims, along with actions to ensure ongoing fidelity to the chosen model. In this chapter, I describe the practice of assuring model fidelity, an essential component in the success of dual language programs.[1] In the first section of this chapter, I discuss selecting a service delivery model and establishing fidelity assurances to guide the school through stages of implementation. Next, I apply these ideas by sharing the story of my experiences working with one Two-Way Immersion Network for Catholic Schools (TWIN-CS) school as it transitioned from monolingual English instruction to bilingual instruction through a two-way immersion (TWI) program. Finally, I discuss lessons learned from these experiences, and share ideas for how educational leaders can apply these to the practice of assuring model fidelity in other contexts.

ASSURING MODEL FIDELITY

Engaging in the practice of assuring model fidelity requires that you iden-tify your service delivery model. Generally speaking, service delivery models define how students who are designated English Learners (ELs) will receive support services that provide them with equitable opportunities to learn (see table 1.1). Some service delivery models promote bilingualism and bil-iteracy (columns A and B), while others solely promote English language and literacy, either by incorporating some home language of students who are designated ELs (column C) or by focusing only on English (columns D and E).[2] If the service delivery model is to provide the school community clear direction on its journey of transformation, it must advance the three goals of culturally and linguistically responsive schools: building students' sociocultural competence, respecting and cultivating proficiency in home and community languages in addition to English, and promoting all students' academic achievement. Service delivery models that promote bilingualism and biliteracy (columns A and B) align most closely with these goals.

Committing to a service delivery model does not just answer questions—it also raises them. Educational leaders guiding the process must help their school community navigate complex and at times contentious questions: Which general model is most appropriate for this school community given the current student demographics, projected demographics, and school cul-ture and identity? In this context, which specific model do we think will be most effective from an academic and linguistic perspective? After a model has been selected, questions about implementation then arise: How much instructional time will be provided through the partner language? How will instructional time be allocated across the two program languages? Will one teacher provide instruction through both languages, or will two teachers work together as a team?[3]

When selecting a service delivery model, an important place to start is examining the cultural and linguistic characteristics of your students. For instance, all of the bilingual models in table 1.1 require concentrations of desig-nated ELs that share the same home language. Among those models, TWI (see column B) is the only one that integrates students from English-monolingual or English-dominant homes as well as those from bilingual homes with those from partner-language dominant or monolingual homes. In the ideal TWI model, classrooms are "linguistically balanced," with no more than two-thirds of the student population being composed of a single home language group.[4]

In keeping with an asset-based orientation, TWI views each student's native language as a strength, and organizes curriculum and instruction to capitalize on this in educating all students. Because of the linguistic integration inherent in the TWI model, all students have the opportunity to be positioned as both learners and leaders, learning from their peers while working in their less-developed language, and providing support to their peers while working in their dominant language. Students that enter the school already bilingual can serve as "brokers" between the Spanish-dominant and the English-dominant students, and can therefore potentially be positioned as leaders throughout the day. Moreover, successful TWI programs strive to help students understand and value language variation, and therefore choose curricular materials that reflect multiple registers and varieties of both program languages, as well as bilingual materials that incorporate the use of both program languages.[5]

Selecting the general model—such as TWI—frees you to turn your attention to resolving important details about implementation. For instance, in the context of implementing a TWI program, one important detail to resolve is how to allocate instructional time in each language. Some schools choose to implement a 90/10 program, which provides the majority of instruction in the primary grades (90 percent) in the partner language (Spanish, Mandarin, etc.), with the percentage of English instruction steadily increasing each year until it reaches a ratio of 50 percent instructional time in each language by about third or fourth grade. Alternatively, some schools choose to provide equal amounts of instruction in both program languages at all grade levels through a 50/50 model. Navigating the 90/10 versus 50/50 decision is a complex leadership challenge, since the decision can be affected by different, and at times competing, factors. For instance, some research points toward 90/10 as a stronger model for ensuring that all students from all home language backgrounds develop higher levels of bilingualism and biliteracy. This is because there are no differences in ultimate English attainment across models, but there are often differences in attainment of the partner language that favor the students in 90/10 programs.[6] However, it is often the case that a variety of stakeholders (administrators, parents, teachers) are more comfortable with the 50/50 model, in large part because of the accountability system that is based on high-stakes standardized testing, which is primarily carried out in English as early as third grade.

Another factor that affects this decision involves staffing. In both approaches, the best staffing includes bilingually certified teachers with high levels of proficiency in the partner language as well as English, technical teaching skills, and positive dispositions about their students and their families.[7] However, finding bilingual certified teachers with these qualifications is a major challenge, as there is a chronic national shortage of bilingual teachers.[8] This shortage favors the implementation of a 50/50 model, as fewer bilingual teachers are needed since the instructional time in the partner language is less than it is in the 90/10 model. To maximize the skills of the bilingual teachers, most 50/50 programs use a "team teacher" approach, in which a bilingual teacher who is proficient in the partner language shares teaching responsibilities with an English-speaking teacher. In this approach, the two teachers are jointly responsible for providing instruction to two classes of students that alternate between the partner language teacher's classroom and the English teacher's classroom, thus changing the language of instruction every day, every other day, or every week. Additionally, looking at the team-teaching approach from a capacity-building and financially sound perspective is worthwhile. This approach eliminates the need to hire extra teachers. In self-contained, or one-teacher models, only half the number of students could be served. Therefore, for those schools committed to reaching out to include larger numbers of students to ensure equitable access, the team-teacher model is preferable.

Establishing Fidelity Assurances

After deciding on the appropriate service delivery model, educational leaders must adjust the school's strategic plan to implement this. This planning should include considering how it will ensure fidelity to the chosen model by explicitly establishing *fidelity assurances*. Fidelity assurances are tools that provide guidance for implementing a particular model as it is intended. To illustrate fidelity assurances, I return to the example of TWI. Various resources provide guidance for implementing a TWI service delivery model with fidelity. Some are general checklists that identify the basic tenets of this service delivery model, and others go into more detail. At the "simple and straightforward" end of the spectrum of fidelity assurances are Thomas and Collier's three "non-negotiables." [9] In their book *Dual Language Education for a Transformed World,* they enumerate three essential components of well-implemented, research-based dual language education:

- At least 50 percent of the instructional time must be taught in the non-English (partner) language.
- The two languages for instruction should be taught separately.
- The program should commit to a minimum of five years, and ideally extend from elementary through secondary.

An advantage of starting with simple fidelity assurances like Thomas and Collier's non-negotiables is that they are clear and concise. They are grounded in research showing that students designated as ELs in TWI programs score as well or better than their non-EL peers when taking state and norm-referenced tests in English. A disadvantage of such an articulation of fidelity assurances is that they oversimplify and lack a developmental framework. Thomas and Collier imply that either a school is a dual language school or it isn't. If any of the three non-negotiables are not in place, or are in dispute, then the program should simply not call itself a dual language program.

At the other end of the spectrum are fidelity assurances that are detailed and elaborate. Take, for instance, the *Guiding Principles for Dual Language Education.*[10] *Guiding Principles* provides a comprehensive synthesis of research on developing a TWI model, alongside tools for moving from an initial implementation to a mature, well-developed model. *Guiding Principles* identifies seven strands: program structure, curriculum, instruction, assessment/accountability, quality/professional development, family/community, and support/resources. Each strand includes a relevant research summary that supports the guidance provided in that section, followed by several guiding principles, each with a series of key points that allow for evaluation using a rubric ranging from minimal alignment to exemplary evidence. It is a useful framework that can be used by schools at any stage of implementation given its layout and reflective nature. Importantly, the rubrics encourage evidence-based assessments of current practice.

There are many versions of fidelity assurances that lie somewhere in between these two poles on the spectrum—the concise Thomas and Collier non-negotiables and the extensive *Guiding Principles*. Utah has developed an example of this. In 2008 Utah embarked on a concerted, statewide effort to promote bilingual service delivery models. That year the legislature created a funding stream for bilingual service delivery that focused on one-way and two-way models called dual language immersion. As of 2019, 43,000 students are enrolled in programs that use English for 50 percent of the time alongside partner languages: Chinese, French, German, Portuguese, Russian, or Spanish.[11] With such a large-scale project to implement, the Utah State Board of Education knew it needed to create systems that could be applied across contexts. For evaluation and guidance of the non-negotiables, they published the dual language immersion program fidelity assurances for elementary and middle schools.[12] These guidelines, which are periodically updated, articulate essential assurances of fidelity to the model, evidence sources, and evaluation criteria. Not surprisingly, other schools and districts have adapted Utah's model to their particular contexts. Fidelity assurances can provide guidance to the community in implementing the selected program model.

In short, fidelity assurances can vary across a spectrum—from being relatively simplistic to quite detailed. Establishing fidelity assurances is an important step in the practice of assuring high levels of commitment to a research-based model. The final consideration of this practice is to notice how the fidelity assurances unfold across stages of implementation.

Progressing Through Stages of Implementation

The process of creating a school that is culturally and linguistically responsive can seem overwhelming. When considering the practice of assuring model fidelity, it can be helpful to step back and remember that implementing a dramatic change happens not all at once, but in stages. The National Implementation Research Network describes four stages through which all large-scale implementation processes move: exploration, installation, initial implementation, and full implementation.[13] Understanding these stages can help schools navigate the journey from selecting an appropriate service delivery model to establishing fidelity assurances and finally assuring model fidelity. I describe each stage in turn.

The *exploration* stage is the entry point to a transformative idea. It is during this stage that schools must first decide if there is a need for change from current practice and consider how shifting to a more culturally and linguistically responsive service delivery model (refer to table 1.1) would fit within the context of the organization. An important part of the exploration stage is establishing an implementation team to conduct the work. The implementation team analyzes the evidence regarding a need to change and the options for potential changes. This analysis includes both identifying the costs and benefits of adopting a new service delivery model and identifying the organization's capacity to support the change. The importance of establishing scaffolded networks starts in this stage and continues throughout the remaining stages. Identifying other schools that are further along in the stages of implementation and conducting in-person or even virtual field trips help the implementation team visualize the end product. Listening to other schools share their successes and challenges helps the beginners anticipate roadblocks. Finally, assessing the resources (e.g., funding, staffing) and soliciting input from stakeholders (including teachers, students, and parent and community members) lead the implementation team's decision to either move into the next stage or abandon their idea. A common time frame for the implementation team to conduct this task is six to twelve months.

If the implementation team decides to move forward with a new service delivery model—such as launching a TWI program—it moves to the *installation* stage. The main goal of this stage is to figure out the details of how to put the new model into place. This involves both establishing fidelity assurances (as described above) and attaining and organizing resources that will allow schools to adhere to these fidelity assurances. In the case of launching a new TWI service delivery model, these resource needs are abundant. For instance, the implementation team must select and develop culturally responsive, authentic materials for curriculum, instruction, and assessment. The teaching and learning environment of the school needs to be adjusted to fit the new model. This includes altering the layout of classrooms and revising scheduling in manners that will allow teachers to work with one another to implement the model with fidelity. Recruiting and selecting teachers and support staff is one of the most daunting tasks of the installation stage, alongside planning and delivering the appropriate professional development.

Perhaps the most important aspect of the *installation stage* is securing student enrollment and buy-in from parents who will be unfamiliar with this transformational approach to creating bilingual and biliterate graduates. Parent informational nights, tours of the school, social media, and press releases are just a few of the ideas that are launched during this stage. A comprehensive public relations and marketing plan will help create a "buzz" around a new program that builds until that first day of school.

When the doors open on that exciting first day, the *initial implementation* stage begins. This stage is the most fragile of all. Establishing additional time for the implementation team to evaluate how the new model is functioning within the fidelity assurances is an absolute necessity during this stage. Additional support measures need to be readily available for difficulties that will arise, as all those involved are venturing into new territory. As is often the case when moving outside of a comfort zone, the implementation team must have a robust system in place to mentor and coach teachers that are implementing the new program model. If support is not sufficient, many practitioners will resort to prior practices because they are more comfortable. Administrators need to be prepared to support the new model with facts and evidence to convince those who question the change or are searching for answers to many questions. The implementation team must be aware of challenges that arise and be ready to address them. At times, this could require making unexpected changes to address unanticipated issues. It is crucial the implementation teams maintain their scaffolded networks with other schools who have already gone through this initial implementation. New principals can learn from more veteran administrators just as new TWI teachers can learn from those that have already implemented the model for several years.

Once more than half of the school is participating in the model, the scales tip and the *full implementation* stage begins. At this point, fears and uncertainties tend to subside. Yet the implementation team must remain vigilant and continue to deepen their understanding of the fidelity assurances. It is during this stage that the team must work to systematize the service delivery model in order to protect it from changes in administration or teaching staff. Identifying a tiered professional development approach can help meet the needs of new and existing teachers. It is essential to conduct walkthroughs with a fidelity instrument or an observation checklist to observe students using English and the partner language and to determine whether there is evidence that they are meeting the targeted proficiency levels. Establishing a system of exploring, applying, recording results, and reflecting can result in a systematic approach to on-going growth throughout the organization during this stage.

To recap, in this section I have talked about the practice of assuring model fidelity in the process of transformation. I have discussed how implementation moves through clear stages as one selects a service delivery model, establishes fidelity assurances, and launches a culturally and linguistically responsive program. In the following section, I illustrate this practice by recounting my experiences as a mentor working with a TWIN-CS member school as it selected its service delivery model, established fidelity assurances, and moved through the stages of implementation.

ASSURING MODEL FIDELITY IN TWIN-CS: THE STORY OF ST. MATTHEW CATHOLIC SCHOOL

As a mentor working with St. Matthew Catholic School (SMCS) in Phoenix, Arizona, I helped directly with their process of transformation. I use the story of SMCS to illustrate the practice of assuring model fidelity and the importance of developing scaffolded networks. I organize this story by discussing the movement through the stages of implementation—from exploration, in which a service delivery model was chosen, to installation, in which fidelity assurances were established, through implementation.

Exploration

During the 2008–09 school year, the principal of SMCS, Gena McGowan, reached out to me. She asked to meet me in Cave Creek Unified School District in Arizona, where I served as the coordinator for a one-way Spanish immersion program. Prior to the passage of the English-only laws in Arizona, I had managed several TWI and maintenance bilingual programs, so I was very familiar with different service delivery models for emergent bilinguals. As we discussed the context of SMCS, I immediately recognized that Principal McGowan's school had the perfect demographic profile for a TWI program, since nearly all its students were Latinx (99 percent), half of whom were designated ELs.[14] Moreover, being a Catholic school, it did not have the programmatic restrictions imposed on Arizona public schools because of the English-only legislation. By reaching out to me, Principal McGowan established the first network between our schools and left the meeting encouraged to look more closely at TWI. The exploration stage had begun for SMCS.

Over the subsequent year, as Principal McGowan learned more about dual language service delivery models, including TWI, she sent several of her teachers to observe and network with local teachers working in different types of bilingual settings as well as with me. This careful, methodical networking approach grew the base of knowledge among her staff and allowed them to arrive at their own conclusions regarding what model would best serve their linguistically and culturally diverse population.[15] Given the school's economically disadvantaged demographics and its low achievement data, it became apparent that the English-only service delivery model that SMCS was implementing at the time was not the best choice. At the end of this year-long process, the team had reached the decisive conclusion to replace their English-only approach to service delivery with TWI.

Installation

Once SMCS committed to adopt the TWI model, the school moved into the installation stage. During this period—which lasted approximately six months—Principal McGowan and the rest of the SMCS implementation team wrestled with the many details of how to enact this new model. Part of this involved securing the buy-in and support from key stakeholders through a marketing/public relations focus. Principal McGowan played the leading role in contacting and meeting with colleagues across SMCS as well as reaching out to parents and students. She engaged others in helping in many of these meetings. For instance, she asked me to help provide parents with an overview of TWI that summarized its goals and benefits. By finding multiple ways to educate her stakeholders, Principal McGowan built the capacity needed to gather momentum through this crucial stage.

As is necessary during the installation stage, the implementation team worked diligently to identify the structural supports that were needed. Principal McGowan began to hire teachers with high levels of academic Spanish proficiency who could become the partner language teachers to work alongside the already present English teachers. Local talent was also identified in current bilingual SMCS teachers and paraprofessionals with a grow-your-own attitude toward teacher certification. The implementation team also spent time discerning different ways to organize curriculum and instruction. After considering different options, they landed on a two-teacher model where a Spanish teacher taught kindergarten in the morning and first grade in the afternoon, while the English team teacher did the reverse. These teacher pairs at the kindergarten and the first-grade levels each shared two classrooms of students. The implementation team established a plan to add a new grade level every year, growing the TWI model through eighth grade. Principal McGowan provided these grade-level teacher pairs release time to visit local schools implementing TWI in the Phoenix valley. This applied professional development helped them appreciate the importance of working closely together, and also helped them establish important networks of support.

As the installation stage continued in SMCS, I worked with the implementation team to help teachers coordinate their curriculum, instruction, and assessment. We created a document, which we called the TWI team planning guide, to serve as our first version of a fidelity assurance tool. The purpose of the TWI team planning guide was to scaffold this coordination among the English/Spanish TWI teacher teams, ensuring that expectations and accountability structures were clearly in place. The process of completing the guide involved the TWI teacher team sitting together to discuss the different components, adding their joint reflections and answers to one document. This helped build a sense of team with discussion of critical topics in the process of implementing the TWI model.

One area the TWI team planning guide helped clarify was classroom arrangement. In the primary grades, having team teachers map out their classrooms and place carpets, word walls, work tables, homework bins, and other features in the same place helped students feel like their two classrooms were in sync. Having K–1 students start the year sitting in the same place in both classrooms also eased some of the confusion that could arise when young students moved between two rooms and two teachers during the daily switch at lunchtime. Those inaugural groups followed a roller-coaster schedule, meaning that wherever a group ended the day was the same classroom that they would return to in the morning until the time came to switch classrooms again midday.

Relatedly, the TWI team planning guide described mirroring classroom procedures. In this section, teachers were to jointly decide on similar procedures in both languages with identical hand signals. They considered everything from a common "May I go to the bathroom?" signal to deciding what an appropriate "quiet" signal could be for both classrooms. Identifying a place for teachers to share parent concerns or changes to how students would go home was also crucial. This section of the planning guide helped the two teachers put systems in place to make their management of two classes as seamless as possible.

Since a critical dimension of this service delivery model involves supporting students in developing bilingualism and biliteracy, the TWI team planning guide detailed language usage policies. This involved prompting the teacher team to decide on important linguistic considerations that would keep them in line with Thomas and Collier's second non-negotiable, that the two languages for instruction should be taught separately. The team had to commit to using their respective instructional language 100 percent of the time with each class. Additionally, they had to think of clever ways to encourage the students to use the language of that classroom with each other. A bilingual zone in each classroom was also identified to provide a clear space for students to use both languages as necessary, and clear language expectations for other adults that might enter the classroom were also agreed upon and shared.

The implementation team applied this concept of each teacher staying in one language beyond the classroom as well. For example, this meant that sometimes, depending on who was on lunch duty leading the prayer, the entire student body would be following a Spanish teacher in Spanish or, conversely, an English teacher in English. What emerged once they had applied this concept to every area of the school, from walking into the front office to greet the bilingual receptionist to playing on the basketball court at recess, was a school that truly functioned in a linguistically and culturally equitable manner. Each person's heritage language was valued and accepted by others. While the implementation team participated in a book study during a subsequent stage, *Dual Language Education for a Transformed World*, we felt that it would have been the perfect installation stage activity. This book further strengthened the SMCS implementation team's understanding of linguistic equity and the commitment to fidelity required by dual language education.[16]

The TWI team planning guide also described broader issues. For instance, one section on grade-level planning and communication emphasized the importance of team building and of the teacher pairs working closely together to manage the same group of students. Another section asked the teachers to outline curriculum and instruction, identifying which content areas they were primarily responsible for teaching and which ones they would help support or "bridge" from the other language.[17] This also prompted teachers to map curriculum to standards.

In short, the TWI team planning guide was a tool for establishing fidelity assurances that helped the initial grade teacher team proceed through the installation stage with greater clarity and confidence. A byproduct of the teamwork was that each set of two teachers got to know each other and their respective working styles. By the fall of 2009, SMCS was ready to begin implementation with many of the details around classroom design and routines already in place.

Implementation

In August 2009, the first students in kindergarten and first grade entered TWI classes in SMCS, marking the launch of the initial implementation stage. Although the older students in the school (second through eighth grade) were still receiving monolingual English instruction, SMCS had gone from exploring the idea of a new service delivery model to actually implementing this change. As the implementation team attempted to introduce a new grade level each year to the TWI model, they experienced some difficulties in finding qualified Spanish-speaking teachers. Regardless, each new team coming in drew on the TWI team planning guide to help establish fidelity assurances to the model. Year by year, enrollment increased and all stakeholders began to see the fruits of their labor.

During these initial years of implementation, the community at SMCS was largely working on their own in figuring out this implementation with only a few local scaffolded networks in place. This all changed in the spring of 2012 when Principal McGowan learned about the launch of TWIN-CS and was invited to apply to join. Consulting with the implementation team, SMCS eagerly accepted, as it was the only Catholic school in all of Arizona implementing a TWI model.

I attended the inaugural TWIN-CS summer academy with the SMCS implementation team in 2013. Here, for the first time, we met other Catholic schools and mentors engaged in the change process. A central feature of this summer academy that focused on the practice of assuring model fidelity was using the *Guiding Principles for Dual Language Education*, a publication of the Center for Applied Linguistics.[18] The TWIN-CS design team introduced all member schools to this resource as a comprehensive tool to scaffold movement through the stages of implementing TWI.

The SMCS implementation team was eager to dig into the *Guiding Principles*, which was much more elaborate than the TWI team planning guide that we had been using. Since we were already implementing TWI, we hoped this would help us refine our model within the context of fidelity. We all wondered, "Is TWI in our school in line with what the *Guiding Principles* defines as exemplary practice?" As I sat with the implementation team and we all took our first glances at the extensive rubrics, a hush fell around the table. We began to comb through the comprehensive guide. As the details washed over us—seven different strands, thirty-one specific principles, and individual evaluation rubrics—people quickly became overwhelmed. Questions about how to approach the *Guiding Principles* began to surface: Which principle should SMCS concentrate on first? How would the process be shared with the rest of the school's stakeholders? What type of evidence would need to be provided if all of the principles were to be evaluated using the rubrics?

As the academy continued, we realized that we were not alone. Questions about how to use a tool like the *Guiding Principles* to guide implementation and assure fidelity to the TWI model were common across all the member schools. While the TWIN-CS schools shared a common framework of being Catholic elementary schools at different stages of implementing their TWI model, the logistics of the models were quite diverse. TWIN-CS member schools had wide-ranging demographic profiles, goals, and challenges. When schools at that first summer academy introduced their TWI models, the explanations of specific models ranged far and wide. For example, some schools explained that they separated students for native language literacy as in the Gómez and Gómez model.[19] Others used translation methods to aid in instruction, and still others believed in simultaneous biliteracy. Some had a one-teacher, self-contained, bilingual model, while others separated the languages by teacher and classroom. Additionally, many schools were at completely different stages of implementation, which made it difficult for TWIN-CS schools to find others like themselves with which to establish networks. If schools did set up strategic networks among themselves, they soon realized that they did not have a common way to share their experiences or to ensure fidelity to the model. Clearly, the practice of assuring model fidelity was going to be complex!

When we returned home from the academy, I began searching for a way to help us move forward with implementation. While the initial tool to assure fidelity—the TWI team planning guide—was a useful start, we learned that there was so much more that we needed to consider, as the *Guiding Principles* articulated. However, we also knew that we could not do everything at once and needed to find an entry point into a more comprehensive fidelity assurance tool. I began working on a tool that would be accessible to the SMCS teachers and administrators and applicable to our context. I began comparing the very general fidelity assurance of Thomas and Collier's three non-negotiables with the very comprehensive *Guiding Principles*. I saw overlap in the two tools: the three non-negotiables were encompassed in the *Principles*, but the rubrics offered a much better job of articulating evidence. I decided to engage the SMCS teachers in a hands-on activity, where we would work together to identify evidence that their practices were indeed in the exemplary range of the rubrics.

The implementation team embraced the process using Thomas and Collier's first non-negotiable, that at least 50 percent of instruction be taught in the partner language. They saw that this aligned with the program model in the *Guiding Principles*. We recognized that this was something that we had spelled out years before in our TWI team planning guide, but realized this was not something that we carefully monitored. Asking teachers to calculate their instructional minutes proved to be quite difficult and time-consuming, but the final results came in the form of a clear pie chart for each grade level (see figure 4.1). The process of inputting the number of minutes into a

FIGURE 4.1

Time allocations by language

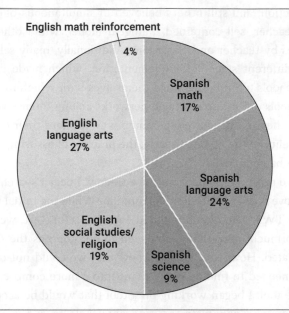

English math reinforcement

4%

Spanish math
17%

English language arts
27%

Spanish language arts
24%

English social studies/ religion
19%

Spanish science
9%

spreadsheet and then clicking the button to turn it into a pie chart allowed grade levels to continue to play with the minutes in order to get the chart to show 50 percent English and 50 percent Spanish instruction. However, once completed, these grade-level pie charts gave the SMCS program legitimacy and also held the teachers accountable to the selected model.

Once the pie chart was complete, we turned to the next two non-negotiables from Thomas and Collier, then consulted the guidance articulated in the *Guiding Principles*. The second non-negotiable, the separation of languages, led to intense discussions for the SMCS implementation team. This required teachers to not only look at how the program was set up (one self-contained teacher versus two team teachers) but also consider their use of translation during instruction. Ultimately, a two-teacher model was established to make it easier for one teacher to focus on certain subject areas in English and the other to do the same in Spanish. The teachers also chose to interpret the "separation of languages" so that the Spanish teacher would consistently use Spanish in the classroom and around the school while the English teacher would likewise use only English at all times and in all contexts. Through this process, the teachers and principal created meaningful and workable fidelity assurances that enabled them to strengthen their program.

Moving Fidelity Assurances Through Strategic and Scaffolded Networks

By the 2014–15 academic year, SMCS had implemented TWI in the K–4 grades. The implementation team had worked through the questions that had percolated at the summer academy the previous year during conversations with other school teams and had continued to refine their fidelity assurances. We had studied the nine assurances and decided to add one more assurance related to the National Standards and Benchmarks for Effective Catholic Schools to make the total number ten.[20] As the mentor to SMCS, I suggested that if the implementation team committed to focusing on one fidelity assurance topic per month, the task of providing evidence would not feel as overwhelming. The team also noticed that six of the assurances were tailored more for teachers and the remaining four spoke more to administration. This made the process even more manageable. The design team took notice of this guided approach during its monthly consultation calls and asked SMCS to present a fidelity assurances workshop at the 2015 summer academy. This evidence-based approach to fidelity assurances, while simpler than the guiding principles, resonated with many other TWIN-CS schools that needed a simpler starting point for defining their model and organizing their professional development around an initial framework. (see figure 4.2).

SMCS learned to value the scaffolded networks that were created and developed within TWIN-CS peer institutions at the summer academies. Back in Arizona, SMCS joined yet another regional network of dual language schools. A federal Office of English Language Acquisition grant called the Teachers of Language Learners Learning Community, based at Mesa Community College, started a network of Arizona dual language immersion institutions that refined and further pushed ten fidelity assurances out to schools that were looking for an implementation guidance tool. This exposed SMCS

71

FIGURE 4.2
Handout for implementation team on ten fidelity assurances

1 INSTRUCTIONAL MODEL	2 TEACHER MODEL	3 TEACHER PARTNER LANGUAGE USE	4 STUDENT PARTNER LANGUAGE USE	5 TEACHER COLLABORATION PLAN
■ Identify your model as 90/10, 80/20, or 50/50 ■ Make a visual (e.g., pie chart) ■ Develop clear goals ■ Set performance towards proficiency targets for each grade level ■ Align to partner language report card	■ Identify your model with one teacher (teaching both languages) or two teachers (separate languages) ■ Set standards for hiring regarding minimum proficiency levels as well as literacy	■ 100% partner language usage in class ■ 100% partner language usage outside of class (when children are present) ■ Both languages are valued equally throughout school (e.g., bilingual signage, announcements)	■ Develop clear expectations per grade level for students to use the partner language in the classroom with the teachers as well as with other students in the class	■ Establish daily/ weekly planning time for teachers (especially team teachers) ■ Establish parameters for reinforcement of academic content from one language to the other (sometimes identified as "bridging")

6 PROFESSIONAL DEVELOPMENT PLAN	7 ADMINISTRATION COMMITMENT *(School & District Level)*	8 OPEN ENROLLMENT FOR ALL	9 COMMUNITY EDUCATION AND MARKETING PLAN	10 *For SMCS only:* CATHOLIC IDENTITY *(Western Catholic Educational Association)*
■ TWIN-CS Webinars ■ Conferences (e.g., local, state, national international) ■ Workshops ■ Networking opportunities ■ Visits to other TWI schools ■ Book talks ■ Teacher share days	■ Identify learning opportunities for administrators regarding TWI ■ Start to meet about vertical articulation ■ Review annual evidence of fidelity assurances as a school ■ Provide regular programmatic updates to administration and stakeholders	■ Articulate a clear and consistent enrollment policy (e.g., lotteries, first come first serve) ■ Establish a late entry procedure including what support looks like) ■ Include special needs students while respecting the pull-out time during the partner language	■ Invite stakeholders for visitation and tour days (have student ambassadors lead) ■ Publish a parent education calendar for different topics and student showcase events ■ Conduct stakeholder surveys for program quality	■ Catechetics: Clear Catholic teaching ■ Worship opportunities in two languages ■ Participation in the Sacraments ■ Evangelization and Service

to even more schools that were interested in the same change process and helped the dual language immersion community in Arizona begin to use similar terminology and fidelity assurances, and networking began yielding more positive results.

Once a school has implemented TWI in over 50 percent of its classrooms, it moves into the final stage of full implementation. This is the case with SMCS, currently in its tenth year of implementation and seventh year with TWIN-CS. SMCS continues to refine its fidelity assurance instruments and processes to systematize the program, resulting in concomitant gains in enrollment, student learning outcomes, and student and parent satisfaction. Continuing to look back at these instruments with a reflective lens is the hard work of this stage, because TWI and school in general seem to be moving along so smoothly. Asking the key question of *what evidence do we have to support each assurance?* might seem redundant at this stage but is a necessary one. Now that the SMCS implementation team has progressed through all four implementation stages with an increasingly complex set of fidelity assurances, they are giving back to the TWIN-CS organization by coaching other schools that are in the exploration, installation, or even initial implementation stages. Their efforts include webinars, mentoring, blog posts, summer academy presentations, and networking. This is a testament to the scaffolded networks behind TWIN-CS schools that continue to push the field into new and better evaluation cycles.

ASSURING MODEL FIDELITY ACROSS CONTEXTS

The journey toward culturally and linguistically responsive schooling is complex. The key to leading this journey is the practice of assuring model fidelity as defined by a school's context. I began this chapter describing the process of selecting a model, establishing fidelity assurances, and progressing through stages of implementation. I then drew from my experiences as a mentor in TWIN-CS to illustrate these points. In this final section, I discuss how assuring model fidelity applies across other contexts.

The central lesson here is that the practice of assuring model fidelity is a personalized, dynamic, and ongoing process. SMCS began with one tool to scaffold fidelity assurance—the TWI team planning guide. At the time, this served a purpose in helping the teachers coordinate the initial implementation at the teacher team level. However, over time, as the school community became more comfortable with the implementation process, it was open to developing and refining its tools. Moreover, the SMCS implementation team has agency in this process of development. Building from different resources, they have designed their own fidelity assurances for their context. Educational leaders in other contexts show similar agency. An example of a school district in the full implementation stage is Seattle Public Schools, boasting twenty years of experience with one-way and two-way language immersion programs. International education administrator Michele Aoki crosswalked fidelity assurances being used across the United States and developed a set specific to Seattle. Furthermore, in 2016, the establishment of a task force to "gather, analyze, review and consider information and data and to prepare a report to the Superintendent of Schools . . . to make recommendations to the School Board" for future changes showed their deep commitment to fidelity to evidence-based outcomes.[21]

In this dynamic process of defining and refining fidelity assurances, educational leaders across contexts need to draw evidence from diverse sources. One of the lessons learned from the Arizona English-only story was the importance of being able to articulate how well students were progressing in their English- and Spanish-language development. To accomplish this, I facilitated professional development that helped teachers set initial proficiency targets within the SMCS program. Two-way programs can find this especially challenging given the wide range of language proficiencies that students possess, and SMCS was no exception. Consequently, the implementation team decided to set a minimum target that everyone at a grade level needed to reach and to then address the need to differentiate for those who only approached the target as well as those who exceeded it. The same approach was created for English-proficiency targets. Teachers began to have a common language to discuss students' linguistic progress. They could all bring writing samples, and as a school team we could engage in inter-rater reliability work, which in turn assisted our vertical articulation process. Not surprisingly, parents began to appreciate getting more meaningful feedback about what students could do in the language from a developmental perspective.

Finally, this process of developing and refining ways to assure fidelity need not be a solitary endeavor, but one that is assisted through networking. The TWIN-CS design team led SMCS to *Guiding Principles,* which provides much more sophisticated tools than the implementation team guide with which they had started. While SMCS developed scaffolded networks nearby, TWIN-CS became a lifeline outside of Arizona for SMCS. Being able to connect during the school year with other TWIN-CS members through webinars, online contact, and the summer academy propelled their movement toward full implementation as they rolled their program up one grade level per year. Starting with simple non-negotiables, shared terminology, and evidence-based practices, they slowly evolved to becoming a TWI school.

Whether a school is ready to use a sophisticated guide or a simplified version more suited to initial conversations, identifying instruments and networking with others using those same instruments is key. Today, additional versions of fidelity assurances are appearing as evidence-based outcomes become a standard expectation. Organizations and entire states are taking existing versions of fidelity assurances and adapting them to their own individual contexts. The concluding factor is to identify some type of foundational pillars that can support a successful program for a culturally and linguistically diverse school. Turning those pillars into a set of fidelity assurances sends a message that those key features are important and need to be continually revisited as the model evolves through the different stages of implementation. No school or organization will progress through transformation at the same pace and manner, but assuring fidelity to the model will keep them focused on the ultimate goal of delivering high-quality culturally and linguistically responsive programs to all students.

Leveraging Networks for Coordinated Professional Development

BRIDGET YADEN

AS SCHOOLS STRIVE to be culturally and linguistically responsive—whether by taking on a new service delivery model or by working toward improving their current one—consistent, high-quality, and accessible professional development (PD) is key to success. In this chapter, I illustrate the practice of coordinated PD, featuring a variety of purposefully planned, ongoing PD options offered to the network's staff throughout the year. I explore how these efforts affect organizational learning to support culturally and linguistically responsive schools. As a university professor who trains preservice teachers and provides workshops and courses for educators around the country, I know the value of PD. However, I have seen firsthand how isolated, impractical, and disconnected the learning can often be, limiting its impact on teaching and learning. As a mentor in the Two-Way Immersion Network for Catholic Schools (TWIN-CS), I have seen how coordinated PD through the network helps teachers integrate and apply the learning more directly in the classroom. Drawing from my experiences, I show how PD both within our school and across schools in the network affects organizational learning, with a specific example of how it positively influences instructional practices around assessment of language proficiency. I first discuss coordinated PD in the broader context of culturally and linguistically responsive schools. Next, I describe the practice of coordinated PD through TWIN-CS and how, in our particular case study, the PD helped improve assessment practices around multilingual language assessment. Finally, I discuss implications of our experiences for other educational contexts.

PROFESSIONAL DEVELOPMENT AND ORGANIZATIONAL LEARNING

Highly effective educational programs are committed to ongoing learning and reflection in order to improve. However, many barriers inhibit the knowledge and skills educators build in PD and therefore their ability to transfer this knowledge into meaningful changes in their classrooms and schools. Kennedy describes this as a problem of enactment: "PD programs typically meet with teachers *outside* of their classrooms to talk about teaching, yet they expect their words to alter teachers' behaviors *inside* the classroom."[1] As Kennedy asserts, "in an era in which teachers receive numerous messages about what they should be doing and in which these messages compete for teachers' attention . . . [w]e need to ensure that PD promotes real learning rather than merely adding more noise to their working environment."[2] In a similar vein, Gulamhussein explains that "teachers' greatest challenge comes when they attempt to implement newly learned methods into the classroom. In all forms of learning a new skill, mere knowledge of it, is never as difficult as its implementation."[3]

Complicating the process of transferring learning from PD contexts back to changes in classroom practices is the challenge of cost. While it is tempting to focus on direct monetary costs (e.g., travel expenses, registration fees), time may in fact pose the largest cost of PD for educational leaders to consider. This cost directly relates to the problem of transfer, since the "ideal structure for ongoing professional development is to provide teachers time embedded in the school day."[4] Hence, PD that is most likely to transfer also poses the highest cost to deliver, as it can involve release time for teachers and substitute teachers for the classroom.

However, the practices described in this chapter, such as local workshops, live and recorded webinars, and reading groups, address these challenges innovatively. They provide teachers time to share based on their own experiences, while at the same time reducing costs both in terms of time and travel. Some network-provided PD occurs outside of normal teaching hours yet optimizes transfer by serving as both a learning opportunity and a kind of accountability measure. Thus, coordinated PD can minimize the challenges and draw from practitioners' experiences to advance professional learning that leads to culturally and linguistically responsive teaching practices.

Networking

Ample research shows how organizational learning helps participating members create and apply knowledge to improve practices.[5] Participating in a network can ensure a cycle of continuous learning, foster collective inquiry, and lead to practical application of the learning.[6] Networked learning models inclusivity, as it involves all participants. Bryk and colleagues describe how broad participation "opens up numerous opportunities for individual members to engage with its problem-solving mission."[7] Networking supports intentional learning among similarly minded schools.

Networked learning helps address the challenges of PD when it leads to intentional coordination. This coordination creates opportunities for educators to critically reflect on their current practices and discover opportunities to improve. Such improvement requires that educators bring a growth mindset, both to strengthen their systems and practices for student learning and to model this improvement process for their students.

Tools can help school leaders in this coordination. Howard and colleagues describe a principle of culturally and linguistically responsive schools as "provid[ing] high-quality professional development that is tailored to the needs of dual language educators and support staff."[8] Toward this end, they provide a detailed self-assessment rubric that schools can use to check their effectiveness in many areas, including PD. They describe how an exemplary program in our particular model (two-way immersion, or TWI) includes "a variety of professional development opportunities (e.g., workshops, conferences, peer mentoring, peer observations, critical friends groups, book study groups)." In addition, they identify that in high-quality programs, "staff engage in outreach opportunities within and beyond the district to learn from and support other dual language programs regarding approaches for fostering staff learning and autonomy."[9]

Culturally and linguistically responsive teaching is a must for schools to survive and thrive today, and networked practices of learning to improve and supporting PD can provide the structures to make this happen in any educational setting.[10] I now turn to share my experiences, reflecting on how such practices are supported through and are integral to the success of the structured network of TWIN-CS.[11]

COORDINATED PROFESSIONAL DEVELOPMENT

A key practice of transformation—as illustrated in TWIN-CS—is advancing organizational learning through coordinated PD. As a structured network of schools with similar educational missions, enacting two-way language immersion to support culturally and linguistically diverse student populations, TWIN-CS provides multiple opportunities to engage in this practice. I participate in TWIN-CS as a mentor at Holy Rosary Bilingual Academy (HRBA) in Tacoma, Washington, which has been a member of TWIN-CS since the beginning, in 2012. HRBA's trajectory in PD is one common to many learning communities across TWIN-CS.

HRBA first developed a committee that included administrators, teachers, community members, and parents to begin planning for a new educational model that would attract families looking for high-quality education and boost enrollments to keep the school sustainable. At that time, the committee decided to move from a traditional monolingual school to a two-way Spanish-English immersion program. While we were in the early stages of this major program and curriculum overhaul, we learned of TWIN-CS. Members of the committee—which would become our official implementation team—attended the first summer academy and have participated in the network ever since.

As TWIN-CS schools are at different stages in the change process, we bring varying perspectives and learn to improve together and from each other. In this section, I describe how my work as a mentor coordinating PD at HRBA and through TWIN-CS has affected practices—namely, language assessment—that support our culturally and linguistically diverse school. I describe the various PD opportunities that are facilitated by the TWIN-CS design team, first by describing in detail the annual face-to-face summer academy. I then describe a variety of coordinated PD opportunities throughout the school year that keep the momentum of the academy going, such as on-site workshops, regular webinars, direct consultations by mentors in school-based PD, and book studies. For each PD opportunity, I summarize the experiences and outline some limitations. Finally, I share the story of how HRBA directly benefited from coordinated PD opportunities, as an example of how educational leaders seeking to support culturally and linguistically diverse schools in other contexts can apply their learning.

TWIN-CS Summer Academy

The annual summer academy is the main event in TWIN-CS promoting coordinated PD.[12] This is a face-to-face event, lasting four to five days, in a retreat center near the network's home institution of Boston College. The academy is one example of scaffolding communities of practice, combining time for teachers and principals to work together, networking with colleagues as well as with outside experts. This kind of foundational experience within a network of practitioners can provide focused, relevant, and participant-centered organizational learning in a face-to-face environment that also builds trust and social capital within the network.

School teams who attend the academy invest a great deal of time and money, so in order for the learning to be relevant and focused, the design team plans for the academy carefully throughout the year. The planners take into consideration participant surveys from previous years and listen to participants' questions and needs throughout the year. The academy has provided space for participants to engage in guided reflection on topics that they deem important, such as data analysis to support systems changes. Participants also learn from other member schools' experiences, sharing as critical, but not competitive, friends. In this way, over the years, the academy has served as a scaffolded "data retreat" experience of sorts. Our team analyzes assessment data at the academy and consults with assessment experts to interpret the data. Such data sharing can be incredibly productive to advance organizational learning. Our school's team, for example, learned both practical tips for conducting specific language assessments and ways to use the results to make systems changes, including curriculum and program design changes. As Bryk and colleagues describe, "comparing one's results to those of others can create a sense of moral urgency—if others can accomplish this, we can and should be able to do better too. This positive response stands in sharp contrast to the defensiveness that comparative data tend to generate in high-stakes accountability contexts."[13]

As coordinated PD, the academy serves as a space to facilitate the sharing of ideas among people from diverse contexts. Participants, including our own teachers, share ideas from other professional conferences and workshops they have attended as well, incorporating outside expertise and experiences to strengthen the learning. Mentors like me support the PD of our school as well as of schools across the network of TWIN-CS by brokering connections to other organizations and resources. For example, as a mentor, at the academy a few years ago I shared my involvement in world language proficiency assessment, describing a project that allows students to earn competency-based credits on their high school transcript. Having attended several national workshops on language assessments, I was able to incorporate this outside expertise into the academy. Sharing experiences at the academy laid the foundation as the HRBA implementation team crafted our own assessment plan, which we piloted for two years, shared across the network, and now have fully implemented during the last two years.

In addition to providing time, space, and guidance for narrowly focusing on areas such as bilingual assessment, the academy also provokes creative thinking. For instance, there is time for hands-on exploration and learning that is called *makerspace*, a collaborative workspace where participants can try out new physical tools and digital and print resources, and experiment with various materials such as sample assessments and curriculum sets. PD that provides this kind of engagement with the material makes the learning immediately applicable. Creativity is also fostered via the many opportunities for socializing, which strengthen relationships and trust across the network. These opportunities are often semistructured, such as field trips and scavenger hunts in town, as well as cultural events including salsa dancing lessons and calligraphy. One teacher who has participated in the network since the beginning described the value of this type of networking:

> The TWIN network gave us the opportunity to meet with other schools that were starting up their two-way immersion programs at their schools. We were able to share how to promote the program to our school community and look at curriculum options for the different grade levels rolling out the program. We were also able to listen and learn from experts in the field with the latest research on second language acquisition.[14]

At the end of each day of learning, the academy builds in bridging time where groups of teams come together, share, and reflect on the learning of the day.

Opportunities for coordinated partnerships among members of the network directly grow from the academy. Through the community built during the academy, participants make social and professional connections that then facilitate more effective and interactive face-to-face PD opportunities throughout the school year at both the local and regional levels. For example, HRBA teachers were able to get to know well the staff from the only other network school in our state, which is about forty miles from our school. Building on social and professional relationships forged during the academy, we have come together for face-to-face PD when schedules have allowed, mainly on the topic of assessment. This has allowed colleagues at both schools to leverage a wealth of expertise.

In these ways the academy has helped HRBA—and other member schools—foster trust among a community of learners that maximizes participation and engagement. The TWIN-CS design team insists that schools send teams to the academy, not just administrators or individual teachers. Although this can be a challenge given budget constrictions, travel time, and schedules, the intention behind this requirement is that upon returning to their schools, participants share their learning with others so that it transfers to truly influence teaching and learning.

In addition to improving our networking within TWIN-CS, in my role as mentor I have also seen participants benefit from bridging with schools and organizations from outside TWIN-CS, including other schools implementing

TWI as well as language teacher organizations. For example, our HRBA teachers have collaborated with a local public TWI program by sending a team to the school as well as hosting a team visit to our school to explore and share program models, staffing, and curriculum. From my perspective, the coordinated PD that is modeled within TWIN-CS provides a springboard for other learning and growth opportunities outside of the network.

These coordinated partnerships in PD—both within TWIN-CS and beyond—have helped shift HRBA educators from being only receivers of the PD learning to becoming providers of it as well. An important example of this was the opportunity for our implementation team to share their bilingual assessment work at a national bilingual education conference outside of TWIN-CS. We received great questions and feedback from bilingual teachers from around the country who attended our session, which cycled back into our improved thinking about assessment going forward. We have presented on our program at local world language and national bilingual conferences, with a specific emphasis on our assessment work. In addition, our teachers have expanded their PD opportunities by participating in these conferences and others. In turn, we have become PD providers to TWIN-CS by facilitating a webinar and sessions at the academy. As these examples demonstrate, coordinated PD through the network has led to both structured and serendipitous opportunities for growth and improvement.

While the academy has many strengths, it still confronts the two challenges of PD described at the beginning of this chapter: transfer and cost. Implementation team members can come back from the summer academy with lots of great ideas and feel inspired and ready to implement them. However, we can often lose momentum as we strive to transfer that knowledge and apply our learning to actionable work. In addition, member schools have limited financial resources to support participation in the PD offered at the academy. TWIN-CS schools are private Catholic schools that depend heavily on tuition yet strive to be accessible to all students, regardless of their ability to pay. Although the design team works hard to keep costs down, travel to the academy can be a financial burden on already tight school budgets.

The academy can also improve by more fully supporting bilingualism and biliteracy among the educators, as the bilingual capacity of our members has not been harnessed to its fullest. For instance, despite the fact that many of the administrators, teachers, mentors, and other staff attending the academy are bilingual (English-Spanish or English-Mandarin), we dedicate little time to providing bilingual PD. Although year by year the amount of bilingualism in the PD at the academy has risen, this remains an area that can continue to improve. We need to model multilingualism more regularly and normalize it in order to truly be examples of culturally and linguistically diverse educators.

As described in this section, the academy provides coordinated PD that is focused, relevant, and participant-centered. This PD is the springboard for a wide variety of other coordinated PD opportunities throughout the school year, to which we now turn. These varied opportunities address the challenges of transfer and cost associated with the summer academy but also serve as tools to keep the learning momentum going, to produce actual implementation of the learning, and to inspire changes in practices to support culturally and linguistically diverse schools.

Strategies for Maintaining Momentum

Clearly, a powerful experience like the academy contributes to coordinating PD in a manner that advances organizational learning. However, a central challenge of PD design is the difficulty of maintaining momentum and transferring learning into changes in curriculum, instruction, and assessment. The TWIN-CS design team addresses this by providing infrastructure and accountability measures throughout the entire school year. In this section, I describe tools for fostering and facilitating collaboration within and across our communities of practice. Some have been more effective than others in coordinating PD to advance learning and systems changes. The opportunities for PD and the technological tools described here could be piloted and used by any educational network hoping to strengthen PD through expanded choices and opportunities for learning. The more resources and tools we utilize, the more effective we will be in meeting different learning styles and needs for the culturally and linguistically diverse teachers in our network.

Webinars

One way in which TWIN-CS coordinates and sustains PD through the year is through free monthly webinars. Topics for webinars range widely and often stem from themes presented during the academy, from the big picture (e.g., "Improving Systems") to the cultural (e.g., "Catholic Identity," "Bilingual and Bicultural Holiday Celebration Ideas") to the nuts and bolts of teaching and learning (e.g., "Assessment," "Data Driven Instruction"). Webinars are offered at different times, and since PD is more effective when the educators participate collaboratively, member schools are encouraged to watch the webinars with teams of teachers, administrators, and their mentors. All webinars are recorded so that participants can watch afterward if they are unable to participate live.

The TWIN-CS design team has encountered several hurdles that inhibit the efficacy of webinar tools. For instance, various video-conferencing tools (such as Adobe Connect and Zoom) differ in the ease of access to live and recorded workshops that they provide. Another challenge has been finding a time that works for most participants. Member schools have different schedules and are spread across four time zones. For our school on the West Coast, for example, the majority of the webinars were originally scheduled in the middle of the school day (1:00 pm), so teachers could not participate live unless substitute teachers could cover their classes. In response, the design team has experimented with different times and held regional webinars. Currently each webinar is repeated four times, providing teams with multiple options for participation.

An opportunity for TWIN-CS webinars to more effectively coordinate PD that advances organizational learning for culturally and linguistically responsive schools is to incorporate more fully the linguistic assets within the network. TWIN-CS teachers, mentors, and principals who are bilingual could offer full webinars entirely in the non-English language, rather than just allowing for questions or clarification in that language if needed. Such a coordinated approach might help teachers who speak English as a second language feel even more welcomed and valued to both participate and access resources in their native languages. This would also affirm their roles as leaders who provide valuable insight and learning to the network.

In sum, webinars are a key tool for coordinating and sustaining PD through the year, serving as an example of how, according to Bryk and colleagues, effective networks "nurture social capital across the network."[15] This is important because, as these authors observed, as network participants "come to know, respect, and trust one another, they are more likely to adopt the innovations of their colleagues and test and refine these innovations in their own contexts."[16] These multilingual practices are central to transforming to a culturally and linguistically responsive school and network.

Design team infrastructure and support

In addition to the regular webinars, the design team provides a host of infrastructure and support to foster learning and systems improvement. It has leveraged cloud tools to promote participant-developed resources, many of which are first started during the academy and then expanded during the school year. Member schools share curriculum ideas and lesson plans through a shared cloud drive during the year. During webinars, implementation teams often use a Google Doc to collaboratively keep notes and share ideas for future reference.

The design team maintains a website with a password-protected "Resources for Member Schools" section. This contains presentations, documents, and recordings from both the academy and webinars, so that those who cannot attend the academy or those who miss a webinar can easily access these high-quality learning resources. These resources move beyond PD and include tools for parent engagement and marketing of our schools. The website has expanded its non-password-protected area to include a resources library for parents, superintendents, and network supporters.

As the number of culturally and linguistically diverse TWIN-CS schools has grown, the design team has worked to hire more staff who are bilingual and who have experience with TWI. Networks such as ours should strive to, as best they can, align their goals with their hiring profiles both to model the cultural and linguistic diversity we support and to provide the most experienced experts to the network as a resource. The network strives to be more intentional in developing and designating resources that are in the non-English languages spoken by its members (currently, Spanish and Mandarin).

Book study is a tool that the design team has leveraged for PD. We were all provided with a copy of Bryk and colleague's *Learning to Improve* during an academy a few years ago, and then during that school year we had an on-site book study that was supplemented with network webinars. Our school team that had attended the academy met monthly, and each month a different team member took the lead on one chapter. That member first facilitated a discussion of the content of the chapter and then encouraged the team to apply the ideas to specific issues at our school. We came away with a deeper understanding of the systems at our school and how to develop problem-specific and user-centered solutions. In particular, we focused on issues of gaps in assessments. Subsequently, we had a network book study of Howard and colleagues' *Guiding Principles for Dual Language Education.*[17] During the school year, we had network-wide webinar discussions of the text. At the following academy, we were honored to have presentations in person by one of the authors (Dr. Liz Howard). We had the opportunity to sign up for consultations with her, and we were each given a digital copy of the newest edition of her book. This book provides a detailed rubric for program self-assessment, which is aligned with the specific goals and mission of our school's academic program. As a result of our in-depth exploration of this book, we established the goal of focusing on one principle each year. Thanks to this particular book study, which is specific to our educational context (TWI), HRBA has been able to set program goals and assess our curriculum, which has also been very helpful in accreditation and regular program review.

More recently, the design team has started a blog that serves as yet another tool for networked PD. Blogs, by their nature, are written in a more personal tone, are often shorter, and can come out on a regular basis. In fact, the blog currently has a new post almost daily. It often provides updates and news regarding the academy and other coordinated PD opportunities, but it is also used regularly to push PD tidbits related to TWI out to participants, such as short TED Talks and links to other blog posts. Different members of the network, such as mentors, principals, and teachers, are invited to contribute to the blog.

Networked peer mentors

Formal and informal mentoring is another way to coordinate PD to advance organizational learning. TWIN-CS mentors directly support the coordination of PD and advance organizational learning in their member schools. At the beginning of each school year, the mentor meets with the principal and outlines a plan for the year, articulating program target areas and objectives for the mentor-school partnership. This plan is then submitted to the design team for approval. At the end of the year, the mentor provides a brief report on the achievements relative to the goals. The mentors attend the academy with their teams, where they also have time to network with other mentors.

These mentors, as outside facilitators and coaches who do not have the evaluative function of a principal, help reduce the perceived risks among the staff for trying something new or asking questions. In other words, they can serve as critical friends to support organizational learning and improved systems. I have found that connections among mentors across TWIN-CS provide additional opportunities to advance organizational learning, as we share our knowledge and experiences with each other that we then bring back to our individual schools. For instance, the official mentors in the network set up an Edmodo site after one academy so that we could have a collaborative space to post questions and share resources. This is a tool that has the features of a social networking site but is specifically designed for educators. This tool can be set up for functional specialization, such as groups interested in assessment or lesson planning, or it can be set up by categorical specialization, such as a group for mentors (as we tried), principals, grade-level teachers, and/or language-specific teachers.

In recent years, the design team has increased support and infrastructure for the mentors. For example, mentors now have monthly check-ins with the design team to provide updates on progress toward goals as well as to ask questions and request support from the network that will affect the individual schools. Principals have similar check-ins with the design team.

THE STORY OF HOLY ROSARY
BILINGUAL ACADEMY

The story of HRBA illustrates how networking has promoted organizational learning. Coordinated PD opportunities begun at the academy and then extended during the year have led to improved Spanish oral and literacy outcomes. Our story, and in particular our bilingual assessment work, serves as an example to any group of educators as to the value of coordinated PD through a network. In this section, I first describe the coordinated network PD opportunities, both formal and informal, that inspired and informed the changes we made at HRBA. I then describe the assessment outcomes that resulted from those changes.

During our first year at the academy, our implementation team attended sessions led by national experts in the area of assessment. The team engaged in many informal opportunities to talk to other schools similar to ours and hear what they were doing (and not doing) with regard to assessment. This helped us develop—alongside our colleagues in other schools—what Bryk and colleagues call "common language and measures to enable social learning," which are "essential for coordinated improvement in complex systems" like schools.[18] For several years the implementation team at HRBA struggled to apply the initial bilingual assessment tool provided by TWIN-CS. Then, an informal lunch conversation at the academy with colleagues from other member schools spurred ideas for trying out new bilingual assessments at several schools in the network. Returning from the Academy, our school continued the conversation with the other member schools in our state, which led to organizing a shared on-site workshop on bilingual assessment. We followed this with phone consultations with other TWIN-CS mentors. As the HRBA mentor, I worked with the principal and staff to develop a Spanish assessment plan, and we piloted a new bilingual assessment tool. I then facilitated a webinar for all of TWIN-CS on our work. This shows how a nascent idea from one school can be developed at the academy and then eventually take off during the coordinated opportunities through the school year.

I have seen how the academy positively and directly affected HRBA's practices supporting culturally and linguistically diverse students, particularly in the area of bilingual assessment. At HRBA, using the assessment plan we developed and the tools we learned about through TWIN-CS, we first assessed the Spanish listening and speaking proficiency of our students using the AAPPL exam (the American Council on the Teaching of Foreign Languages [ACTFL] Assessment of Performance Toward Proficiency in Languages). This was an exam we learned about through TWIN-CS, which other member schools had also piloted. We had mixed results (based on the ACTFL Proficiency Guidelines). The older students had lower results relative to our proficiency goals, as these were the grades for which we experimented with and changed the program model, based in part on models we learned about in TWIN-CS. The younger students had better results, and this can be attributed to the intentional program changes we made, such as adding all-day 100 percent Spanish immersion programs for preK three- and four-year-olds, changing kindergarten from 50/50 (Spanish-English) to 90/10 (Spanish-English), and moving to a language-of-the-day model in which students spend all day in all subject matters in one language, then the next day in all subject areas in the partner language.

In addition to the program model changes described above, we made other improvements based on our first year of Spanish proficiency assessment results. By administering this proficiency test, teachers started to think differently and more intentionally about teaching toward proficiency. I provided a PD workshop on the first round of results and how the results inform instruction. Teachers began to include more opportunities and strategies for students to advance in their proficiency, such as regular thirty-second turn-and-talks to a partner, practice asking for and requesting clarification, and short freewriting and journal writing on a variety of both academic and non-academic topics.

We also learned through TWIN-CS to be intentional about sharing results with parents. We developed a template in Microsoft Word and used the mail-merge tool to import the data from Microsoft Excel. The letter included the student's proficiency score, the entire grade's scores, a narrative describing what the student can do at that level, how parents can support students in moving to the next proficiency level, and who to contact if they have more questions.

This assessment work, inspired and facilitated by the network, led to improved systems in our program model design. The assessment data for Spanish pointed to some linguistic gaps that needed to be remedied. We learned through other schools about different program models that they had tried, which informed our work as we changed our model to increase the amount of Spanish instruction in the earlier grades. These model changes, we believe, have led to improved assessment results, with demonstrable increases in written and oral proficiency in Spanish by both our native and non-native speakers. We benefited from the structure of the network "in which participants engage in disciplined inquiry that supports both individual and collective improvement."[19]

The network has provided a wealth of opportunities for PD in many formats over the years, and these opportunities could be duplicated within any new or continuing network of schools. Specifically, the academy, design team support (including webinars), mentors, and coordinated PD advanced organizational learning. As the assessment examples above have demonstrated, this sustained and articulated PD resulted in organizational learning as demonstrated by improved assessment practices and higher language and literacy outcomes on a variety of assessments at our own school.

IMPLICATIONS FOR EDUCATIONAL LEADERS ACROSS SECTORS

In this chapter, I have described a variety of practices of coordinated PD in TWIN-CS that support and advance our culturally and linguistically diverse educational communities. In this final section, I discuss implications of this for educational leaders across sectors. Whether looking to improve an existing program to serve emergent bilinguals or to completely transform a learning community, coordinated PD is an essential component of success. Networked learning can accelerate learning through the networked communities, as Bryk and colleagues describe: "When many more individuals, operating across diverse contexts, are drawn together in a shared learning enterprise, the capacity grows exponentially."[20] Clearly, member schools have benefitted from the coordinated PD that is facilitated through TWIN-CS. At HRBA, our participation in the network has led to improved assessment practices, particularly related to assessment of our non-English language. This assessment is a specific need of a TWI program, which is why our membership in a network that has a shared academic goal is an effective resource for PD.

Coordinated PD in a network is not without barriers. But these barriers are not insurmountable challenges as long as they are recognized and discussed will full transparency in mind. In fact, through the power of the network, answers to solving the inevitable challenges can be developed by the members themselves.

Any network of educators interested in PD that can lead to systems changes can learn from the examples and models described in this chapter, including face-to-face academies and workshops, webinars, peer mentors, book studies, and design team support. For example, the summer academy provides an opportunity to build relationships and share knowledge from experts and peers in a powerful setting. A variety of PD opportunities throughout the year that branch from the foundational summer academy maintain the momentum and support the continued learning throughout the network.

Educational leaders can use strategic and scaffolded networking to apply these practices of coordinated PD in their specific educational contexts (i.e., non-TWI, non-Catholic, secondary). In the case of HRBA, the networked learning in TWIN-CS advanced coordinated PD with a particular focus on improving assessment practices, which contributed to stronger Spanish proficiency and literacy. For culturally and linguistically responsive schools, high-quality, consistent, timely, and applicable PD is a key factor of success.

6

Building Teacher Capacity
Using Critical Reflection

MARGARITA GÓMEZ ZISSELSBERGER
AND GLORIA RAMOS GONZÁLEZ

BUILDING TEACHER CAPACITY is about teachers examining their learning, then transferring their new knowledge into practice for the benefit of their students' growth.[1] This complex process requires that teachers be cognitively and emotionally invested, and willing to grow as educators. Teachers learn through critically reflecting on their beliefs and practices, then exploring strategies for improvement. Hence, a positive school culture conducive to ongoing reflection and focused on the learning needs of teachers and students is imperative for the development of culturally and linguistically responsive schools.

One way to conceptualize this process is in the form of reflective cycles. Reflective cycles call teachers to be more thoughtful about their practice. In *Teach, Reflect, Learn,* Hall and Simeral note the stages in a reflective cycle: an awareness of teacher practices, then a call to act with intention, next an assessment of the impact of that action, and finally an evaluation of the practice.[2] This cycle invites teachers to study, experiment, and also engage in critical conversations—purposeful dialogues that address conflicts that arise when a school is embarking on a bold change.[3] Critical conversations can help build teacher capacity by providing space to reflect on working conditions, notice the influence of a school's history and staff traditions, and examine factors promoting and inhibiting students' opportunities to learn.[4] These practices allow teachers to analyze the educational needs of their student populations and the expectations of their education systems.

Building teacher capacity is important because it correlates strongly with student achievement.[5] Furthermore, developing skillful teaching practices is particularly important when working with culturally and linguistically diverse student populations, because these students frequently face additional barriers to navigating the school system. While these bilingual students bring unique knowledge and skills to the classroom, understanding how to facilitate language and literacy development requires additional knowledge from the teacher. Unfortunately, these students are often taught by teachers who are unprepared to work with them.[6] Even teachers that have completed relevant preservice training frequently report feeling ill-prepared to work with culturally and linguistically diverse students.[7]

Hence, the goal for this chapter is to present the process for and lessons learned on building teacher capacity, using two schools' efforts to improve writing for students designated as English Learners (ELs) as an example. These schools, located on opposite coasts of the United States, both belong to the Two-Way Immersion Network for Catholic Schools (TWIN-CS). Their work to collaboratively build teacher capacity around dual language writing development illustrates that as a school community grows more culturally and linguistically responsive, critical reflection can simultaneously promote student and teacher learning. We worked with the teachers in these two elementary schools to examine the writing patterns of students designated as ELs by applying a holistic bilingual lens.[8] Holistic bilingualism reflects the belief that the interaction between two or more languages uniquely contributes to the learning process as a whole rather than as separate and independent processes of each language. In this way, a person's lived experiences, abilities, and knowledge are understood as a whole. In keeping with the focus throughout this volume, this chapter explores these schools as part of the broader network of two-way immersion (TWI) Catholic schools in

TWIN-CS. We recount the process involved in building capacity to support the writing development of students designated as ELs, and share how networking contributed to the development of biliteracy instruction for linguistically marginalized students. A central point we emphasize is the professionalism of teachers as key facilitators of their own growth. To provide context, we first discuss research around building teacher capacity when educating students designated as ELs, both generally and in the specific area of writing development.

BUILDING TEACHER CAPACITY IN CULTURALLY AND LINGUISTICALLY RESPONSIVE SCHOOLS

Schools serving large populations of students designated as ELs often face multiple challenges in being culturally and linguistically responsive: building students' sociocultural competence, respecting and cultivating proficiency in home and community languages in addition to English, and promoting all students' academic achievement. This is no small feat, and often teachers are not adequately prepared to do such work.[9]

Language and literacy development entails complex and dynamic processes.[10] This is further compounded when developing two or more languages simultaneously across multiple contexts and content areas.[11] Specific knowledge of second-language acquisition and best practices to bridging between two languages is necessary for successful content-area literacy transitions. Hence, meeting the demands of culturally and linguistically diverse learners can be challenging for teachers as they navigate how to meet students' educational needs while adhering to state standards and curriculum. These are essential components to the goal of culturally and linguistically responsive schooling, in which academic achievement includes respect for cultivating the students' home and community languages in addition to English. In addition, in order to be culturally and linguistically responsive, teachers must also be able to recognize and draw on students' funds of knowledge.[12] Tapping into students' backgrounds validates students' knowledge and informs the teacher about their students' familiarity with the topic. Furthermore, building on students' background knowledge and sociocultural competence enables teachers to connect the curriculum to students' lives in relevant and meaningful ways as part of enacting culturally and linguistically responsive schooling.

Being responsive to culturally and linguistically diverse students' needs also implies scaffolding their learning as they move through various receptive and expressive language development stages (see table 6.1). During the initial stages of language development, young students in particular may receive language input in the form of stories, songs, poems, and chants, but have

TABLE 6.1

Receptive and expressive language stages in second-language acquisition

	RECEPTIVE	EXPRESSIVE
Preproduction	Listening to language input, "active listening" of new vocabulary. Use of visual aids, high-interest materials, music, movement, and artifacts.	Use of gestures. Pointing to pictures (vocabulary). Drawing pictures to communicate.
Early production	Active listening. Comprehensible input in the form of modeling language use (e.g., interactive read-alouds).	Use of one- or two-word statements. Use of yes and no questions and listing questions. Drawing and labeling to communicate written messages.
Speech emergence	Increased listening vocabulary. Use of games, music, discussions, and more complex language play to increase content-area knowledge and language use.	Use of more complex phrases and sentences and engaging in conversations about familiar topics. Writing sentences to communicate understanding.
Intermediate fluency	Demonstration of well-developed vocabulary, comprehension, and fluency. Use of choral and echo reading and read-alouds.	Reading and writing in narrative as well as expository genres. Use of more sophisticated vocabulary. Use of paragraphs and genre structures to communicate written messages.
Advanced fluency	Deep understanding of grammar, syntax, pragmatic, and semantic features of language. Development of complex content knowledge and critical literacy.	Use of more abstract language and concepts. New understandings of content-area information. Use of a variety of genres to communicate new knowledge.

Source: Josefina Villamil Tinajero and Sandra Rollins Hurley, "Assessing Progress in Second-Language Acquisition," in *Literacy Assessment of Second Language Learners*. 1st ed., edited by Sandra Rollins Hurley and Josefina Villamil Tinajero (Boston: Allyn and Bacon, 2001), 27–42.

limited expressive language. As they develop more vocabulary and exposure to the language, they are able to express more through oral and written language, but extended discourse remains one of the most complex language expressions.[13] Hence, teachers fostering bilingualism and biliteracy—such as in TWI contexts—often find it challenging to teach and effectively evaluate oral language and written expression.[14]

Because of the complexity involved in teaching and evaluating expressive language, particularly writing, building teacher capacity in the area of writing is an important goal in addressing language and literacy development. Helping teachers analyze student writing using a broader perspective creates a common understanding about simultaneous bilingual writing and can challenge monolithic language frameworks, in which one language is activated while the other is dormant.[15] Additionally, research shows that teachers have a tendency to focus on the conventions, such as spelling and punctuation, rather than on the more complex traits of writing.[16] This is evident in Hernandez's study of writing with fifth-grade students designated as ELs. The study examined the student writing and the teachers' beliefs about the writing ELs produced. Hernandez found that a teacher's perception of students designated as ELs was influenced by spelling and convention errors.[17] She found that although there were errors, the content and ideas of these students' writing were similar to those of students that spoke English as the home language. However, these perceptions impeded the placement of students designated as ELs in mainstream classrooms. Hernandez's study called for ways to expand the use of these students' home language in supporting the development of English.[18]

In a similar vein, Soltero-González, Escamilla, and Hopewell found that teachers' analysis of writing by students designated as ELs was very different from their own analysis in relation to identifying assets within the writing. Their work found that teachers' evaluation of student writing did not recognize the cross-linguistic strategies employed by ELs.[19] Thus, Soltero-González et al. identified a number of bilingual writing features from a more holistic framework of bilingualism (e.g., inter-and intra-sentential code-switching, biphonetic spelling transfer) and presented these to teachers to build a framework for assessing the writing of bilingual students. Once the teachers understood the framework and features, they were more able to identify the assets found in their bilingual students' writing.[20] Thus, the need to understand bilingualism from a holistic lens versus a parallel monolingual lens is important to building capacity with the goal of creating and sustaining culturally and linguistically responsive schools.[21]

Although bilingual programs provide instruction in English and Spanish, students designated as ELs are often perceived and assessed as a homogenous group with the same needs. Various studies have contested this notion by demonstrating that simultaneous bilingual students, those that learn two languages at the same time,[22] fall into distinct language profiles as early as kindergarten.[23] These findings demonstrate the need to provide differentiated literacy instruction and holistic assessment measures as early as kindergarten in order to meet the individual needs of students designated as ELs.

Furthermore, even in well-intentioned dual language programs, assessments may be biased by grouping native English speakers and students designated as ELs as one entity that progresses through literacy in the same way.[24] This "homogenization" of language learning does not take into account the primary language and how it influences the second language or all the language varieties that exist between being a monolingual English speaker or a monolingual Spanish speaker. Creating assessments and making instructional decisions based on a theoretical framework that positions students as either monolingual English or monolingual Spanish can create deficit perspectives about simultaneous bilinguals even within a bilingual program. Moreover, teachers may form beliefs about achievement and literacy acquisition based on an incomplete portrait of a student's literacy abilities.[25]

Using reflective cycles to build teacher capacity around holistic bilingualism and the writing process is an important facet in becoming more culturally and linguistically responsive. Understanding how learners use their entire cultural and linguistic repertoires to make meaning vis-à-vis writing has the power to change how writing is both assessed and subsequently taught. In the next section, we describe the general collaboration between two TWIN-CS member schools taking up this endeavor. We also discuss in greater detail the professional development process used at the two schools as they engage in reflective cycles to adapt and adopt culturally and linguistically responsive practices toward the teaching of writing to emerging bilinguals.

BUILDING TEACHER CAPACITY IN TWO TWIN-CS MEMBER SCHOOLS

Members of TWIN-CS have the common mission of sustaining culturally and linguistically responsive schools through a dual language service delivery model. As part of a network organizational learning is developed through professional development throughout the school year and during a week-long summer academy. We participate in this network as mentors to two of the schools on opposite coasts. Both schools have been part of the network since its inception in 2012. As mentors in this network, we have specific opportunities to work toward the learning and improvement cycles of the schools and to link common goals among schools. The complex issues surrounding bilingual writing surfaced during our mentor sessions at the 2015 TWIN-CS summer academy. We found that both our schools, Archbishop Borders Catholic School in Baltimore, Maryland, and All Souls World Language Catholic School in Alhambra, California, had teachers in need of resources in order to support their students' writing. Because of our common area of interest in professional development around writing, we decided to work together. After the TWIN-CS summer academy, we began planning how we could address our teachers' needs. We determined a shared priority was helping teachers at Archbishop Borders and All Souls move away from focusing solely on isolated skills and conventions, such as spelling, capitalization, and punctuation, toward a more holistic view of bilingualism as the research recommended.[26] We had bimonthly and later weekly check-ins to facilitate conversations and share professional development ideas across our two settings.

While both Archbishop Borders and All Souls were unique in their makeup, with differing contexts and challenges, a valuable aspect of the collaboration between our schools was identifying current dual language research and resources that could be used in the process of looking at student work. Archbishop Borders is located within an urban area and serves a racially, ethnically, and linguistically diverse community reflected in their student body. Teacher from all grade levels, kindergarten through eighth grade, were part of the professional development sessions, even though the school's Spanish-English TWI program served only kindergarten through fourth grade at the time. Grade-level teams worked together to plan instruction and discuss writing genres and plans for the year.

All Souls is located in California outside a large metropolitan area serving a community rich in racial, ethnic, and linguistic diversity. The school has two TWI language strands, Spanish-English and Mandarin-English. When this writing professional development series was initiated, teachers from transitional kindergarten through second grade worked collaboratively across strands in most subject areas through thematic planning. Most of the language arts instruction was integrated with science or social studies themes that complemented and deepened students' understanding of the content and language.

Despite these differences, as mentors we were able to serve as boundary spanners, facilitating discussions among teachers across grade levels. These conversations were based on this research and were the starting point for developing bilingual writing rubrics. These rubrics reflected an understanding of the holistic bilingual framework and genre-specific pedagogy.[27] Through this collaboration, teachers across the two school sites were able to create a common vocabulary for looking at students' narratives, in the form of informative and persuasive writing samples. The process also allowed teachers to learn about the various holistic writing strategies students designated as EL use while simultaneously acquiring two languages. After analyzing student writing samples, teachers crafted differentiated lessons based on the needs that surfaced. Teachers created common graphic organizers and drafted lesson sequences that could be used for differentiation across several grade-level spans. As mentors, we were able to share the teacher-created rubrics across schools and discuss the ideas for writing lessons.

Building teacher capacity around supporting the writing development of linguistically minoritized students and developing biliteracy evaluation tools was enhanced by TWIN-CS's involvement.[28] Teachers at our two schools had access to more research, resources, and student writing samples to further enhance the teaching and learning in their classrooms. They were also able to participate in developing evaluation tools that they could compare across member schools. The design team provided a pathway for us to develop a community of practice around bilingual writing by facilitating webinars where we shared our writing ideas with other mentors across the network.

In addition to sharing our process virtually, we were also given the opportunity to present our collaborative work at the following summer academy. Here, mentors and teachers from implementation teams across the network were able to learn about our professional development program that analyzed student writing and helped teachers create writing lessons. Having us, the mentors, facilitate the connection between the teachers at All Souls and Archbishop Borders was very effective because many of the teachers and administrators were either too new to dual immersion or too overwhelmed with daily tasks to initiate a school-wide collaboration with another school across the country. This approach to school change and program development was effective not only in encouraging collaboration but in combining resources to bring a more comprehensive understanding to their professional development sessions. What's more, we were able to use lessons learned from the TWIN-CS collaboration to present at relevant national conferences and take our work to a broader audience that also works with culturally and linguistically diverse students.

Building Capacity Around Writing Development: The Professional Development Sessions

We now turn to describe the process of professional development for the reflective cycles on the teaching of writing to students designated as ELs. Each professional development session was part of a writing lesson sequence we outlined to address the academic and sociocultural aspects of writing at each school. We focus here on the steps we used in developing sessions to best meet the writing needs of our students.

Grounding conversations in research on bilingual writing

In order to develop a common understanding of the different ideologies that guide working with students designated as ELs, our initial professional development session explored different bilingual frameworks. Through our conversations, the notion of parallel bilingualism, in which a bilingual is seen as two monolinguals, was critically analyzed and viewed as unfit to address the needs of many of our simultaneous bilinguals. During this session, we introduced contrasting theories that highlighted a more holistic perspective of bilinguals[29] and included developing broader conceptualizations of

103

simultaneous bilinguals. Teachers explored the idea of bilinguals consistently drawing on all their language resources regardless of the linguistic task. For example, we displayed student work written primarily in Spanish with the exception of one or two words that were borrowed from English, also known as intersentential code-switching.[30] Then we discussed how switching between languages within a writing piece is common when acquiring a second language. We talked about the need to honor this bilingual strategy by noting it in the writing rubric and providing feedback to the student that would help further develop their writing.

Collecting baseline data

To create a common school experience to analyze writing and see how these theories applied to a natural classroom setting, we decided as mentors to administer a narrative writing prompt for the entire school.[31] Collecting baseline data for this was important.

The first prompts were created by us, the mentors, and discussed with design team members from TWIN-CS to ensure its applicability to the writing analysis (see table 6.2). The two narrative prompts varied slightly, to ensure that students were not translating directly from one language to the other as suggested by Soltero-González and colleagues.[32] The narrative prompts were adapted in Spanish and Mandarin so that they encompassed a similar narrative topic, which related to their thematic units. As mentors, we translated the prompts into Spanish, and provided guidance for teachers translating them into Mandarin. This first writing prompt was given to the students with little instruction or guidance. The goal was to create a baseline narrative writing sample for each student that would be used as a basis for our initial bilingual writing analysis.[33]

Analyzing and reflecting on baseline data: Creating common vocabulary

Each school administered the prompts independently. Once all students had completed a baseline narrative writing sample, we worked with the teachers to analyze the student writing. As mentors, we had had many phone conversations discussing how to lead professional development with the goal of developing a common protocol for looking at student writing. Although each

TABLE 6.2

Initial writing prompts

NARRATIVE FAMILY PROMPT	
English: Spanish:	Tell us in writing/drawing about your most recent family outing or get together. What did you do? Dinos por escrito/dibujo acerca de una salida o reunión con tu familia. ¿Adónde fueron? ¿Qué hicieron?

NARRATIVE FRIEND PROMPT	
English:	Write/tell about a fun outing with your friends. Where did you go? What did you do?
Spanish:	Cuéntenos/Escribe acerca de una excursion de diversion o un tiempo divertido que has tenido con tu amigo(s). ¿Adónde fueron? ¿Qué hicieron?

school did this analysis separately, they followed the same protocol. Teachers at each grade level brought in all their student narrative writing responding to the prompt. Before analyzing the writing, we facilitated a discussion about the narrative writing expectations at each grade level. To inform our writing criteria, we reviewed research on narrative writing features.[34] What surfaced from reading the research was a need to separate general writing conventions from the specific genre descriptors and to be specific about the language needed to complete the genre's purpose. For example, teachers examined the difference between writing a sequence of events and writing a narrative story that included all the elements of character, setting, problem, events, and resolution. Then they analyzed the key features of a good narrative by writing their own personal narrative. After each teacher wrote their own response to the prompts, they discussed the areas they felt were important to include in the writing rubric. The teachers concluded that the criteria presented here in table 6.3 needed to be part of the narrative writing rubric.

During this time, we began to refine a writing rubric that described bilingual writing strategies, writing conventions, and grammar, as well as the specific genre features. Although the rubric was not finalized, it gave the teachers a roadmap for feedback they needed to give students about their writing. As they began using it, we encouraged teachers to adapt it to better meet their language and grade-level needs.

TABLE 6.3

Initial writing rubric

LEVEL	CRITERIA
4	Feels complete—presents a clear sequence of events (beginning/middle/end) with details (introduction, and conclusion for fluent writers)
3	Uses effective transitions (first, then, after, etc.)
2	Describes two ideas: who is in the narrative and/or what action is taken
1	Describes one idea through pictures, labels, or lists of words
Prewriting	Only scribbles or draws unrelated pictures

After outlining the narrative writing expectations, we analyzed the student baseline samples to see if they were congruent with the expectations we had delineated. During our first writing analysis, we referenced the holistic biliteracy research.[35] We highlighted the bilingual strategies that surfaced in the student writing samples, such as code-switching, switching between languages within the same phrase or sentence, and bidirectional phonetic transfer, using knowledge about the phonics of one language and applying it in the same way in the other language. During these teacher conversations, teachers frequently referenced code-switching as "interfering" with language development. In response, we asked teachers to reread the research on writing for students designated as EL, and then reflect on how it applied to what we were seeing in the student writing. We specifically had the teachers reread and discuss the sections of Soltero-González and colleagues' study that describe code-switching as a holistic bilingual strategy within their biliteracy development. This encouraged the teachers to engage in a reflective cycle where they developed an awareness of their practices, then decided on an action.[36] For example, some teachers decided they wanted to be more intentional about noting the code-switching on the student writing rubric as a bilingual strategy, and discussed it with all their students.[37]

After examining student writing schoolwide at both schools, teachers noted several patterns: first, students used limited vocabulary, which was evident in the need to directly translate or "borrow" from the other language (e.g., *monkey bars* as *baras de monos*) and invented words (e.g., *ansemra* for *encima*); second, students used limited transition words in both languages (e.g., *and/y*); and third, students used basic characters and settings and did not include details about either (e.g., *I, me/yo, mi; friends/amigos; family/familia; house/casa; park/parque*). For example, one student wrote "My family is good" and then listed where they went for a birthday with no further descriptions about family members or the places visited.

After a few more professional development sessions analyzing student writing samples, teachers began to identify this bilingual writing strategy as bidirectional phonetic transfer and not merely spelling errors. These bilingual writing patterns were discussed in depth, and instructional implications were addressed. The iterative reflective cycle helped teachers ask important questions about spelling patterns rather than just correcting the spelling and seeing it as an error. Teachers were excited to see students using these strategies, and as a result teachers identified and generated lessons to expand vocabulary, focus on idea development and descriptive language, use genre elements such as narrative character and setting development, and use sentence fluency.

Creating goals and a plan of action

After each session, grade-level teams separated to create a lesson sequence that addressed the narrative bilingual writing needs that surfaced in their grade level within each language. They referenced their thematic units to ensure that writing lessons were congruent with the content-area instructional targets and provided lesson ideas that could be incorporated during their whole-group writers' workshop. Each language teacher discussed adaptations that needed to be made to assist students designated as ELs in the writing process. For example, a second-grade teacher engaged in teaching procedural genres recognized the need to bring in ingredients and model why more specific details were a necessary part of the writing process. She asked each child to individually describe how to make a taco and then made the taco according to each student's specifications. When a student stated, "You get a tortilla and put lettuce and some meat," the teacher responded by giving the student a plate with a tortilla, a head of lettuce, and ground beef that was still in the packaging. The students in the class quickly learned that specific details with the relevant vocabulary were necessary for the recipe and for teaching others.[38] When the teacher realized that students were borrowing words from their native language for the target language, she responded by creating anchor charts with common vocabulary that the students could use to write the recipe for making tacos, thus identifying and being responsive to the features and needs of students in her classroom designated as EL. The teacher was able to create anchor charts of the content words needed for the recipe (e.g., tortilla, tomato, shredded lettuce, shredded cheese, cooked ground beef with taco seasonings, guacamole), as well as general quantity terms (a small amount, one to two scoops or spoonfuls, a small handful, etc.). Finally, the teacher also created an anchor chart on adverbial terms (gently, carefully, with care, etc.). These were newer additions that were directly responsive to the need for more specific vocabulary for supporting students designated as ELs with this genre of writing. Typical aspects of the unit also included the use of transition words. By the end the unit, students designated as ELs were able to write, "First, you need to place a tortilla on the plate. Then you put in two scoops of cooked ground beef. Next, you add a spoonful of shredded lettuce." This was a marked improvement over the initial oral instructions provided during the initial demonstration lesson.

After grade-level teams completed a draft of their lesson ideas, they shared highlights with the vertical teams. Vertical teams included teachers from each grade level in order to plan and sequence lessons with a focus on the different developmental levels across each grade. Many lessons were shared across the staff to address the students' multiple language and literacy needs. For example, after the second-grade teacher shared the power of providing word banks with visuals as well as sentence frames as ways to support early writing, the third- and fourth-grade teachers at Archbishop Borders were able to use these structures and improve their lessons when they instructed students to write about how to build a snowman. They also shared how frontloading key vocabulary for the topic extended academic word usage and varied sentences. These practices developed at both schools. Another result from the teacher collaboration was the effort to unify the graphic organizers introduced for each genre. Graphic organizers helped structure the writing ideas and organized the students' thinking. At the end of each session, grade-level teams discussed how to create the next writing prompt so that it would fit into the thematic unit they were teaching, and shared the graphic organizer they all planned on using to teach the next genre. They also scheduled times for the following weeks to monitor the lesson delivery and share lesson resources with a new holistic framework in mind. Using reflective cycles helped teachers build their capacity not only to teach genres of writing but also to specifically adapt their instruction to meet the needs of their students and subsequently act as resources for each other.

This approach stands in sharp contrast to the methods that look at only one language, either monolingual English or monolingual Spanish writing standards rather than as a bilingual drawing on both language systems. Rather than measure second language writing using standards developed for monolingual speakers, the teachers began to notice their practices and anticipate ways to scaffold language development with more of a developmental bilingual perspective. Initial discussion about using holistic bilingual rubrics made some teachers feel uneasy about evaluating student writing. Several of them explained that they had limited experience evaluating bilingual writing, and had writing rubrics and lesson plans only for monolingual students. As a result of this self-reflection, we spent time listing ways to adapt a writing rubric that addressed not only the narrative writing criteria but bilingual writing strategies as well. We wanted to ensure teachers were measuring students against language-development standards created for emerging bilinguals.[39] This also appealed to their desire to honor the knowledge that their students designated as EL were bringing to the task of writing.

This writing-analysis process allowed teachers to see how their students interacted with both language systems within their writing and gave teachers explicit tools they could use to provide feedback to students. By the end of the sessions, teachers had more knowledge about holistic scoring and were sensitive to the way they provided feedback to students about their writing. Developing this sensitivity helped create a more culturally and linguistically responsive school atmosphere during the subsequent professional development sessions.

Collecting and analyzing of summative data

Six to eight weeks later, a second writing sample was collected. The comparative student writing samples demonstrated many of the features of narrative writing. The improvement was significant across all grade levels. For example, first-grade students wrote about a Christmas family outing in Spanish/Mandarin and then wrote about a Thanksgiving outing in English. In both samples, the students demonstrated transition words and showed a clear sequence of events. They also had clear topic sentences and good word choices with more varied academic vocabulary. Despite students receiving instruction in two languages, with two teachers, many of the narrative writing features were evident in both their English and target-language writing pieces. Another helpful aspect of the writing-analysis process was that teachers from both schools were able to see student work from students at the other school and could see similarities and differences among the students designated as ELs at both schools. Given that there is only one classroom per grade level per school, it was of great benefit to the teachers to see samples from their students' same-grade-level peers across the country. Teachers valued having the opportunity to collaborate with another bilingual teacher and described feeling validated in seeing the same writing features surface in their students' writing despite being in another state. They also liked having the opportunity to connect with other grade-level colleagues to share teaching experiences and felt that this network contributed to building their capacity around understanding and teaching writing to students designated as ELs.

As the school year progressed, teachers began taking more ownership of their learning and often led segments of each meeting. For example, each teacher at All Souls had to present a writing lesson to the entire staff, showing how the lesson could be adapted to varying developmental levels across each grade, which helped provide ideas to differentiate lessons. Because each grade level shared how they went about teaching their lessons, the entire staff was given ideas on how to adapt the upcoming writing lesson to a lower or higher level. Teachers across grade levels shared lesson adaptations for students who were still struggling with writing. This collaboration among teachers provided more ideas and added rigor and quality to the students' writing.

This writing-analysis process continued until the end of the school year for various genres (see figure 6.1). As a result of this work, bilingual writing samples were collected from each grade level to use as exemplars for the upcoming year. The writing rubric itself was helpful in reviewing the student

FIGURE 6.1
Writing analysis process

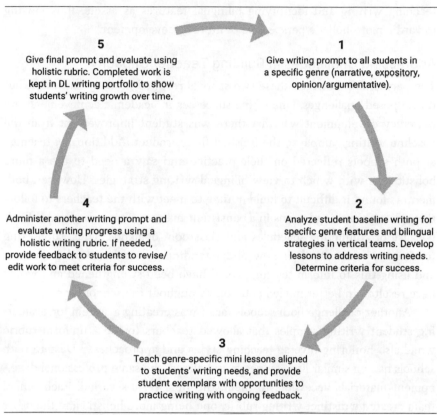

5
Give final prompt and evaluate using holistic rubric. Completed work is kept in DL writing portfolio to show students' writing growth over time.

1
Give writing prompt to all students in a specific genre (narrative, expository, opinion/argumentative).

4
Administer another writing prompt and evaluate writing progress using a holistic writing rubric. If needed, provide feedback to students to revise/edit work to meet criteria for success.

2
Analyze student baseline writing for specific genre features and bilingual strategies in vertical teams. Develop lessons to address writing needs. Determine criteria for success.

3
Teach genre-specific mini lessons aligned to students' writing needs, and provide student exemplars with opportunities to practice writing with ongoing feedback.

work, but also required further adaptation to meet the various grade-level and developmental and linguistic needs of the students.

One of the successes of this collaboration was seeing students' academic achievement and biliteracy development improve from the baseline writing sample to the finished final product. Teachers subsequently developed writing lessons and evaluation tools that promoted students' biliteracy skills. As a result of the writing-analysis process and ongoing professional development, a bilingual assessment tool was created to monitor bilingual writing growth across both school sites. Additionally, the collaboration and reflection cycle across schools resulted in teachers at both sites feeling more confident about teaching writing and identifying bilingual features as assets, thus moving toward a more holistic perspective of literacy development.

Addressing Challenges in Building Teacher Capacity

The partnership between these two schools resulted in many successes, but it also posed challenges. One of the successes in academic achievement and biliteracy development was that there was student improvement from the baseline writing sample to the finished final product. Additionally, teachers at both schools reflected on their practice and saw a need to use a more holistic lens with which to view bilingual writing strategies. However, both mentors found it difficult to build in time to meet with the teachers to follow through with writing lessons in a consistent manner. This was often difficult because of conflicting schedules and classroom demands. Thus, supporting teachers to reconcile their new understandings about holistic bilingualism and using this to inform teaching could have been strengthened and would have resulted in better implementation throughout the school year.

Another challenge both schools faced was creating a system for evaluating student writing samples that allowed teachers to use a uniform rubric while also honoring diverse teaching styles and approaches.[40] Despite both schools having similar literacy needs and almost the same professional development materials accessible to them, the final results varied. Each school team created a distinct writing rubric, one being more holistic and the other using more of the analytic rubric structure that included features of the writing of students designated as ELs. Teachers also varied in their implementation and use of the new rubric. At All Souls, for example, many of the teachers did not use the rubrics to consistently provide feedback to students. They felt the writing lesson ideas were valuable but said there was not enough time to confer with each student using the rubric.

We also found it difficult to visit all the classrooms in a consistent manner to ensure that the professional development recommendations were implemented. Additionally, we found that despite the training sessions, teachers varied in their understanding of how to use writing rubrics to analyze and evaluate writing. Consequently, the consistent use of the rubric was a challenge at both schools. Moreover, there were misunderstandings around how holistic features affected the way teachers perceive and score students' bilingual writing. For example, if a student was relying on their home language discourse patterns, this could affect the organization of the writing. Addressing this trait would require discussing how to organize ideas in different languages. This was sometimes challenging for teachers since it required that they shift their mind-set from a deficit perspective to an asset-based perspective and learn how to honor the cultural language style.

BUILDING TEACHER CAPACITY USING REFLECTIVE CYCLES: LESSONS LEARNED

As demonstrated through the two schools' reflective cycles, building teacher capacity to transform schools to be culturally and linguistically responsive requires a development of knowledge and skills specifically geared toward respecting students' home and community languages while they are in the process of learning a second language. Teachers need to explore ideologies around holistic bilingualism in order to provide quality instruction that promotes academic achievement, including those that support writing development. As part of a networked community of learners with the same mission, Archbishop Borders and All Souls worked together to facilitate the reflection and critical inquiry that propelled the necessary learning.

This joint effort holds several valuable lessons for educational leaders engaged in the process of transformation. Three areas emerged as important aspects of the practice of developing reflective cycles to promote culturally and linguistically responsive schools. The first involves using research to ground discussions and to promote an asset-based orientation when working with diverse student populations. The second is using baseline data to analyze an issue and develop a plan of action, and the last is designing an ongoing process to monitor, refine, and document growth.

Beginning professional development sessions with research that promotes an asset-based orientation when working with culturally and linguistically diverse students is critical to promoting a responsive school. Grounding conversations in research not only creates a common vocabulary to discuss the issue but also develops a foundational understanding around the professional development topic. Focusing the initial conversations around best practices and research within the field helps create cohesion and provides a resource to draw on when differences of opinions or questions arise. Furthermore, it brings a level of awareness and lays the foundation for deeper connections to the topic, as the research on building teacher capacity recommends.[41] In addition, using research and creating discussion norms that move participants to a more asset-based orientation alleviates the danger of falling into deficit thinking about working with diverse learners.[42] It may also help in connecting to previous schemas and funds of knowledge that not only honor the learners' experiences but also use those experiences as assets in their learning.[43] Lastly, using research literature to initiate professional development discussions can also surface what participants know about the subject, and help the facilitator tailor the session.

The next key area is collecting baseline data. It is important to use students' data when implementing a new practice. More specifically, when gathering information about what learners know at the start, you can develop a plan that is relevant and meaningful and takes participants to the next level. Documenting a baseline helps you know where to begin your lesson, and it also provides evidence to reference when monitoring growth.[44] Additionally, it provides time to reflect and assists in determining next steps. This reflective time also facilitates an analysis that may highlight the strengths and the areas that need growth.[45] This information can lead to creating goals and a plan of action to reach those goals. Incorporating other teachers' voices when creating goals and identifying the steps necessary to achieve them is vital. Next, ensure that the plan of action is aligned to the baseline data collected and the areas identified as needing growth. Within your plan of action, design a professional development/lesson sequence to address goals and provide ample time for teachers to reflect, analyze, and receive in-service information and coaching to help implement changes. This will take time; hence short-and long-term goals should be outlined.

The last area we identified is designing an ongoing process to monitor, refine, and document growth. This revision cycle should provide time to collect formative data across the year to inform the subsequent professional development plan. Teachers need time to review, adjust, and provide/receive feedback.[46] At the end of the revision cycle, collect summative data to analyze growth and see whether goals were achieved. Recognize successful outcomes and/or exemplars and disseminate them as evidence of having accomplished goals, and create a system to share this data with stakeholders. Documenting results and creating an archive for exemplars helps validate your efforts for yourself and teachers, which may make them more sustainable over time.

Many of the features outlined in the professional development sequence are congruent with best practices in the field with respect to building teacher capacity. Teachers at the schools were involved in learning about holistic features of bilingual writers and in finding ways to acknowledge these features as assets in the writing process. Teachers were able to learn more about writing development for students designated as ELs. They were also able to look at rubrics to assess other features of writing and to develop instruction that was culturally and linguistically responsive to the specific needs of students designated as ELs.

In conclusion, building teacher capacity through reflecting on writing is often seen as a challenge requiring a lot of rigor, given that writing is one of the most complex forms of language expression. However, in order to develop excellent communicators who can demonstrate their knowledge and understanding, schools need to effectively teach students to communicate orally and in writing. Selecting writing across the disciplines as a school focus ensures that educators are providing rigorous instruction. Exemplary writing requires students to master many literacy subskills but also builds their confidence in their writing voice, which is closely tied to their cultural and linguistic identity. Hence, writing across the disciplines challenges both teachers and students to work toward mastering very high standards while honoring and sustaining diversity in learning.

Moreover, incorporating a more holistic assessment lens in analyzing student writing encourages teachers to be more culturally and linguistically responsive. Teachers working with culturally and linguistically diverse students need to question monolingual writing expectations, which often misidentify linguistically minoritized students as deficient. In using a more holistic, asset-based lens, teachers can broaden their understanding and view many of the bilingual strategies as contributing to a student's linguistic repertoire. Schools need to be sensitive and respectful of diverse learning trajectories yet provide the explicit tools necessary to take students to the next step in their literacy growth. Providing a broader literacy approach and using reflective cycles encourages teachers and administrators to view linguistically diverse students as having different literacy trajectories rather than literacy deficiencies. When teachers and administrators build capacity in teaching culturally and linguistically diverse learners, it communicates to diverse students that they are honored for who they are and where they are in their literacy journey, and that they, like any student, are capable of reaching high academic performance.

Cultivating Family Engagement

AMIE SARKER

FAMILY ENGAGEMENT CAN BE an elusive endeavor when working in culturally and linguistically marginalized contexts. Yet effectively catalyzing and empowering families and community members can create significant opportunities for developing culturally and linguistically responsive instruction. As a mentor in the Two-Way Immersion Network for Catholic Schools (TWIN-CS), I have experienced how networked learning can both inspire and facilitate this process. In this chapter I examine key practices that create authentic partnerships and facilitate family engagement—building relationships, fostering asset orientations, and integrating funds of knowledge. Beginning with a brief discussion of certain essential practices for cultivating family engagement in schools serving linguistically minoritized students, I then present an example from my experience in TWIN-CS of how parents' funds of knowledge were explored, valued, and harnessed to build relationships and foster students' language and literacy development. I close by discussing implications of these practices for educational leaders engaged in the process of transformation across various contexts.

INVOLVING FAMILIES AND COMMUNITY IN CULTURALLY AND LINGUISTICALLY RESPONSIVE SCHOOLS

Researchers and practitioners have traditionally found value in fostering parent and community involvement as a means to improve student achievement.[1] Converging evidence points toward several practices that higher-performing schools successfully employ when engaging families from diverse cultural and linguistic heritages:

- building trusting collaborative relationships between educators, families, and community members
- demonstrating awareness of and respect for differences in class and culture while addressing the needs of all families
- embracing shared power and responsibility as a guiding philosophy of partnership[2]

These practices of building strong, authentic community and family partnerships can advance culturally and linguistically responsive schooling through opportunities for sociocultural integration, cultivation of language proficiency, and promotion of academic achievement. Such efforts among linguistically marginalized, culturally and linguistically diverse populations also demonstrate a commitment to social justice.

Auerbach argues that for partnerships among schools, families, and communities to be truly beneficial, they must go beyond the instrumental.[3] Schools engage in the formation of authentic partnerships by honoring the democratic principles inherent to American education and demonstrating a commitment to seeking the common good and social justice. Auerbach defines authentic partnerships as "respectful alliances among educators, families, and community groups that value relationship building, dialogue across difference, and sharing power in pursuit of common purpose in socially just, democratic schools."[4] Her meta-analysis examining leadership practices and their impact on student learning outcomes revealed that relatively little is known about *how* leaders work strategically with family and community members. Auerbach offers a continuum of leadership practices that range from preventing partnerships, to nominal partnerships, followed by traditional partnerships, and then finally authentic partnerships (table 7.1).

Three aspects of authentic relationships that are particularly important for leadership in culturally and linguistically responsive schools are fostering asset orientations, cultivating funds of knowledge, and building relationships. One way to conceptualize the relationships among the three is as a series of nested circles. The broadest one—building relationships—would be the widest circle. Fostering asset orientations is a smaller circle, representing one strategy of building relationships. Finally, the specific practice of cultivating funds of knowledge would lie in the innermost circle, as one approach to fostering asset orientations.

Building Relationships

Authentic partnerships build relationships as a precursor to fostering productive dialogue with families and communities. Culturally and linguistically responsive schools are a social frontier where different worlds collide while creating intersections of shared interest.[5] A foundational component of relationship building is understanding how parents prefer to relate to schools, understanding their educational orientations.[6] Together, school administrators and teachers alongside family and community members negotiate varied conceptual frameworks for teaching and learning processes. Educators must make it a priority to get to know their students' families, eliciting their concerns and interests for cooperative action. For educators to know families, safe spaces must also be created to facilitate dialogue across differences. In the process of creating a shared community of practice on a school campus, dialogue, inquiry, and storytelling aid the reciprocal learning process.[7]

There are a number of concrete approaches that can be used to promote this type of reciprocal learning, such as home visits. Home visits are not a new idea for fostering relational networks, but they can be very effective in engaging marginalized populations and generating more insight into a family's funds of knowledge.[8] However, without adequate preparation and opportunities to reflect on and process the experience, home visits can actually reinforce deficit orientations teachers have about families and communities. Since many aspects of culture are hidden below the surface and therefore not

TABLE 7.1

Continuum of leadership practice

	LEADERSHIP PREVENTING PARTNERSHIPS	LEADERSHIP FOR NOMINAL PARTNERSHIPS	LEADERSHIP FOR TRADITIONAL PARTNERSHIPS	LEADERSHIP FOR AUTHENTIC PARTNERSHIPS
Goals	Maintain control. Protect school from outside influence.	Maintain control. Comply with mandates. Improve achievement.	Improve achievement and school climate. Meet family and community needs.	Work toward various goals based on mutual interests. Equity, social justice, dialogue, empowerment.
Position of families and community members	Outsiders. Deficit view of family/community members.	Clients, visitors, supporters. Deficit view of family/community members. Community members provide resources and services.	Supporters, allies, limited partners. Mix of deficit and assets views of family/community members. Community members provide resources and services. "Funds of knowledge" contributors to curriculum.[a]	Full partners, advocates, leaders. Assets view of family/community members. Cultural brokers.
Related models	Transactional. Leader as buffer. Closed system.	Leader as potential bridge. School to home transmission. Traditional PR approach.	Leader as bridge, listener. Coordination with community partners (e.g., full-service schools). Participation.	Transformative. Collaborative. Social justice. Two-way accommodation. Reciprocal learning.
Power relations with families and community groups	Unilateral "power over."[b] Large power differential.	Unilateral "power over." Large power differential.	Mix of unilateral "power over" and relational "power to." Moderate power differential.	Relational "power to." Minimized power differential.

Source: Adapted from Susan Auerbach, *School Leadership for Authentic Family and Community Partnerships: Research Perspectives for Transforming Practice* (New York: Routledge, 2012).

[a] Luis Moll et al., "Funds of Knowledge for Teaching: Using a Qualitative Approach to Connect Homes and Classrooms," *Theory into Practice* 31, no. 2 (1992): 132–142.

[b] "Leaders seek "power over" families and communities, or subordination vs. seeking to empower them by working together to achieve common goals ("power to").

as observable (such as values, expectations, assumptions, and thought patterns), such elements can be easily misinterpreted or overlooked, particularly when interacting with culturally diverse and linguistically marginalized populations. To avoid such problems, educational leaders may find Johnson's home visit protocol helpful for scaffolding, including guidance for before, during, and after such experiences.[9] Additionally, Frank's "Notetaking-Notemaking" observational approach, which she describes in *Ethnographic Eyes*, can be a useful tool in this process, along with Diller and Moule's Self-Assessment for Cultural Competence, which helps facilitate teachers' awareness, interpretation, and goal setting.[10]

A barrier to building relationships is when schools are singularly focused on their own agenda and expect deferential support from parents rather than true collaboration. Auerbach brings to light the concern that "despite the rhetoric of partnership, the literature suggests that many educators do not want parents or community groups as equal partners with agency and voice."[11] Authentic partnerships, while time-consuming and challenging, involve co-constructing the school through culturally responsive parent involvement. In practice, this means fostering a climate of belonging where all stakeholders feel welcome, minimizing bureaucracy and nurturing a family-friendly environment. In culturally and linguistically diverse communities, affirmation of language identities includes translations as well as strategies for affirming and integrating the linguistic and cultural capital families contribute. School activities for parents may include time for informal interaction both with educators and among the families themselves, a space for sharing their hopes and dreams for their children. Auerbach describes how, "guided by an ethic of care," educators listen attentively to what these parents have to say and respond with their own stories through encounters that are more authentic than scripted, further building relationships of trust and understanding.[12]

Auerbach argues further that authentic partnerships extend to sharing power, "learning to lead from within a web of relationships by empowering rather than controlling others."[13] The development of parent leadership is a critical component of this process in culturally and linguistically minoritized communities. For parents to have a meaningful role in the decision-making process, they need training in curriculum, policy, and operations to help them navigate the language of education and rules of engagement.

School leaders have the opportunity to become boundary spanners and border crossers as they develop authentic partnerships to create more socially just and democratic schools. Scanlan and Johnson describe boundaries as middle grounds, ambiguous spaces where much remains apart. Yet common interests create a social frontier with points of intersection.[14] Boundaries are at times permeable, allowing an individual to bridge or link two boundaries at once, as though with one foot in both worlds. Drawing on Miller's characterization of boundary-spanning leaders as "institutional infiltrators organizing for community advancement,"[15] Scanlan and Johnson suggest that boundaries are also at times more like borders. This border-crossing conceptualization requires that a leader abandon personal "assumptions, privileges, and expectations in order to enter a new space."[16] In order for school leaders to effectively navigate the process of boundary spanning, border crossing, and advocacy, they must develop particular knowledge, skills, and dispositions.

Fostering Asset Orientations

A second and critical element of effective family engagement that promotes culturally and linguistically responsive schooling is fostering asset orientations. In order to build respectful alliances in culturally and linguistically diverse contexts, educators must first examine their own beliefs. Differences can exist among educators and the culturally and linguistically diverse communities that they serve in regard to school expectations, discourse patterns, and perceptions about what count as "appropriate" literacy practices. In some cases, differences can lead to misunderstandings and tensions (see table 7.2).[17]

McKenzie and Scheurich identified particular equity traps, or conscious and unconscious behaviors and patterns of thinking that prevent educators from creating equitable schools.[18] One trap to be dismantled, for example, is deficit thinking about linguistically minoritized, immigrant, and/or poor families and communities. Such thinking presents a major barrier to forming respectful, constructive alliances. Presuming parents' deficiencies leads to communication that goes in only one direction, from school to home. Deficit views purport a view of parents solely in instrumental terms—as "empty vessels" requiring training from school experts, as problems who challenge the school culture, or as exemplars to point to as reinforcing the expected

TABLE 7.2

Differences between mainstream American teachers'
expectations and language-minoritized parents' expectations

MAINSTREAM AMERICAN TEACHERS' EXPECTATIONS	LANGUAGE-MINORITIZED PARENTS' EXPECTATIONS
Students should participate in classroom activities/discussion	Students should be quiet and obedient, observing more than participating
Students should be creative	Students should be told what to do
Students learn through inquiries and debate	Students learn through memorization and observation
Students should do their own work	Students should help one another
Creativity and fantasy should be encouraged	Factual information is important; fantasy is not
Reading is a way of discovering	Reading is the decoding of information and facts
Children should state their opinions even when they contradict the teacher's	Teachers are not to be challenged
Students need to ask questions	Students should not ask a lot of questions

Source: Adapted from Nancy Hadaway, Sylvia Vardell, and Terrell Young, *What Every Teacher Should Know About English Language Learners* (Boston: Pearson, 2004); Robin Scarcella, *Teaching Language Minority Students in the Multicultural Classroom* (Upper Saddle River, NJ: Prentice Hall, 1990).

behaviors.[19] In contrast, asset orientations affirm families' cultures and honor their contributions.[20] Scanlan and Johnson suggest that a practical way to replace deficit orientations with asset orientations is to create counternarratives through practices such as recrafting outdoor spaces at schools for community use and offering continuing education like English for Speakers of Other Languages classes, wellness workshops, and/or legal clinics on topics related to immigration for family and community members.[21]

Similarly, community walks raise educators' level of understanding about assets and challenges present in the communities they serve with community residents acting as cultural brokers to help educators look at the neighborhood through a new lens.[22] During a community walk a small group of educators physically walk through and explore the school community neighborhood with community residents as "guides," allowing educators to gain new insights into understanding housing issues and the roles of religious institutions, businesses, and other organizations within the life of the community. Story mapping is another effective tool whereby educators can "uncover, recover, and retell the stories and assets of community members in order to develop a road map for future advocacy."[23] During the story mapping process, local residents interview other community members while educators serve as the notetakers during the interviews. This process allows school leaders to respond to local community member leadership in identifying the complexities of issues that are important to the school community. At the same time, school leaders can explore advocacy opportunities for educators to implement in this context. Short one-page summaries are then developed and circulated across groups for reflection and action. Community-based equity audits can be powerful tools in transforming culturally and linguistically marginalized schools and neighborhoods in that they assist school leaders in better understanding and acting in solidarity with community stakeholders. Drawing on the reflections of aspiring principals, Green describes a four-phase process of disrupting deficit views about community, conducting initial community inquiry and shared community experiences, establishing a community leadership team, and collecting equity, asset-based community data for action. Practices such as these guide educational leaders in constructing equitable solutions to school-community issues that are context-specific.[24]

Cultivating Funds of Knowledge

A third key tenet of effective family engagement that is particularly important for leadership advancing culturally and linguistically responsive schools is cultivating funds of knowledge. Economically poor families have often been perceived as socially disorganized and even intellectually deficient, but Moll and others challenge this notion.[25] *Funds of knowledge* refer to the "historically accumulated and culturally developed bodies of knowledge and skills essential for household or individual functioning and well-being."[26] The work of Moll and colleagues examined the working class Mexican-American context in Tucson, Arizona, where classroom teachers and ethnographers together identified home and community resources to integrate into the curriculum as learning opportunities. Teachers conducted home visits and engaged in observations and open-ended interviews with the families of students in their classes. Teachers were supported in executing these practices through afterschool study groups, part of a larger inquiry project in which they explored life histories and case studies.

Educators counteracted deficit views with asset orientations by recognizing and integrating the funds of knowledge that students bring from home to the classroom.[27] Too often, educators view students from "poor" households as also lacking in their quality of experiences.[28] Engaging in "ethnographically informed classroom practices" can help educators develop a deeper understanding of the sociocultural contexts in which their students live, including the following:

- history of that geographical region (such as the border region between Texas and Mexico)
- sociopolitical and economic context of the households
- social history of the households (including their origins and development in this country)
- labor history of the families (which reveals accumulated bodies of knowledge passed down from elders)[29]

These households have certain social networks that strategically facilitate the development of knowledge, skills, and dispositions and the exchange of resources. The experiences of culturally and linguistically minoritized students may be different from those of "mainstream" students, but their home-based language, traditions, values, and literacy-related practices are rich resources for developing content knowledge as well as bilingual and biliteracy skills. Educators rarely draw on the resources available to students outside the classroom walls, but households and community-based organizations can assist teachers in becoming cultural brokers between schools and families.

Educators in Moll and colleagues' study found increasing value for the resources family and community members contributed, such as children being viewed as international travelers as they journeyed across the border during vacation, engaging in international commerce as they sold candy they brought back from Mexico. With the background knowledge these students possessed they exhibited greater interest in studying economic issues and were poised to better understand the complexities of different systems of law, both topics in the sixth-grade curriculum. This led to the creation of culturally responsive units, such as a sixth-grade inquiry on the topic of candy in which a mother came to demonstrate and explain the steps involved in making *pipitoria,* a Mexican candy, discussing nutritional concepts and differences in food production and consumption between the United States and Mexico. By exploring and accessing the resources in culturally and linguistically minoritized communities, a reciprocal exchange took place that fostered authentic partnership. Parents were motivated and empowered to bring their voices to the school setting, and educators were better equipped to sensitively navigate collaboration with students designated as English Learners (ELs) and their families.

These three practices—building relationships, fostering asset orientations, and cultivating funds of knowledge—are vital for educational leaders forging authentic relationships with families as they transform their schools to be culturally and linguistically responsive. In the next section, I draw from my experiences in TWIN-CS to describe how these practices strengthened family engagement and moved a school community along in the continuum toward authentic partnerships.

ENVISIONING A TRANSFORMATIONAL FAMILY ENGAGEMENT PROJECT THROUGH NETWORKED LEARNING

During my first year with TWIN-CS, I served as a mentor for two urban school campuses in our large metroplex area in the southern United States. My first exposure to the full TWIN-CS network came through the opportunity to attend the annual summer academy at a retreat center in Massachusetts. Not only was this a unique opportunity to get to know my school teams and other mentors better both professionally and personally, it was an introduction to an incredibly valuable space for germinating ideas that would grow into multifaceted opportunities to develop the language and literacy skills of the students and families we served.

During this first summer academy, a couple of the presentations in particular resonated with me and sowed the seeds of ideas that would grow into a family literacy project. First, one presentation on engaging families in supporting dual language learners' language and literacy skills prompted my thinking about ways to better foster family and community involvement within the schools I was working with. The presentation drew on Páez and Tabors's research linking home and school curriculum implemented with the Kindergarten Language Study and Vocabulary Instruction and Assessment for Spanish Speakers.[30] The project included equipping parents to engage in focused read-alouds with appropriate response activities at home with their children. I recall follow-up discussions with one of the principals and her teachers during the summer academy where they determined a goal for the year was to better engage families in understanding and participating in the dual language program through home-based and school activities. This was one example of how strategic networking helped to develop my thinking, and our approach to this initiative. This time to dialogue and discover shared values and goals prompted my more focused attention on ways we could engage our linguistically minoritized families with school-related activities, and specifically with the biliteracy development of the students.

A second presentation during that summer academy that helped set this project in motion focused on school climate and identity as a part of the sociocultural strand of the two-way immersion (TWI) program. The session included discussions about communities of practice and how our shared values, vocabulary, discourse patterns, and other facets of identity are enacted in the school culture. Individuals from teams across TWIN-CS stood up to share elements of their school's identity with the whole group. I was struck by the common threads of certain values and funds of knowledge that the various teams possessed, among them Latinx cultural heritage and traditions, Catholic identity and values, bilingualism and biculturalism, and multicultural symbols of various kinds. Their sharing reminded me how certain knowledge, skills, and dispositions cultivated outside of the school setting can be reinforced and accessed as catalysts for deeper learning. For example, strong Spanish literacy models at home help to foster oral and written language development in Spanish, which also supports literacy development in English. Religious funds of knowledge could include moral and ethical values and church-based literacy practices, not to mention catechism and knowledge of saints and biblical characters that have allusions in literature. Celebration of Latinx culture and traditions would be a natural way to show value for the families represented at the school, motivating parents to share their funds of knowledge and increase their involvement in efforts that would move toward the formation of authentic partnerships.[31]

In addition to these presentations, a culminating activity at the summer academy was a collaborative discussion with the school teams on revisioning the mission statement in light of a closer look at identity and school culture. Working with my member school's implementation team, we first brainstormed key ideas and phrases that represented the identity, values, and goals of our school's stakeholders. Then we grouped them semantically to generate common themes. We prioritized which were most important to the team and which we felt were also most important to the families at the school. In talking with the principal and teachers, the themes of affirming the bilingual and cultural (including religious) identities of students and engaging families continued to surface.[32] These became two primary goals for next school year.

To scaffold the networking that started at that summer academy throughout the year, as a mentor I continued working with the implementation team to flesh out ideas and apply them in our local context. In my role as a university professor, my teaching focuses on equipping current and future teachers to use English as a Second Language and second language literacy methods. Hence, I am always on the lookout for ways to better support the learning of culturally and linguistically minoritized students. Returning from the summer academy and preparing for the fall semester, I came across an article by Schrodt and colleagues in *The Reading Teacher*, "Exploring Culturally Relevant Texts with Kindergartners and Their Families," which described a "Family Backpack Project."[33] For this project, teachers and researchers selected high-quality children's picture books and shared them with families "as a launching pad to illuminate the stories" of students designated as ELs and their families, empowering them to contribute to the curriculum.[34] The guiding principles of the project state:

Provide physical and linguistic access to books.

Respect children's home language(s).

Value and use family funds of knowledge.

Preschoolers learn to read and write through participation in reading and
writing events.

Book reading involves the extended family.

Meaning making is multimodal.

Home reading can help children learn concepts and vocabulary needed in school instruction.

Children and families connect to texts with positive depictions of diversity, a global perspective, and culturally relevant topics.

Promote two-way sharing of texts (school-to-home and home-to-school).[35]

The article explored how teachers tapped into the varied cultures and voices of students and their families through sharing diverse children's literature in the home and responding to it through journals in which families could share their connections and other reactions to the texts they read together.

Launching "Faith and *Familia* as Funds of Knowledge"

Coming away from the TWIN-CS summer academy experiences, I was struck by the opportunity to meld ideas from the sessions described above. After I shared the Family Backpack Project article with another TWIN-CS mentor, principal, and teachers, we began brainstorming the possibility of piloting a project that compiled theme-based sets of culturally relevant children's literature to be shared both in the classroom and at home through family read-alouds and associated response activities. To advance the goals we set at the summer academy of strengthening both family engagement and culturally responsive instruction, we modeled the project after the family story backpack projects designed by Kathy G. Short and the CREATE (Communities as Resources in Early Childhood Teacher Education) team, which are described in the article by Schrodt and colleagues.[36] Building from ideas explored at the summer academy, we planned our project to harness the common funds of knowledge for our particular culturally and linguistically diverse community of practice. Through discussions with another mentor at the academy, our implementation team brainstormed a title for the project and came up with "Faith and *Familia* as Funds of Knowledge," as the first themes would relate to familiar family practices and faith traditions, threads of identity reflecting an asset orientation that were highlighted at the academy.

As our planning continued, we crafted four objectives for our "Faith and *Familia* as Funds of Knowledge" project:

- develop methods for effectively integrating culturally relevant children's literature into classroom instruction and home-based literacy activities
- increase the time family members spend reading, writing, and talking about literature together
- create more home-school connections through activities that engage families and harness faith and family traditions and stories for cultural appreciation and language development
- incorporate strategies for increasing L1 (first language) and L2 (second language) use at home

In the last couple of weeks before the school year began, I finalized the logistics of the potential project with two TWIN-CS member school principals I was working with as a mentor. Both gave their blessing to go forward, and we launched later that fall in six classrooms at two schools in the TWIN-CS network that were implementing TWI service delivery.

Another mentor worked with me to complete all the preparation. Together we selected texts and decided to start with the themes of family and Navidad (Christmas). An important selection criterion for the children's literature was how culturally authentic and culturally relevant the texts were. The students in these schools were predominantly of Latinx heritage with both Spanish-dominant and English-dominant speakers, so we made a particular effort to include bilingual books or those with a Spanish or English translation, drawing on strong language models in both languages as we also sought to tap into the funds of knowledge and values held by this community. We sought culturally relevant literature by exploring Pura Belpré Award winners, works by notable Latinx authors, recommendations from Latinx individuals, and research-based book reviews such as those on WOWlit.org. We also examined cultural markers in the content (i.e., accurate depictions of traditions and holidays), text (i.e., authentic language patterns and use of dialect or L1), and illustrations (i.e., skin tone, facial features, and clothing), checking for accuracy, relevancy, and any stereotypes or biases. Additionally, we collaborated on developing appropriate literature response activities to share with the teachers.

As might be expected, our launch of the project that fall was a bit messy. Early in the semester, I met with the teachers to explain procedures for the project, and in a follow-up meeting later in the fall I introduced the books and materials. I prepared a tub for each teacher (preK three-year-olds through first grade) with a set of books (multiple copies of each title in the theme), several backpacks (for at least a third if not half of the students to take home books at one time), and journals in folders for each student, which included example pages of possible literature response ideas for parents. I did not have any direct contact with the parents, so I relied on letters to the parents that would go home in English and Spanish and communication from the teachers. I provided teachers with interactive read-aloud discussion and response ideas for many of the books they read in class (that they later sent home).

The plan was for teachers to introduce the texts effectively in class so that students could build on that initial exposure as they reread and enjoyed them at home with family members. Backpacks that were sent home on a rotating basis included a book pairing (English and Spanish versions of a title or books on a similar topic and/or bilingual texts), students' corresponding response journals (a folder with lined and unlined pages for responses), and crayons or "artifacts" related to the text(s) that may stimulate meaningful family discussion and involvement. The journal included instructions for possible book responses we had prepared along with color examples of journal entries created by other families who had completed similar family story backpack projects (a source available online through CREATE).

We had some great family responses in classes across the two school campuses. Journals came back with pictures of families doing various activities, narratives of family stories related to the content in the books, varied pleasant and comical responses to the texts written by different immediate and extended family members in English and Spanish, and student illustrations and poems about their family traditions and experiences. For example, one family drew their own family tree discussing the origin of the child's two last names as a response to *René Has Two Last Names/René tiene dos apellidos* (René Colato Laínez). Several families connected with *Too Many Tamales/¡Qué Montón de Tamales!* (Gary Soto) by sharing pictures and stories of their traditions associated with making tamales together with family at

Christmastime. It was encouraging to see families sharing their responses in the language they felt most comfortable with. It might be a mother or brother writing in English or a grandmother or uncle writing in Spanish, but rich oral language and transmission of cultural values were cultivated, further demonstrating the importance of and support for the emerging bilingual, biliterate identities of students designated as ELs. Through this project we saw how family members' storytelling opened up a space for the "reciprocal learning" process, further building relationships, developing asset orientations among the teachers, and honoring the funds of knowledge families contributed.[37]

I found that the success of the project on both campuses had a lot to do with the buy-in from the teacher. Those that attended the summer academy were in general much more engaged, active, and successful with the project. While the teachers who were sent to the summer academy may have been selected because of their dedication and leadership potential to a certain extent, I believe the time together provided a scaffold and was important to the success of the project. Discussing the school's identity and mission and the importance of parent involvement along with other elements of culturally and linguistically responsive schooling helped build their interest in this new project.

Growing "Faith and *Familia* as Funds of Knowledge"

This initial implementation provided many lessons on how to improve the "Faith and *Familia* as Funds of Knowledge" project. For instance, we learned that more detailed response-idea instructions for families (and teachers) could be beneficial in helping them build intertextual connections. We also received feedback from teachers who pointed to other adjustments and enhancements we should make, such as implementing a tracking system for the books and backpacks so that they didn't get lost at home and never returned. We discussed the possibility of the two campuses collaborating when implementing the project, and the principals and teachers were in favor of that. However, limited communication took place, as it was difficult logistically to arrange time for the teachers to really dialogue. Therefore, the project continued across the first academic year in more of a parallel, isolated fashion.

The following year, we decided to continue and expand the program, including making the improvements discussed above. For instance, during a parent orientation night I introduced the project and answered questions. One of the lead bilingual teachers and I presented the project rationale and instructions together in English and Spanish. This helped clarify the process for a few classes. During the second year, we encountered new challenges as new teachers and grade levels were added. Orienting new teachers to the project while also extending and selecting new books for the additional grade levels was complex because of the expanding scope, logistics, and time involved. Another difficulty was creating a good tracking system for the books, as we discovered some of the books did not return after the first or second cycle of going home in backpacks if the teacher did not monitor the check-in/check-out system closely.

Other aspects of the project were easier the second time. For instance, a fellow mentor in TWIN-CS and I found that by collaborating, we both got better at analyzing children's literature selections and creating response ideas for teachers and families. We continued to expand the themes and text sets that were offered to the various grade levels. Once our initial preparation work was done, the framework was in place, making it easier for teachers to implement the project.

News of the success of the "Faith and *Familia* as Funds of Knowledge" project in engaging families in meaningful ways began to spread across TWIN-CS. The design team invited me to share a workshop about the project at the summer academy the following year. This allowed me to connect with dozens of teachers across the network to share the resources and processes we had compiled for this project and to engage linguistically minoritized families in the learning process. Many expressed excitement for learning about culturally relevant texts that were available to them as well as other ideas for fostering family involvement through the backpack project.

FOSTERING AUTHENTIC ENGAGEMENT ACROSS CONTEXTS

The "Faith and *Familia* as Funds of Knowledge" project was an example of building relationships, valuing families' cultural and linguistic assets, and integrating such resources in order to foster culturally and linguistically responsive instruction. This project could easily be implemented and/or modified for other contexts to foster authentic family and community engagement. Although it was implemented in a TWI faith-based setting, the strategies are applicable across public and private, faith-based and secular contexts.

Many different text-set themes could be relevant for varied contexts. Drawing on the funds of knowledge that families bring to a particular school community is vital to the success of a project like this. By tapping into resources for quality multicultural literature, related projects touching on varied cultural experiences (African-American, Vietnamese-American, refugees and newcomers, etc.) could be implemented within multiple culturally and linguistically minoritized communities.

In addition, care should be taken in evaluating the cultural authenticity and relevance of the literature shared through such a project. Educational leaders can invite parents and community members to participate in the evaluation process. This provides yet another opportunity to foster relationship building and a sense of shared power.[38] While the preparation requires time and effort, the payoff is worth it, including increased family engagement and sociocultural integration, all while affirming the diverse funds of knowledge that linguistically minoritized students and families bring to the classroom and beyond.

Greater family engagement is correlated with higher student achievement.[39] Projects like the "Faith and *Familia* as Funds of Knowledge" project demonstrate respect and value for home cultures and traditions, which we believe were key reasons we found increased family engagement. Meaningful home-based literacy practices foster not only sociocultural integration but also academic achievement and language proficiency. Relationships of trust are developed as family stories are shared, further developing authentic partnerships with parents.[40]

Through my research I was also able to introduce this project to a first-grade public school classroom on the West Coast, which was a similar urban Latinx setting. The teacher I worked with enjoyed exploring new children's literature selections that her student population was able to connect with and appreciate, seeing their traditions and language represented in a positive manner. This teacher experienced mixed success her first year with the project. Some of the same families who typically participated in home-based activities were more active with this project, and importantly, a couple of additional families that were previously unresponsive were encouragingly responsive with this approach. With normally limited access to children's literature, this project opened culturally relevant avenues for expression and biliteracy appreciation.

The "Faith and *Familia* as Funds of Knowledge" project both directly and indirectly spread in TWIN-CS, with other schools taking and modifying it for their own contexts. Reflecting on lessons learned through my experience with TWIN-CS, I am reminded of how important the "safety" of the learning environment is for both students and adults. TWIN-CS fosters community and a truly effective professional learning network. The structure and design of the summer academy affirms the diverse schemas and skill sets that individual educators and implementation teams bring while scaffolding us all in our zones of proximal development.[41] The design team often encourages us to take the stance of a "critical friend" to help develop best practices and innovations in culturally and linguistically responsive pedagogy.

Particularly when multicultural communities interact, there can be miscommunication and misunderstanding, ethnocentrism and linguicism. However, the annual summer academies and networking activities during the school year are very intentional about valuing the multicultural nature of the participants and the networking endeavor. I experienced how cultural and linguistic diversity in this network yielded mutual edification rather than discord.

The culture of the network allowed individuals to converse freely and in varied languages (such as including signs and encouraging discourse in English, Spanish, and Mandarin, and not necessarily in that order). By valuing bilingualism, biculturalism, and biliteracy from the top down, each facet of the network felt that their contribution and their identity had value. As a result, I was able to learn from insights provided not only through presentations but also from collaborations with other mentors, principals, and teachers in the network. Members of the network felt comfortable and were motivated to share ideas (including successes and failures) about curriculum development, sociocultural integration, assessment, and other aspects of implementing a dual language program.

The network provided professional resources not just at the academy but also through online resources and other methods throughout the school year.

Rather than a "one shot" professional development session that soon falls by the wayside, the ongoing support provided through the network kept key principles in the forefront, revisiting and refining the development of best practices. Through webinars and video conferencing I had opportunities to learn from what other mentors were doing as well as to share our campus's successes and challenges, fostering problem-solving and innovation. Through a book study on *Learning to Improve* facilitated by the network, we were able to take a closer look at how the "Faith and *Familia* as Funds of Knowledge" project was going, as well as other issues our campus faced, by making our work problem-specific, measurable, and engaged in disciplined inquiry.[42]

Engaging family members effectively can be transformative for students and classrooms, particularly for culturally and linguistically diverse communities. Through a project like "Faith and *Familia* as Funds of Knowledge," campus leaders can tap into the funds of knowledge available in their diverse campus community while affirming and actively engaging all families in the learning process. This project brings together efforts that value the language skills, identities, and culturally based experiences of family members while integrating culturally relevant instructional practices. Through the professional learning community created by TWIN-CS, this practice developed and in turn catalyzed the principal, teachers, and mentor to collaboratively energize their parent-engagement strategy as a whole.

Educational leaders in other contexts can similarly use strategic and scaffolded networking that is grounded in an asset-based orientation to meaningfully engage families and develop authentic partnerships.[43] Teachers benefit from scaffolded experiences, time, and space to explore the funds of knowledge their students and their families possess. These help to dismantle equity traps as deficit orientations are replaced with asset orientations.[44] As discussed with the home-visit strategy in the first section of this chapter, time and support in processing such experiences, such as through a strategic, scaffolded network, allow teachers to clarify their understandings of their school communities, with colleagues and community cultural brokers as a valuable part of the learning experience. Intentional discussion and opportunities to brainstorm about the key values and resources of their school's community members can facilitate integration of rich funds of knowledge into the curriculum.

Strategic and scaffolded networking strengthens learning communities within and across schools for the advancement of culturally and linguistically responsive schooling. When a networking framework is applied to increasing authentic family engagement, such networks serve to equip, catalyze, and sustain effective practices so that culturally and linguistically responsive learning communities flourish..

8

Distributing Leadership

ILIANA ALANÍS AND MARIELA A. RODRÍGUEZ

EDUCATIONAL LEADERS who advance culturally responsive schooling serve as change agents who provide equity for their students and the families they represent. These leaders provide "emancipatory spaces for students, parents, teachers, and other constituents."[1] Effective administrators strive to empower all stakeholders to advance a shared vision for culturally sustaining student learning.[2]

In this chapter, we first describe how culturally and linguistically responsive leadership connects to distributed leadership.[3] We then focus on two member schools in the Two-Way Immersion Network for Catholic Schools (TWIN-CS) where we have worked as mentors. We describe the processes each school's principal used to distribute leadership in manners that advanced teachers' knowledge, skills, and dispositions toward culturally and linguistically responsive schooling. We highlight how networking facilitated bridging among key stakeholders. We close this chapter with implications for how leaders can promote transformation within a broad range of educational contexts by using strategic networking to foster distributed leadership.

CULTURALLY AND LINGUISTICALLY
RESPONSIVE LEADERSHIP

Distributed leadership posits that successful educational leadership practices are often not restricted to the work of an individual but instead distributed across the school context through key stakeholders. While each individual leader's knowledge, skills, and dispositions are important, a range of individuals share expertise and enact practices.[4] The concept of distributed leadership, while continuing to evolve and develop, has strongly influenced thinking in the field of educational leadership.[5]

Distributed leadership is important when working with linguistically minoritized students, as this type of leadership reflects a productive way for schools to advance educational equity when becoming culturally and linguistically responsive.[6] As discussed throughout this book, leaders of culturally and linguistically responsive schools do three things: build students' sociocultural competence, respect and cultivate proficiency in home and community languages in addition to English, and promote all students' academic achievement.[7] Culturally and linguistically responsive leadership practices are *distributed* to the degree that they incorporate collaborative efforts. This entails everything from determining the service delivery model offered to coordinating the delivery of professional development and securing and allocating resources.

In culturally and linguistically responsive schools, culture plays a significant role, in particular when it comes to leadership practices. In Latinx-dominant schools and districts along the US–Mexico border, López, González, and Fierro found that Latinx leaders understand that linguistically minoritized students often encounter borders. These borders can be physical, as those immigrant students might face, or experiential, such as challenges posed within school systems to students' cultural and linguistic identities. Leaders who engage in culturally and linguistically responsive practices attend to these borders, determine their root, and then act as bridge builders, identifying ways to counter or eliminate such challenges through distributed leadership. For instance, one way that Latinx leaders engage in distributive leadership that enacts social justice educational agendas is by participating in school-university partnerships.[8] These partnerships lead to reciprocal relationships between the school and community with a shared vision of excellence for students. Additionally, Latinx leaders' cultural positionality fuels their commitment to equity for working-class Latinx students and families located within their neighborhood schools.[9] This personal and professional belief system is necessary when principals work to become cultural change agents for social justice and eliminate boundaries caused by language and cultural differences.

While the example above spoke of Latinx leaders specifically, this cultural work is important for all school leaders, regardless of their race or ethnicity. Effective principals are highly skilled in human relations, and able to confront racial tensions and work with people with ingrained negative attitudes.[10] Culturally and linguistically responsive leaders model the behavior they seek from teachers and staff within their schools and consistently engage all staff members in inclusive practices so that such practices become the high-quality standard required for successful schools. It is critical for school leaders to maintain a "supportive school-wide climate" and a willingness to develop professionally with their teachers as they supervise "quality implementation and improvement," thus fostering ownership of a shared vision among faculty and staff.[11]

As cultural workers, school leaders within culturally and linguistically responsive schools advocate for those silenced by "the hegemony of English" that perpetuates English as the sole language of academic instruction.[12] They ground their decision-making in instructional practices that serve all students, resisting sociopolitical pressure to place students designated as English Learners (ELs) into classrooms that affirm only English and ignore the assets of other languages. Educational leaders need to think and act in revolutionary ways to meet the needs of all students.[13] This means campus leaders must be advocates for students and their families, engage stakeholders in multiple levels of collaborative planning, support their teachers with the necessary professional development, and secure appropriate curricular resources.[14]

Distributed leadership to advance culturally and linguistically responsive schooling is relationship-centered. It emphasizes collaboration and participation in decision-making processes and involves multiple voices in developing positive school performance.[15] This is neither an easy nor a solitary endeavor.

It requires a team who shares a common vision and calls for leaders to foster critical conversations around culture, language, race, and power.

Having discussed the connection between distributed leadership and culturally and linguistically responsive schooling, we now turn to describe our experiences in two member schools in TWIN-CS. We focus on how distributed leadership helped them become culturally and linguistically responsive schools.

DISTRIBUTED LEADERSHIP IN TWIN-CS

In this section, we share the experiences from St. Mary Magdalen (SMM) and St. Leo the Great (SLG), the two network schools where we served as TWIN-CS mentors for three years. Our work as mentors begins with our role as university faculty whose research focuses on dual language education for Latinx children. Principals at SMM and SLG contacted us to work with school principals and their implementation teams to support students' development of bilingualism and biliteracy within the TWIN-CS model. Both principals began with limited knowledge of two-way immersion (TWI). Their commitment to equity and access for working-class Latinx students and families, however, resulted in their need to use their local and national networks to nurture an understanding of this philosophy among their staff. This eventually led to distributed leadership at their campus and among the members of TWIN-CS.

Situated within San Antonio, the seventh largest city in Texas, leaders at SMM and SLG engaged in a process to realign and restructure their educational program to meet the needs of their communities. Both serve students from predominantly Latinx, working-class families of Mexican descent. According to William Daily, the campus principal at SMM, "families are predominately third- or fourth-generation who want their children to regain their Spanish language." Many of the students classified as Spanish speakers in the classrooms at SMM and SLG are more proficient in English than their mother tongue. As young heritage language learners, children arrive at the school with a strong command of English while in the process of regaining their Spanish language through the TWI program.

Adopting the TWI program was a calculated risk for both SMM and SLG. Although principals believed the community would support the new program, the lack of other Catholic schools implementing such a model led to doubt and uncertainty. Nonetheless, campus leaders forged ahead, blazing new trails for Catholic education. In describing our experiences of how distributed leadership helped these schools in the process of transformation, we focus on how various leaders within these schools and across the network shared leadership. Formal leaders in these schools include the members of the implementation teams—both administrators (principal and assistant principal, the academic dean) and teachers. Leadership was also distributed to us as mentors, and with the TWIN-CS design team.

We focus on three key ways leadership was distributed: between administrators and teachers; between administrators and TWIN-CS mentors; and among administrators, families, and communities. We illustrate how these practices of distributed leadership, assisted by strategic and scaffolded networking, advanced culturally and linguistically responsive schooling.

Distributed Leadership Between Administrators and Teachers

A key structure for distributed leadership between administrators and teachers was the implementation team. Composed of principals, assistant principals, academic deans, and lead teachers, the implementation team brought together stakeholders and formed bridges of support in each school. The implementation team led the implementation of the TWI model and maintained ongoing responsibility for ensuring fidelity.[16] In both SMM and SLG, the principals led their implementation teams' efforts to empower teachers to shape and reform their teaching and learning environment and fostered relational trust among their staff.[17]

Distributing leadership within implementation teams and between implementation team members and the rest of the school staff required building trust and respect on existing relationships. Personal relationships are an important factor in schools' success and unfold in a particular manner in Catholic school contexts.[18] The experience of working together helped build a strong relationship among school leaders and their leadership team. They worked closely day in and day out, most times meeting long after the school day ended and on weekends. During these times, leadership teams engaged in curriculum alignment, class scheduling, strategies for parental communication in Spanish and English, and resource allocation to support their TWI programs. Working together, for extended periods, allowed the principal and leadership team to understand each other's leadership style and ways they could complement and support each other. It is important for each school to find common values that join them as a team. In the case of our Catholic schools, leaders built mutual trust and respect through shared values and beliefs rooted in the tenets of Catholicism and spiritual capital.[19] This shared religious community served as a critical point of connection for all of these educational leaders.

Professional development

An important way the implementation team distributed leadership between administrators and teachers was through professional development. The shift from a monolingual school to the TWI model required extensive training, both in the philosophy and pedagogy of TWI. Implementation teams were supported by four types of professional development offered by the network design team: the annual summer academies (a five-day working conference for teams from each member school), bimonthly webinars providing focused professional development for teachers, internet-based support (shared online resources), and personal consultations. Principals attended these sessions and learned alongside their staff. Following trainings, teachers shared new ideas with their colleagues, and teams then brainstormed how they could implement these ideas within the daily schedule. These conversations served to shift teachers and administrators from norms of isolation to collaboration.

To share evidence of fidelity assurance, the principal at SMM asked members of the implementation team, including the TWIN-CS mentor, the school's academic dean, and several teachers, to meet monthly for professional development. Implementation teams worked to design professional development sessions that clearly aligned with teacher needs, pedagogy, and curricula. For instance, a significant component of any culturally responsive TWI program is to respect and cultivate proficiency in the home and community languages in addition to English. Based on input from the implementation team, teachers received extensive professional development around processes for promoting active use of both languages in their classrooms. These sessions, led by the mentor, included practices related to specific components of the TWI model. These included word walls for new vocabulary, bilingual classroom labeling, and alphabets that were created by students. The principal and teachers visited classrooms to see where word walls and student-generated alphabets were implemented within the lesson cycle. Then, teachers met in grade-level teams to discuss how these practices were helping children attain biliteracy.

Additionally, early childhood teachers in the preK three-year-old class through second grade created learning centers in a minimum of four core areas (reading, mathematics, science, and social studies). Teachers designed centers to facilitate academic and linguistic proficiency in two languages through developmentally appropriate practices. As a result, teachers at SMM shared ideas for instruction and creating their learning environment with other TWI teachers from other network schools through virtual visits.

Another example involves monthly professional development sessions around the use of journal writing to develop first- and second-language reading and writing skills across grade levels. Preschool and kindergarten teachers brought student writing samples in English and Spanish to monthly meetings with the mentor. These samples of authentic writing highlighted what young children were capable of when teachers scaffolded for them. This system of exploring results and reflecting on students' biliteracy development resulted in a systematic, shared approach to professional development for teachers and administrators. It also kept a focus on the TWI goals for their school, leading to improved culturally and linguistically responsive practices that were evident in teachers' lesson plans and teaching practices.

Designated lead teachers

Along with establishing an implementation team and advancing professional development, another pattern of distributed leadership between administrators and teachers in SMM and SLG was with lead teachers. In both member schools, the principals understood that teachers were important resources to help build each school's capacity for the TWI implementation. School principals selected lead teachers from the core group of teachers who had demonstrated success in the classroom and had received professional development in the summer academies. To be efficient, they designated lead teachers to grade clusters: one for the prekindergarten classrooms, a second for the kindergarten to second-grade classrooms, and a third for the third and fourth grades. They gave lead teachers added responsibilities including coordinating grade-level meetings, developing lesson plans, and serving as grade-level liaisons to the administrative team. Distributing leadership in this manner gave lead teachers opportunities to engage in a role that extended beyond their classrooms, thus developing their leadership skills.

Administrators tasked lead teachers in targeted ways, such as helping develop their skills in curriculum development, communication, and mentorship. Lead teachers built on curriculum development that supported implementation of the program for all involved. Part of this process included the use of assessment data to inform instruction. For example, the TWIN-CS design team advised all network schools to conduct language assessments for all students in the program. Lead teachers facilitated this process for their teachers. They coordinated the administration of the assessment and led discussions on how to best use this information to improve instruction.

Lead teachers served as boundary spanners, connecting teachers who might otherwise remain isolated from each other. Coordinating communication is a key mechanism for addressing misconceptions and sharing relevant and important information about the TWI program. Communication channels ranged widely, from informal hallway, telephone, and email conversations, to formal, scheduled meetings. A lead teacher, for example, would sometimes email questions developed at grade-level meetings to the mentor, or at times ask clarifying questions when the mentor walked in for a classroom visit. Lead teachers would then share guidance provided by the mentor with other teachers.

Lead teachers advised novice teachers on teaching strategies and classroom management. For example, new kindergarten and first-grade teachers at SMM looked to a seasoned first-grade TWI teacher for suggestions about writing development. They gathered in the lead teacher's classroom to observe her teach mini-lessons, and then tried out the strategies she modeled with their own classes. Teachers would share samples of student work with the lead teacher and evaluate next steps for students. In this sense, lead teachers' experience was elevated when their peers viewed them as experts in their respective areas.

Lead teachers also helped teachers and principals navigate tensions. There were times during the shift to TWI when teachers and the school principal disagreed on how to resolve an issue. For example, some teachers believed staff were speaking more English than Spanish throughout the day. Teachers asked the principal to visit the classrooms more often to offer feedback. At times, the principal would invite the TWIN-CS mentors and all would meet with the teacher to offer their suggestions. In these instances, each listened to the other with respect, valued what was said, and worked to understand other perspectives. Ultimately, school principals made decisions in concert with their lead teachers and mentors. Allowing teachers to engage in these processes helped them share responsibility for school change.

In sum, by establishing implementation teams, designing professional development, and designating lead teachers, the school principals we worked with established a culture of learning where teachers and administrators learned from one another and shared in problem solving. Each principal stressed the need for leadership that encouraged dialogue and reflection through mutual respect. Together they developed their understanding of the TWI model, the significance of quality instruction in two languages, and the need to mentor each other through the process. This process allowed them to nurture and sustain a strong community that was responsive to students' cultural and linguistic needs.

Distributed Leadership Between Administrators and TWIN-CS Mentors

Yet another manifestation of distributed leadership is how these school leaders worked with us as their TWIN-CS mentors to facilitate implementation of the new TWI model. In both campuses, the principal introduced us to teachers and parents as the dual language experts who were there to help their school make the transition from a monolingual English campus to a TWI campus. Although as mentors we were not regular school staff, from the onset we were welcomed as part of the school family. Teachers frequently expressed their gratitude for our expertise, time, and collegiality.

To build a culture of learning and to augment teachers' understanding of bilingual pedagogy, school principals asked us to provide in-class coaching. We coordinated visits with each teacher to determine needs, conducted in-class observations, and completed post-observation debriefings on a monthly basis. These regular classroom visits created a culture where teachers and administrators felt free to ask questions, take risks, and try our suggestions. Over time, these professional relationships built the collective capacity as everyone worked toward the shared goals of the TWI program.

Alongside these classroom visits, school principals invited us to participate in a wide array of meetings, including program-planning meetings, monthly parent-information sessions, and grade-level planning meetings. Grade-level planning meetings were particularly productive and focused. As mentors, we used this time to address questions or concerns, share best practices for students, and validate teachers' efforts. These meetings also provided an opportunity for teachers to highlight what students were learning in their classrooms. For instance, we encouraged teachers to share samples of students' writing, ideas for learning centers, and classroom-management strategies.

Mentors in TWIN-CS regularly facilitate in-service trainings for staff prior to and throughout the school year. During these trainings, mentors provide teachers with children's books, classroom materials, and online resources. For instance, at SMM we introduced teachers to a free online curriculum for children ages two through eight that included animated activities in English and Spanish, each teaching a specific learning topic. After becoming familiar with what the site had to offer, teachers asked for additional training to develop these online activities for parents to engage with their child at home. Teachers in turn trained parents on how to use the online curriculum to augment children's emergent literacy skills. The teachers felt this helped develop their knowledge and understanding of early literacy for culturally and linguistically minoritized students as well as their capacity to advocate for school-home connections.

Mentors also help distribute leadership by serving as liaisons between the TWI teachers and the school principal. For example, on several occasions teachers expressed concerns about various issues, including scheduling, lack of planning time, and classroom rosters. We in turn shared these with the school principal, who worked with us to address the concerns in a reasonable manner. This was evident when both English- and Spanish-speaking parents at SMM struggled with assisting their children with homework in an unfamiliar language. Mentors and teachers discussed strategies to respond, such as providing parents with instructions for homework assignments in their native language, differentiating for language levels, and making sure students could do homework independently. While parents reported concerns directly to the school principal, he stepped back and encouraged teachers to work with families to problem-solve. This established a culture that empowered teachers to shape their teaching and learning community. Whether explaining differences between basic language acquisition and academic language proficiency or providing specific instructional practices to promote biliteracy, TWI teachers became strong advocates for the program, themselves, and their students.

Similarly, school principals sometimes expressed their concerns to us as mentors. These included questions over the correct amount of classroom instruction to conduct in Spanish, and best instructional practices for TWI settings. We then used these questions to develop future professional development sessions for teachers and administrative teams.

Importantly, our experiences have shown us that we as TWIN-CS mentors were also in need of mentoring. Along with other fellow TWIN-CS mentors, we often raise questions to problem-solve together. This occurs through phone calls, emails, and monthly webinars hosted by the design team, where mentors across the network meet virtually to ask questions, share ideas for best practices, and encourage each other through the process.

This distributed leadership between school administrators and mentors, facilitated by the TWIN-CS design team, has promoted a culture of learning and support as everyone learns how to work together toward a shared vision. By making a concerted effort to help teachers remain current around best practices for second-language learners, school principals demonstrated leadership. Importantly, the principals feel that this has led to culturally responsive instructional practices in classrooms. Principals have also reported higher student performance on a variety of school and standardized language and literacy assessments, which we believe may be correlated with the improved classroom strategies and outcomes.

Distributed Leadership Among Families

Another form of distributed leadership occurs between schools and the families they serve. In the process of moving to the TWI model, the principals of SMM and SLG recognized that the assets of a school community extend to the parents and caregivers and their broader communities. There was a strong commitment on behalf of the TWI teachers and principals to nurture relationships with their students' families through open door policies, family/school events, and afterschool activities. This was critical, as outreach between school and home should be a continuous and authentic process.

One of the first ways school principals in SMM and SLG built relationships with families was by providing space and time for parents to learn about the new TWI approach prior to and during their schools' adoption of the model. This included informal meetings, classroom visits, and information sessions throughout the academic year. Principals did not lead the formal information sessions by themselves, but instead drew on mentor leadership and teacher support. Mentors were able to speak directly to the families, explaining the program to them in Spanish and English. This was critical to gain the trust and support of families and community members. Mentors used these sessions to share research related to TWI and emphasize the goals and structure of the TWI program. School principals also asked TWI teachers to present at these sessions. Teachers highlighted student success, presented new initiatives, and answered questions.

These information sessions provided a forum for parents to express their concerns, ask questions, or debunk misconceptions or myths about learning in two languages. Parents of different linguistic and cultural identities raised concerns. In some cases, English-dominant parents had difficulty understanding the TWI program expectations. For example, many did not understand the length of time required for languages to develop. Some questioned why their child was not fluent in the second language after one or two years in the program. School principals encouraged teachers to engage in discussions with parents about their concerns but to continue advocating for maintenance of a child's first language as children gained proficiency in the second.

Although the SMM and SLG principals are White, native English speakers, both developed competency in Spanish to engage with families and students. Mrs. Carol Johnson, principal at SLG, used herself as a model when talking with students about the value of bilingualism. Principals demonstrated this asset-based mind-set toward language learning in their use of Spanish and English for parent meetings, signage displayed in the halls, and expectations for language use within the classrooms. Principals also reflected this mind-set in their strategic use of networking and distributed leadership for professional development opportunities and the designation of lead TWI teachers.

An important component of distributing leadership among families involves interrogating policies and procedures that perpetuate social inequalities. As scholars in the field, we know that in many TWI programs, the hegemony of English leads to a focus on English success.[20] We ensured that school principals were aware of the way the English language is frequently elevated as the language of power. Principals worked to implement linguistic equity in classrooms to avoid English dominance and the marginalization of Spanish. For example, when parents at SMM echoed teachers' concern over the minimal Spanish children were learning, the school principal and the TWI teachers worked to alleviate those concerns. Together, they decided to allocate more time in Spanish for their prekindergarten classrooms, moving from 50 percent of the school day in Spanish to 90 percent of the school day in Spanish.

This change was complicated by the lack of academic materials in Spanish. As mentors, we knew that this challenge was not unique to the TWI classrooms in these schools, as many teachers across the country report their frustration with the lack of Spanish materials.[21] These teachers, however, were highly creative and resourceful. They shared ideas and materials with each other. As their mentors, we reached out to the broader TWIN-CS network for support, and contacted book companies to donate books and related materials for the teachers' use.

The principals were likewise resourceful. Each used professional and social capital as a lever for developing partnerships with local universities and the city government, building coalitions with culturally and linguistically diverse groups in order to work toward educational equity. In the fall of 2015, for example, SMM partnered with a large four-year state university for research initiatives. This networking facilitated research within the TWI classrooms and led to school-home collaborations that facilitated children's early writing and math development in the preschool classrooms.[22]

Members within the neighborhood community also need to feel connected to the school. Like most TWIN-CS schools, SMM and SLG have a church and parish closely associated with the school. School principals and teachers invited the community to attend multiple fiestas, fairs, and masses with the elementary school children. The teachers and students coordinated these frequent events, allowing the community to see the benefit of bilingualism as students worshiped and praised in two languages. In turn, members of the parish became TWI program advocates and helped recruit students to their parish school, including students of other religious backgrounds.

Essentially, through a shared commitment and collective capacity, key stakeholders were able to sustain a program of enriched linguistic and cultural learning for their students. Through distributive leadership practices, principals at SMM and SLG promoted ownership, respect, and advocacy for students and their families. This collaboration facilitated the (re)creation of their schools' service delivery models to foster high levels of bilingualism, biliteracy, and biculturalism for all students. Through intentional collaboration where all had an influence on the TWI model, these school leaders shaped the school culture and recognized the valuable resources that schools have in teachers, families, and the surrounding community, eliminating boundaries between and among key stakeholders.

IMPLICATIONS FOR EDUCATIONAL LEADERS

In this chapter, we have described how culturally and linguistically responsive leadership and distributed leadership are connected, drawing on our experiences with TWIN-CS as illustrative. We have found that collaboration among educators advanced these schools' organizational learning, in these contexts helping the schools become more culturally and linguistically responsive. Although these experiences have occurred in private, faith-based institutions transforming from monolingual to TWI service delivery models, the lessons apply to multiple settings and other educational models. These two schools share features with neighborhood, magnet, and charter schools serving culturally and linguistically diverse populations of students. As such, their story has several implications for all school leaders seeking to make their schools more culturally and linguistically responsive.

First, regardless of school context, leadership must go beyond the formal leader and depend equally on the collaboration, participation, and commitment of their teachers. Additionally, leaders must recognize the power of distributed leadership as better able to ensure strong curricular and instructional practices are taking place within their school.[23] This requires designating lead teachers to work with novice teachers when new initiatives are taking place or reaching out to others who can work with staff to implement new initiatives.

Second, all school principals must embrace the linguistic and cultural richness that children bring to school and accept the magnitude of collaboration needed among families and communities for students to succeed. Regardless of school setting, it is critical when working in culturally responsive settings to take a holistic communal approach to maintain families' cultural wealth and to mobilize initiatives by working with parents and community members. This approach can lead to programs, strategies, and efforts that are tailored to the needs of the students and their communities. This requires the integration of all who work with children in and outside the school and ensures that the learning does not stop the moment children leave school grounds but rather continues into the community and inside children's homes.[24]

Third, through a shared commitment of transformative schooling, leaders must identify community-based partnerships that empower all stakeholders and lead to the maintenance of cultural community wealth. Leaders who engage in culturally and linguistically responsive practices act as bridge builders who identify ways to counter or eliminate challenges to students' native language and culture. For instance, schools can identify and implement partnerships with outside resources such as universities or youth groups that are appropriate and effective for the population they serve. Establishing school-community partnerships that align with the goals of the school promotes equity-oriented and socially just practices that lead to culturally relevant work.

In conclusion, school leaders working toward culturally responsive schooling must be cultural change agents who think in revolutionary ways and engage in distributive leadership practices. There must be a culture of learning and support for risk taking and experimentation as individuals and entities learn how to best work together. When administrators create situations for teachers to build their leadership capacity, they create a culture of learning that reflects shared vision and collaboration. Acknowledging areas for growth allows administrators to engage in strategic guidance from colleagues, mentors, and content-area experts who can advance their understanding of culturally and linguistically responsive schooling. This requires a commitment to advocate for academic and linguistic equity, ensure access to high-quality curriculum and resources, and promote equitable learning environments for all students. As educators continue to engage in this critical work, distributed leadership that values partnerships among teachers, families, and communities must be at the forefront of this process of transformation.

PART THREE

IMPLICATIONS

9

Transforming Communities of
Practice Through Networks

MARTIN SCANLAN, KRISTIN BARSTOW MELLEY,
MATIAS PLACENCIO-CASTRO, AND LARRY LUDLOW

THE THEORY OF ACTION illustrated by the Two-Way Immersion Network for Catholic Schools (TWIN-CS) is that strategic and scaffolded networking that is grounded in an asset-based orientation advances culturally and linguistically responsive schooling. This theory of action is grounded in literature on culturally and linguistically responsive schools and organizational learning. It applies the sociocultural learning theory of communities of practice (COPs) to the context of schools serving linguistically minoritized students. This chapter discusses how the COPs that have spurred the organizational learning within each TWIN-CS member school have evolved over the past five years. Certain aspects of this evolution—what has spurred it, what has impeded it, how it has unfolded unevenly—can be instructive to educational leaders seeking to apply this theory of action and foster transformation in their own contexts. We begin by discussing the COPs at the network level of TWIN-CS. We then discuss how they affect organizational learning, both

157

in the context of Catholic schools and with regard to culturally and linguistically responsive schooling.

UNFOLDING COMMUNITIES OF PRACTICE

The theory of COPs holds that we make meaning of experiences, develop our knowledge and skills, and form our sense of identity through interactions with others. It holds that we learn socially, participating in both formal and informal manners. A COP is present when people are mutually engaged in a joint enterprise, sharing a repertoire of practices. While learning can take place in many places and manners, Wenger writes in a foundational description of COPs, "learning that is most personally transformative turns out to be the learning that involves membership in these communities of practice."[1]

Clearly formal groups, from a social club to a committee to a political party, could be described as having the three characteristics of COPs—mutual engagement, a joint enterprise, and a shared repertoire. However, the theory of COP provides a broader lens for analyzing the process of learning:

> For *individuals*, it means that learning is an issue of engaging in and contributing to the practices of their communities . . . For *communities*, it means that learning is an issue of refining their practice and ensuring new generations of members . . . For *organizations*, it means that learning is an issue of sustaining the interconnected communities of practice through which an organization knows what it knows and thus becomes effective and valuable as an organization.[2]

Thus, there is not one hard and fast rule for defining the parameters of a COP. Instead, the concept is flexible. This flexibility is precisely what makes the COP lens useful for helping educational leaders notice—and ideally support—productive interactions to advance this learning.[3]

A strategy for identifying COPs is examining the *relational networks* among educators. Research shows that relational networks are central to transformational leadership, and that understanding that these relationships can help educational leaders advances organizational learning. For instance, principals exhibit transformational leadership when they engage and support teachers in conceptualizing and enacting changes.[4] Principals with strong relational networks within schools are able to enact transformational leadership and foster innovative climates.[5] Integrated leadership—transformational leadership coupled with shared instructional leadership—helps organizations "learn and perform at high levels."[6] Conversely, as Daly and colleagues note, negative interactions among educators can be mutually reinforcing: "As leaders interact with one another, they form predictable patterns for how each will respond to another. If the response is negative, then the leader is likely to also respond in a negative manner."[7]

Since relational networks are what create COPs, illuminating these relationships is helpful. Social network analysis provides an approach to do so. Social network analysis is an evolving research strategy to describe relational networks.[8] Relationships vary across multiple dimensions, including number (some individuals have many relationships, others are isolated), stability (some relationships are deep and enduring, others ephemeral), and quality (relationships involve exchanging various levels of expertise, knowledge, and information). To examine relational networks, social network analysis involves identifying the range of individuals who compose a given network, measuring the direction and flow of communications among these individuals ("degree centrality")[9] and the relative strength of their communications with others ("network cohesion").[10] Boundary spanners are people who are identified as having multiple relationships, particularly in linking individuals who would otherwise be isolated from each other.

If these concepts are applied to examine the relational networks in TWIN-CS, we might find that members of an implementation team in a school have high levels of degree centrality, in that they communicate among themselves often. A given implementation team might also have strong network cohesion, in that the communication is meaningful. However, as a group, they might be relatively isolated from implementation teams in other member schools, or from the design team. The mentor for this school (who coaches the implementation team) might serve as a boundary spanner, helping broker communication between this implementation team and others, perhaps by communicating with fellow mentors. The mentor might also be a bridge back to the design team.

The theory of COPs holds that learning is happening among different individuals—members of an implementation team, the mentor, and the design team—within their particular relational networks, both within and across member schools. Within one school, this networking creates a COP among members of the implementation team, their mentor, and the design team (figure 2.2). Across multiple schools, the networking creates other COPs, both among many schools brokered by the design team and directly between schools—such as among implementation teams or among mentors (figure 2.3).

A tangible example of these different COPs can be seen in the curriculum development between two TWIN-CS schools, All Souls and Archbishop Borders.[11] Here, select teachers in each school engaged with their respective mentors in developing a new approach to curriculum, instruction, and assessment in the area of writing. From one angle, these could be viewed as distinct COPs—one comprising select teachers and the mentor in All Souls, another comprising select teachers and the mentor in Archbishop Borders. From another angle, this could be considered a broader COP, encompassing participants from both schools.

Studying Communities of Practice in TWIN-CS

To better understand the COPs within TWIN-CS, three studies have been conducted using social network analysis. These drew on data from surveys of participants in TWIN-CS (the design team, teachers and administrators in member schools, and their mentors), interviews with select boundary spanners that emerged from the survey, and archival documentation. The first of these studies examined leadership practices germane to the formation of relational networks during the first year and a half of TWIN-CS.[12] The second and third studies took closer looks into the compositions of the social networking within TWIN-CS during 2014–15 and 2016–17.[13] Drawing from data similar to those gathered during the initial study, these follow-up studies looked more systematically at the relational networks across TWIN-CS, conducting statistical analysis of the network structure, and measured degree centrality and network cohesion.[14] These studies considered three types of communication, ranging in specificity from broad (general communication), to narrower (general advice on the two-way immersion [TWI] model) to narrowest (specific advice on an issue related to TWI).

160

One key finding of these studies is that within a network such as TWIN-CS, multiple intersecting COPs unfold over time, not all at once. Initially, the emergent COPs—primarily at the level of individual member schools—were extemporaneous, tentative, and localized. The composition and communication patterns of implementation teams varied markedly during the early years, despite the design team's attempts to orchestrate similar approaches across TWIN-CS. Even within schools, the educators differed markedly in how they perceived the process of adapting to the new TWI service delivery model. For instance, in one school, the mentor commented, "Overall teaming is weak and structures are inconsistent; there is not a schedule/structure for ongoing work." At the same time, a teacher in this school reported, "We are always discussing best practices and assessment results. We work to provide our students with rich cultural experiences and find ways to get our parents involved."[15] Educators primarily connected with colleagues that worked closely with them. During the first year, "relational network survey data indicated that 80% of all communications regarding meeting the needs of TWI students occurred within the immediate stakeholders of schools, not with other member schools or the TWIN-CS Design Team members."[16]

The second and third studies provide additional evidence into how the networking developed and matured into multiple overlapping and intersecting COPs. During the 2014–15 year a whole-network COP was characterized by a core-and-periphery structure, where design team members functioned as information hubs brokering connections among implementation team members across schools. Two years later, while the network maintained a core-periphery structure with the design team located in the inner core, an external core layer emerged, comprising mentors and principals surrounding the design team. The relational networks were growing more complex, with multiple boundary spanners emerging.

Sociograms are helpful for visualizing these shifts. Consider how general communications over the whole network are illustrated in figures 9.1 and 9.2. Individuals are represented as shapes that correspond to their roles (e.g., mentor), and lines represent communication between two individuals. In the sociogram for 2014–15, one distinct hub is evident, comprising design team members (highlighted with a shaded oval in figure 9.1). The preponderance of communication from members across the network is with members in

FIGURE 9.1

2014–15 general communication network structure

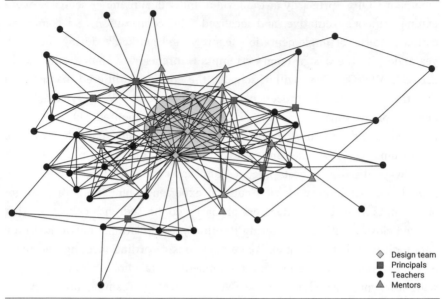

◇ Design team
■ Principals
● Teachers
▲ Mentors

Source: Martin Scanlan, Minsong Kim, and Larry Ludlow, "Affordances and Constraints of Communities of Practice to Promote Bilingual Schooling," *Journal of Professional Capital and Community* 4 (2019): 82–106.

this hub. In the 2016–17 sociogram, the communication patterns are more complicated, with at least two distinct hubs evident (highlighted with two shaded ovals in figure 9.2). Instead of the preponderance of communication occurring with one group, the patterns of communication grew more complex. One way to interpret this is by considering the network as one large COP, in which the core members began expanding from one group (figure 9.1) to include more individuals (figure 9.2). Another way to interpret this is as multiple COPs emerging within the overarching network. The point is not that one interpretation is "better" or "correct"—but rather that they represent different perspectives to understand how learning is unfolding across the network.

Along with this, although teachers are in peripheral locations in both 2014–15 and 2016–17 (represented by the circles in figures 9.1 and 9.2),

FIGURE 9.2
2016–17 general communication network structure

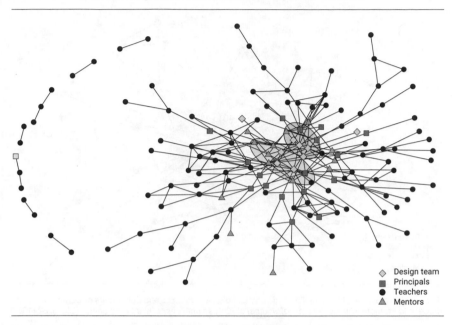

◇ Design team
■ Principals
● Teachers
▲ Mentors

Source: Martin Scanlan, Minsong Kim, and Larry Ludlow, "Affordances and Constraints of Communities of Practice to Promote Bilingual Schooling," *Journal of Professional Capital and Community* 4 (2019): 82–106.

the number of connections among teachers is increasing.[17] This suggests that relational networks among teachers are becoming denser in 2016–17. There are several paths composed by only three, four, or five teachers, and some of them are even isolated from the main network component. Again, consider the implication of this for COPs; this suggests that teachers are increasingly sharing with one another practices, experiences, and common challenges.

While these sociograms illustrate general levels of communication among educators, the multiple COPs that emerge over time become more evident in sociograms illustrating how educators across TWIN-CS reach out to one another seeking specific advice (figures 9.3 and 9.4).

In 2014–15, the design team again served as the core of the COP (see shaded oval in figure 9.3), with principals connecting to it most directly, followed by mentors, with teachers at the periphery. As the network of

FIGURE 9.3

2014–15 specific advice network structure

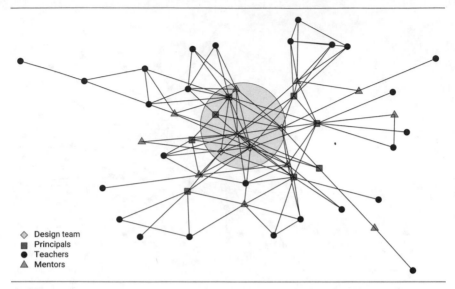

◇ Design team
■ Principals
● Teachers
▲ Mentors

Source: Martin Scanlan, Minsong Kim, and Larry Ludlow, "Affordances and Constraints of Communities of Practice to Promote Bilingual Schooling," *Journal of Professional Capital and Community* 4 (2019): 82–106.

TWIN-CS was still in the early stages of emergence at this point, the heavy reliance on the centrality of the design team was somewhat expected. Two years later, though the design team remained at the center of the network (see shaded oval in figure 9.4), relational networks were growing increasingly sophisticated. First, the composition of the hub became more complex, including not only design team members but also members of implementation teams (including mentors and a principal). In addition, distinct branches became evident (see five ribbons in figure 9.4), suggesting the rise of multiple COPs. Within each of these distinct groups, two or three boundary spanners functioned in bridging roles connecting back to the core. This pattern shows that educators' relevance within the network depends not only on the number of connections but also on their relative locations. Here several individuals, mainly mentors, are located in strategic bridging positions and playing the role of boundary spanners. In this way, they have great control

FIGURE 9.4
2016–17 specific advice network structure

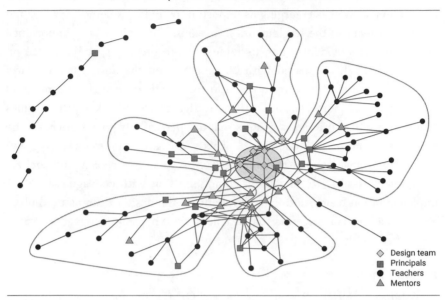

◇ Design team
■ Principals
● Teachers
▲ Mentors

Source: Martin Scanlan, Minsong Kim, and Larry Ludlow, "Affordances and Constraints of Communities of Practice to Promote Bilingual Schooling," *Journal of Professional Capital and Community* 4 (2019): 82–106.

over the information flows and could play an important role in the operation and future development of the network.

Our understanding of the shifting COPs that these sociograms illustrate is deepened by further analysis of the direction and flow of communication, as well as the relative strength of this communication, among the three key actors in TWIN-CS: the TWIN-CS design team (based at Boston College), school-based implementation teams, and school-specific mentors. During 2014–15, the design team was by far the central communicator—both in terms of sending information out and being sought out for answers. This was the case across all types of communication, ranging from general communication, to general advice, to specific advice. Using the community of practice framework, this centrality of the design team suggests that the learning among the educators participating in TWIN-CS primarily occurred in one large COP at this time, operating at the whole-network level.

Two years later, the evidence shows more complex relational networks. Mentors, for instance, became more active in initiating and receiving communication, as well as emerging as important boundary spanners connecting the design team to the implementation teams. This shift in the importance of mentors was evident when individuals were seeking specific advice on an issue in TWI. Compared with 2014–15, when the design team clearly exercised greater control over the information flow, in 2016–17 mentors were two times more central than the design team and almost three times more central than principals, results that are particularly consistent with the branches structure of the network.[18] This suggests that mentors were growing in importance as core members of COPs. As another example, teachers were far more likely to engage in communication with colleagues in other implementation teams, and far less reliant on the design team as the hub of all information. This suggests that teachers were becoming engaged in more diversified COPs.

Implications

The shifts in TWIN-CS from one large COP (i.e., all members of the network) to multiple intersecting COPs have two implications for educational leaders seeking to advance culturally and linguistically responsive schooling. One implication is the critical role that a core hub plays in *seeding* transformation. In the case of TWIN-CS, the design team was clearly a central catalyst to provide coherence and direction at the outset of this initiative. The hub provides strategic direction. It directs members of the network in how to engage in the process of adapting a new service delivery model, such as guiding principles for aligning curriculum to standards. The hub also provides scaffolding to network members, adjusting materials based on where they are in the process. For instance, in the case of TWIN-CS, some schools were already in the process of implementing a TWI model in several grades when they joined the network, while others were in the planning stages of the transition, and others still were start-up schools beginning from scratch. As a hub, the design team was well positioned to provide scaffolding across these different contexts.

A second implication of the shift from a large COP to multiple intersecting ones is less apparent, but equally important: micro-hubs are critical in *growing* transformation. While the central hub of the design team was a necessary catalyst to launch TWIN-CS, it soon became apparent that the network would benefit from balancing the strong central hub with dispersed responsibilities within the network. Developing outside expertise beyond the hub was an intentional goal of the design team. As mentors and principals grew more comfortable and confident in their roles, they came to play boundary-spanning roles with more novice members of the growing network.

Thus, the lessons of these two implications for educational leaders are twofold. For networking to be productive, a hub can serve to unify and catalyze initial efforts, but diversifying control over time is a valuable follow-up strategy, since reliance on an overly centralized COP may create a communication bottleneck and stifle ongoing innovation and adaptation across the network.

ORGANIZATIONAL LEARNING IN THE CATHOLIC CONTEXT

When considering the big picture of organizational learning across TWIN-CS, context matters. As described in chapter 2, three distinctive features of the context of Catholic schooling that ground this story are mission, governance, and resources. Several studies have examined how these dimensions are affecting the organizational learning in this particular context.[19]

Regarding mission, the evidence suggests that participating in the network catalyzed and scaffolded a mission revision. For instance, one study found that networking helped member schools systematically "strengthen the congruence of their TWI model with their school missions."[20] An illustration of this is how the language in mission statements changed after implementation teams worked on these at a summer academy. Figure 9.5 illustrates a content analysis of the language in mission statements across member schools. After revising their mission statements, implementation teams incorporated much more explicit language referencing a commitment to linguistically minoritized students, particularly by addressing cultural and linguistic diversity and social justice/global citizenship.

Relatedly, another study found member school principals describing the shift from a monolingual environment to one embracing bilingualism

FIGURE 9.5

Shifting language in mission statements in member schools

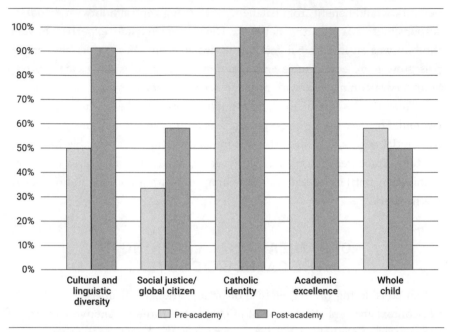

Source: Martin Scanlan et al. "Poco a Poco: Leadership Practices Supporting Productive Communities of Practice in Schools Serving the New Mainstream," *Educational Administration Quarterly* 52, no. 1 (2016), figure 7.

and biliteracy as a dramatic change in mission. For instance, one TWIN-CS principal reported that the former school principal saw it as "her duty" to take an English-only approach to teaching students designated as English Learners (ELs): "Therefore, it was absolutely illegal to speak Spanish . . . You got detention. You got grounded. As a result of that, there was a deep prejudice."[21] This study finds that the transition to the TWI model was one directly connected to these schools' missions: "the implementation of dual language programs in the Catholic schools in this study went to the core of teaching and learning and required a whole school reculturing process."[22]

Regarding governance, evidence shows that participating in the network supported the site-based decision making, while concomitantly reducing the isolation of schools. Dramatically shifting a school's model of educating students designated as ELs, from a monolingual approach to a TWI model fostering bilingualism and biliteracy, takes bold leadership. A study of the member school principals found that they were the key drivers of the change process in TWIN-CS, and that the site-based, top-down decision-making authority allowed these school leaders to initiate the dramatic changes. Some principals reported bold and entrepreneurial approaches to tackling their schools' problems, such as lacking viable enrollment and poor student learning outcomes for linguistically minoritized students. Others described their choices as hasty and reflecting a certain naivete. One principal considered that naivete may have actually helped:

> I know that some of the schools have done a year of planning before they jumped into it. I might have come back and done a year of planning. Maybe if I'd done that, I'd have said, "No. It's too much." Maybe I would've gotten push back from the teachers and they didn't want to do that or the parents. Instead, we just went into it. We barreled into it. We're going forward, and we're going to do it.[23]

Although these school leaders valued their autonomy, they nevertheless were operating under numerous constraints and limitations, including both central office (diocesan) policies and the local authority of the pastor. Thus, these principals' creative management and negotiating skills were central to their abilities to advance meaningful change. In one representative quote, a principal explained, "We're doing the work alone in our Archdiocese. Sometimes I feel like that. Having this [TWIN-CS] network has been so important because we can't do it alone. We have to be part of a community."[24] The social network analyses described above point to how participating in TWIN-CS provided vital connections to distribute this leadership, particularly in drawing on support and guidance from the design team and from mentors.

Finally, networking provided member schools both material and conceptual resources necessary for their transformation. Resource constraints both catalyzed the shift to the TWI model and presented barriers. Schools needed material resources to initiate the shift:

> Mostly, [principals] spoke of low enrollments or the lack of financial resources in the startup stage . . . Moreover, changing from standard monolingual textbooks and materials to dual language materials and curriculum is costly. The demands on teachers can also be overwhelming with little time for extended training or ongoing support in the initial stages.[25]

In multiple studies, school leaders across TWIN-CS report learning new strategies for attaining these material resources by collaborating with peers in the summer academies, the online webinars, and the direct communications and consultations among colleagues across member schools.[26]

Schools also needed conceptual resources. This included guidance on the host of decisions with which implementation teams were wrestling, from selecting a model of TWI for their community, to attaining and developing curricular materials and assessing language development. In addition to the fine-grained description of these practices described in part II of this volume, studies looking at the network as a whole point toward the structures and supports that helped member schools develop these conceptual resources. Again, multiple studies report developing conceptual resources via the networking in TWIN-CS.[27]

Clearly, material and conceptual resources are interconnected, with one informing the other. For instance, the design team directed member schools to ground the change process in both Catholic and TWI standards.[28] These conceptual resources directed the schools in their pursuit of material resources.

Implications

The organizational learning in TWIN-CS, involving the areas of mission, governance, and resources, has implications for educational leaders seeking to foster transformation in other contexts. Regarding mission, in TWIN-CS the school leaders were able to draw on the religious identity of the school— as well as their own affiliation with this faith tradition—as a resource to lead this shift. In secular contexts, school leaders can draw on broader commitments to educational equity to similarly catalyze this movement. School leadership to foster culturally and linguistically responsive schools must foreground mission—and specifically a mission to advance equitable opportunities for all to learn within a pluralistic democracy.

Regarding governance, the experiences in TWIN-CS point toward two lessons. On one hand, the experiences of TWIN-CS echo literature on organizational learning that shows building leaders as drivers of change.[29] While granted considerable autonomy to make decisions in their own school's curriculum and instruction, these principals found counsel, support, and encouragement by participating in a network. On the other hand, the experiences of TWIN-CS show the importance of productively distributing leadership. The nature of the network helped these independent principals reach out to others, receiving anchoring support from the central hub of the design team, critical feedback from their school-level mentors, and support to develop curriculum and professional development from their implementation teams.

Finally, networking can be a tool to creatively confront resource limitations. Strategic collaboration with colleagues across TWIN-CS allowed these Catholic schools to confront limitations in both material and conceptual resources.

ORGANIZATIONAL LEARNING ADVANCING CULTURALLY AND LINGUISTICALLY RESPONSIVE SCHOOLING

This big-picture view of the organizational learning—considering both the communities of practice across the network and the Catholic context—reflects fundamental changes across schools participating in this network that advance culturally and linguistically responsive schooling. Starting as monolingual, English-only environments with few if any supports for students designated as ELs, member schools in TWIN-CS engaged in a dramatic shift when they embraced the TWI model and joined this network. Yet this move resulted in tremendous gains in stability and vitality for some schools. The enrollment trends of the TWIN-CS member schools are markedly divergent from their monolingual English counterparts (see figure 9.6). Eight consecutive years of enrollment data for ten of the original TWIN-CS schools show the trends since TWIN-CS was formally launched in the fall of 2012 and held its first annual summer academy in 2013. The Roche Center for Catholic Education at Boston College, which houses TWIN-CS, tracks enrollment data for member schools and their corresponding dioceses. These

FIGURE 9.6

Enrollment trends in TWIN-CS member schools
compared with respective dioceses

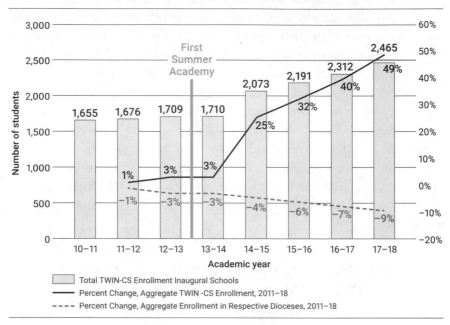

Source: Roche Center for Catholic Education, 2018.

enrollment numbers are represented by the solid and dashed lines, respectively. TWIN-CS member schools show continued enrollment growth despite a declining enrollment trend within each of the dioceses.[30]

Three aspects stand out in these enrollment trends. First, the data suggest that the change within the schools has been steady. As the overarching network evolved, the schools' new culturally and linguistically responsive identity grew more established. In time, this identity defied the downward enrollment trends of the surrounding schools. Second, these data point to the value families are placing on culturally and linguistically responsive schooling. While families have many Catholic schools to choose from in a given diocese, it is those schools that are explicitly culturally and linguistically responsive through their implementation of a TWI program that parents are seeking over those offering a monolingual English model. Third, the data suggest that the strategic and scaffolding networking within TWIN-CS is allowing member schools to overcome constraints on school change. Back in 2012, these schools in many ways resembled other schools in their dioceses in terms of mission, governance structure, and resources. Today, the first two factors remain much the same, while access to resources has drastically changed. As the organized learning of TWIN-CS evolved, member schools accessed necessary resources to manage change and navigate a course very different from their peer schools in their respective dioceses.

Organizational learning in member schools did not only increase the schools' stability and vitality, it also changed the practices of educators related to advancing culturally and linguistically responsive schooling. One study explored how teachers learned to change their practices.[31] It illuminates the complexities of shifting mind-sets and attitudes within a school, and how the support of a network was an important scaffold for this. This study found that while teachers supported the change from a monolingual to TWI model, they themselves paradoxically created barriers to enacting the change. One barrier was their deficit-based perspectives toward linguistic differences. Another was a lack of pedagogical skills to implement the new model. Specific strategies developed through TWIN-CS promoted organizational learning to address these barriers. First, engaging in courageous conversations around race, power, and privilege allowed the teachers to critically reflect on their own stances and develop more affirming, sensitive, and supportive approaches to their students' language and culture. Second, integrating the use of formative assessments allowed teachers to improve instructional practices to advance academic achievement as well as cultivate language proficiency. Both of these practices grew directly out of participation in the network—starting with work done by the implementation team at a summer academy and continuing with the mentor's support and guidance over the following academic year.

Other scholarship has further documented how networking within TWIN-CS has supported organizational learning that has changed educators' practices. One study found that teachers increased their use of formative assessment data to promote literacy development.[32] Another study examined how paired partner work affects children's approaches to mathematical problem solving. It found intentionally pairing students and consistently planning for paired learning to be an important step in fostering cognitive, linguistic, and social development. Partners are most effective when heterogeneous pairs are formed with respect to students' linguistic and cognitive developmental levels.[33]

Finally, the organizational learning to advance culturally and linguistically responsive schooling is dynamic. One manifestation of these dynamic influences is the interplay of interactive participation with the establishment of products and processes. Studies of the communities of practice in TWIN-CS, discussed earlier, conclude that educators learn from one another primarily through interactions. For example, they describe "interactive spaces supporting relational networks via online webinars and a five-day face-to-face Summer Academy . . . [that] helped network members overcome challenges, access new knowledge, and feel and become connected."[34] Initially, these activities were typically facilitated by the design team. This was in keeping with the previous discussion of the centralized COP that characterized the initial structure of TWIN-CS. Moreover, from the launching of the network, the design team orchestrated participation among implementation teams to be collective. It directed member schools to send teachers and administrators from the implementation team as well as their TWIN-CS mentors to the summer academy. Thus, the interactions were designed to be shared, increasing the likelihood of transferring knowledge and skills into institutional routines.

Alongside this interactive participation, products and processes also influence the organizational learning. Some of these products are simply archives of interactions, such as the video recordings of webinars housed on the TWIN-CS website. Others are products to accompany processes, such as planning templates aligned to the Center for Applied Linguistics's *Guiding Principles for Dual Language Education*. The templates were used to structure interactions at the summer academy as well as to provide a documented record of those interactions to be used the following school year. While the studies show that the interactive participation has steadily influenced the organizational learning, they suggest that initially the specific tools and materials that accompany these activities were less effective. Over time, different products and processes have been abandoned or replaced. For instance, initially the design team tried to have member schools across the entire network use a uniform process and product to conduct summative evaluations of student language development. In time, this proved to not be efficient or effective, so instead member teams began employing a menu of options.

Another example of the dynamic influences on organizational learning is the interplay of local and outside influences. For instance, these studies of communities of practice in TWIN-CS collectively point toward mentors helping shape processes of transformation and their role growing increasingly powerful over time. Mentors are, by design, boundary spanners. Being outside the school community, they broker connections to new resources and ideas. They serve the school as consultants, working alongside educators on the implementation team. Thus, they enjoy a degree of membership within the school community as well. In sum, the mentors serve to help implementation teams draw from outside influences and then interpret them into their own context.

Implications

Collectively, the organizational learning across TWIN-CS is building member schools' capacities to be culturally and linguistically responsive. An important aspect of this is how members of the network come from diverse vantages to advance this learning. Working from a central, whole-network perspective, the design team is focused on supporting the development of the network as a whole, advancing the overall program efficacy. In contrast, mentors and implementation teams are concerned first and foremost with their own school's development, and look to the design team and other member schools in TWIN-CS for support and guidance. But while mentors and implementation teams share an interest in a school, they, too, come from different vantages: implementation teams approach the organizational learning as direct members of the school community, while mentors bring outside perspectives as independent scholars and critical friends.

In conclusion, this chapter has described how COPs have unfolded and evolved, influencing the pursuit of culturally and linguistically responsive schooling in TWIN-CS. We discussed the unfolding COPs at the network level, as well as the organizational learning in the context of Catholic schools and with regard to culturally and linguistically responsive schooling. We now turn to our final chapter, where we look forward to the implications across sectors.

10

Looking Forward: Transformation Across Contexts

MARTIN SCANLAN, CRISTINA HUNTER,
AND ELIZABETH R. HOWARD

AS A TRANSFORMATIVE LEADER, you are committed to deepening, expanding, and catalyzing your educational community's journey to becoming culturally and linguistically responsive. Throughout this book, we have described how you can advance culturally and linguistically responsive schooling, specifically drawing on strategic and scaffolded networking that is grounded in an asset-based orientation. In this final chapter, we help you look forward, considering lessons you can take from this story of the Two-Way Immersion Network for Catholic Schools (TWIN-CS) to help you in this journey. We highlight three key lessons for you as an educational leader embarking on the process of transformation in your own context:

- Lesson 1: Affirm diversity through an asset-based orientation
- Lesson 2: Audaciously articulate your theory of action
- Lesson 3: Leverage networking

LESSON 1:
Affirm Diversity Through an Asset-Based Orientation

Culturally and linguistically responsive schooling builds students' sociocultural competence, cultivates their appreciation of and proficiency in multiple languages and language varieties (including but not limited to English), and promotes their academic achievement. A key component of all these goals is to affirm diversity through an asset-based orientation. This is the first lesson.

As has been discussed throughout this book, an asset-based orientation is essential for culturally and linguistically responsive schooling.[1] Such an orientation leads one to recognize that cultural and linguistic diversity benefit both individuals and communities, and that as a consequence, multiculturalism and bilingualism and biliteracy are strengths that should be nourished and fostered.[2] To do this, educators must enact critical consciousness, a mindset and stance of continuously reflecting on and confronting the multiple barriers of marginalization—such as racism—that operate both within us individually and at the institutional level.[3]

Leaders exhibit an asset-based orientation by developing for themselves and instilling in others an appreciation of multiple, divergent, and generative manifestations of capital. This includes professional capital—which integrates individual capacities (human capital), relational networks (social capital), and practical wisdom (decisional capital).[4] Further, it involves more expansive understandings of wealth, such as bilingualism and biliteracy (linguistic capital), cultural knowledge nurtured among kin (familial capital), and knowledge and skills to oppose injustice (resistant capital).[5] An asset-based orientation guides leaders to build authentic partnerships with families and community members.[6] A school culture that is grounded in an asset-based orientation supports the enactment of asset-based pedagogies in the classroom, in which teachers integrate students' cultural and linguistic identities, knowledge, and interests into the teaching and learning environment.[7] When teachers implement asset-based pedagogies, bringing to their curriculum and instruction a critical awareness of sociohistorical contexts, building from students' cultural and linguistic knowledge, and validating students' experiences, they are "more likely to engage in behaviors that are formative in nature . . . [and]

promote the development of ethnic and academic identities of historically marginalized youth."[8]

The stories recounted here show that an asset-based orientation is not an abstract platitude, but manifest in concrete practices. Critical conversations among colleagues inside schools (e.g., on the TWIN-CS implementation teams) and with coaches (e.g., between member school principals and their mentors) create space for nurturing this orientation. Distributing leadership provides a structure for spreading it. Developing and implementing holistic bilingual language assessments and writing rubrics are tools for implementing it, as are partnerships that integrate families' funds of knowledge. These practices can be revolutionary. They allowed member schools of TWIN-CS to move from monolingual approaches to educating students designated as English Learners (ELs) to enacting two-way immersion (TWI) service delivery models, cultivating bilingualism and biliteracy.

As an educational leader, you affirm diversity through an asset-based orientation both *personally* and *structurally*. Personally, you do this by cultivating your dispositions and mind-set. While in the examples of TWIN-CS, the leaders were animated by the Catholic context of the schools, this personal choice is by no means limited to leaders operating within a religious context or from a faith-based perspective. As Byrne-Jiménez and Yoon eloquently explain, educational leaders across contexts are challenged to act with "radical, transformational, and sustained love."[9] Such love is exemplified by being guided by habits of heart, including imagination, harmony, wisdom, and courage.[10]

You affirm diversity through an asset-based orientation at *structural* levels as well. This orientation is reflected in the policies and practices that shape the teaching and learning environment. Educational leaders in the story of TWIN-CS personally developed their asset-based orientations, which motivated and directed their decisions to change their school structures, including shifting their school missions, expanding their decision-making practices, and broadening their resource bases. They determined that a monolingual school structure was failing their linguistically minoritized students and families, and needed to be dramatically changed. In your own context, an asset-based orientation can provide direction to critically reflect on the structures in place. Specific tools can assist this structural analysis, such as school- and community-based equity audits.[11]

LESSON 2:
Audaciously Articulate Your Theory of Action

A second key lesson is that leadership for transformation entails audaciously articulating a theory of action to move your community forward. Our theories of action map our understandings about how the world works and how to enact change. Just as a Global Positioning System can guide our journeys through unfamiliar streets, theories of action help us navigate our educational leadership. To effectively lead a school or district, you must be critically reflective, ambitious, and bold in discerning and proclaiming your theory of action.

The theory of action that we have used to organize this book is that strategic and scaffolded networking that is grounded in an asset-based orientation advances culturally and linguistically responsive schooling. The goal of this theory of action is straightforward: advancing culturally and linguistically responsive schooling. This approach to schooling builds students' sociocultural competence, respects and cultivates proficiency in home and community languages in addition to English, and promotes all students' academic achievement. These three components create coherence for educators embarking on similar journeys.

In addition to being clear, this goal is also audacious. As our schools grow increasingly linguistically and culturally diverse, educational inequities persist. Students designated as ELs remain linguistically minoritized in classrooms, where asset-based pedagogies are the exception rather than the norm. Creating schools and classrooms that embrace and sustain diversity across all dimensions—and in particular across language and culture—is a bold aim that can inspire and energize the entire community.

You can audaciously articulate your theory of action by being at once aspirational, inspirational, and sophisticated. A theory of action is aspirational when it directly confronts and seeks to eliminate the inequities in opportunities to learn. The story of TWIN-CS reflects this. These schools' journeys to reshape monolingual, English-only schools into TWI schools fostering bilingualism and biliteracy and sociocultural competence in addition to academic achievement called for a dramatic change in the entire teaching and learning environment. A theory of action is inspirational when it catalyzes the community to act. In TWIN-CS, member schools reimagined their missions and reconfigured leadership within implementation teams, which allowed them to make these dramatic changes. Moreover, by virtue of the network structure, changes in one school often prompted similar changes in another, as mentors and implementation team members shared success stories and motivated one another to continue to take audacious actions toward linguistically and culturally responsive schooling. Finally, a theory of action is sophisticated when it is grounded in evidence-based practices and theories. In TWIN-CS, the design team and mentors supported such sophistication by guiding implementation teams to ground their journey to TWI programs in the *Guiding Principles of Dual Language Education*,[12] and to do so in a manner respecting the context of these schools, following the National Standards and Benchmarks for Effective Catholic Schools.[13]

As we have argued throughout this book, the point is not for you to replicate the approach of TWIN-CS, but rather to draw from this as one example. You will need to audaciously articulate an aim that is aspirational, inspirational, and sophisticated in a manner that is specific to your context. Contrast the context of a superintendent of a public school district consisting of twenty-five schools, with a diverse population representing fourteen languages and composing 20 percent of the total school population, with the context of a middle school principal in a charter school of two hundred students, 75 percent of whom are Latinx, and 40 percent of whom are designated as ELs. Educational leaders in both of these contexts are called on to audaciously articulate theories of action that advance the three goals of culturally and linguistically responsive schooling. The details of how these theories of action will play out will vary, at times substantially. However, regardless of the contextual variation, school leaders seeking to create more culturally and linguistically responsive cultures by articulating a theory of action must aspire to confront and eliminate educational inequities, inspire the community to action, and be sophisticated in the choice of evidence-based practices and theories that guide the work.

LESSON 3:
Leverage Networking

A third lesson is to leverage the power of networking as you engage in the change process. In our theory of action, we have characterized this networking as strategic and scaffolded. *Strategic* networking is deliberate. Relational networks are initiated and fostered purposefully, in hopes that they will advance organizational learning. *Scaffolded* networking provides differentiated support. Highly constructive criticism that one educator may find helpful and invigorating can overwhelm another, who yearns for a more nuanced blend of nurturing encouragement combined with discreet direction.

Characterizing the networking that happened in TWIN-CS as strategic and scaffolded is a retrospective way to encapsulate a complex process. Certainly, as is shown throughout this book, many dimensions of the network were strategic—such as establishing structures for providing professional development both in person (e.g., the summer academy) and virtually (e.g., webinar), centralizing expertise on the design team, and distributing expertise among mentors for each member school. Moreover, these strategic actions scaffolded the efforts of schools that were at very different stages in their transition from a monolingual approach to educating students in a TWI context by providing ongoing support both collectively and individually to each member school and its staff and community.

However, while the strategic and scaffolded networking included key elements that were consistent for all TWIN-CS member schools, the processes undertaken in those schools were flexible and responsive to local conditions and needs. This can be seen in looking at the big picture—such as the shifting nature of the communities of practice across the network.[14] It can be seen as well when recalling the specific practices described by TWIN-CS mentors in part II of this book. From how schools engaged in critical conversations to how they created authentic partnerships with families, there was not a straightforward process, but rather an iterative and messy one.

Connecting with one another was an essential component to adaptation. It allowed implementation teams, for instance, to move from pioneering a new process of creating fidelity assurances to modeling this process for other member schools. It led teachers from exploring the implementation of a new formative assessment to presenting on this practice at a national conference. Being adaptive means recognizing both the commonalities of shared, macro-level goals and the distinctions of unique, micro-level ones. At the macro-level, all TWIN-CS member schools engaged in advancing culturally and linguistically responsive schooling in the form of the TWI model. At the micro-level, they pursued this in manners particular to each community's context.

Strategic and scaffolded networking reduces isolation and creates opportunities for organizational learning. Regardless of their eagerness and openness to learn from colleagues, teachers and administrators often remain in different orbits, as do educators in rural, suburban, and urban schools. This can even apply to schools that are relatively close in sector and geography, such as two public elementary schools in a common district or two Catholic high schools in a shared diocese. Creating occasions for educators to interact in ongoing, substantive manners and to collaborate in deep and meaningful ways can provide space for them to learn from one another. This strengthens communities of practice, expanding the membership and deepening the exchange of knowledge, skills, and dispositions.

All networking is not created equal, however. As an educational leader, you are interested in making connections purposefully, not randomly. All partnerships are not equally valuable. While well-conceived and implemented partnerships provide substantial benefits to school communities, many fail to deliver on their promises. Thus, leveraging networking should create structures that advance organizational learning. Some of these structures foster internal cohesion, while others foster external connections. TWIN-CS fostered relational networks within schools—such as via the implementation teams—as well as among schools—such as via the summer academy and webinars. Drawing on the power of networking means intentionally fostering organizational learning by supporting communities of practice in both of these manners. Specific structures help in each direction. In TWIN-CS, having a central hub (i.e., the design team), dispersed experts (i.e., mentors), and distributed decision-making bodies (i.e., implementation teams) catalyzed the formation and maturation of multiple overlapping and intersecting communities of practice.[15]

Trends in research on organizational learning point to how communities of practice—such as via networked improvement communities, research-practice partnerships, and design-based research—catalyze organizational learning to sustain improvement.[16] These all explicitly incorporate networking both among educators within and across schools and between educators and colleagues in other organizations, including community-based organizations and universities. The improvements evidenced by TWIN-CS schools support these trends. For instance, sessions at multiple summer academies provided professional development on improvement science and disciplined inquiry cycles. Implementation teams were provided copies of *Learning to Improve*, and mentors led them in discussions about the book during the academic year.[17] Mentors initiated research projects based on problems of practice that surfaced from implementation teams, such as using formative assessments to improve instructional practices.[18]

Finally, leveraging networking means taking initiative. One distinctive feature of the TWIN-CS member schools is that they sought to engage in the process of innovation and change. With neighboring Catholic schools in similar situations, attempting to educate significant numbers of ELs but lacking comprehensive models of service delivery to effectively do so, the member schools in TWIN-CS proactively sought support in changing their models. Taking initiative means not waiting for a clear, set road map to engage in the change process. As has been shown in the story of TWIN-CS recounted here, member schools were not conservative, waiting to have a secure path.

Similarly, your leadership in transformation requires that you take initiative to leverage the power of networking. Taking initiative to forge relationships, particularly across cultural and linguistic borders, is essential. TWIN-CS school leaders took it upon themselves to develop their own bilingualism, demonstrating in tangible ways how they viewed language as an asset. Such initiative can yield novel, unexpected rewards. In TWIN-CS, principals reached out to public school colleagues to arrange site visits for their teachers to observe each other, and mentors led implementation teams from piloting new assessments to presenting on them at national conferences.

MOVING FORWARD

The lessons of affirming diversity through an asset-based orientation, audaciously articulating your theory of action, and leveraging networking will help you move forward in your journey to becoming more culturally and linguistically responsive. In this book, we have focused on this journey to improve equity for linguistically and culturally marginalized students. However, as you are well aware, discrimination and bias are rampant across multiple dimensions of diversity, including not only culture and language but also race, gender, sexual orientation, religion, (dis)ability, and more. The lessons shared in this book can serve your leadership in promoting radical change across these multiple dimensions of diversity. For example, as an elementary school principal, asset-based orientations can shape how you welcome the transgender student in fifth grade. As the dean of students, audaciously articulating your theory of action can guide your work in eliminating the racist disciplinary practices used in your high school. As the district superintendent, leveraging networking can direct your efforts to craft a comprehensive approach to educating students experiencing homelessness.

In this sense, the theory of action that we have used to ground this book—that strategic and scaffolded networking with an asset-based orientation advances culturally and linguistically responsive schooling—can be expanded: strategic and scaffolded networking with an asset-based orientation advances *socially just schooling*. As we hope we have demonstrated throughout this book, while the effort required for transformation is considerable, the rewards are well worth it!

NOTES

PREFACE

1. Donald Hernandez, Nancy Denton, and Suzanne Macartney, "School-Age Children in Immigrant Families: Challenges and Opportunities for America's Schools," Teachers College Record 111, no. 3 (2009): 616–58.
2. Jeffrey Passel and D'Vera Cohn, U.S. Population Projections: 2005–2050 (Washington, DC: Pew Research Center, 2008).
3. Kerry Anne Enright, "Language and Literacy for a New Mainstream," American Educational Research Journal 48, no. 1 (2011): 80–118.
4. Most states have approved the Seal of Biliteracy. See the map published at https://sealofbiliteracy.org/. This is an award from schools or districts given in recognition of students who attain proficiency in two or more languages. It typically appears on the student's transcript and diploma, signaling this accomplishment to employers and college admissions personnel. As we discuss later, however, such efforts have also been criticized as promoting "elite bilingualism" over addressing educational inequities of linguistically marginalized populations. For instance, see Nelson Flores, "How to Dismantle Elite Bilingualism," Education Week 38, no. 17 (2019): 14–15.
5. For instance, a developmental bilingual model is a version of dual language education appropriate when the majority of students share a common language heritage (e.g., a majority of Latinx students with Spanish as a mother tongue). The Sheltered Instruction Observation Protocol (SIOP) Model, an approach to sheltered instruction that focuses on making content comprehensible, is appropriate when students come from a range of linguistic backgrounds (for further resources, see http://www.cal.org/siop/).
6. Rebecca Freeman, Bilingual Education and Social Change. Bilingual Education and Bilingualism 14 (Philadelphia: Multilingual Matters, 1998).

CHAPTER 1

1. For a general overview of developing knowledge, skills, and dispositions, see Linda Darling-Hammond and John Bransford, eds., Preparing Teachers

for a Changing World: What Teachers Should Learn and Be Able to Do (San Francisco: Jossey-Bass, 2005). To look more specifically at students designated as ELs, see George Bunch, "Preparing Mainstream Secondary Content-Area Teachers to Facilitate English Language Learners' Development of Academic Language," National Society for the Study of Education 109, no. 2 (2010): 351–83; and George Bunch, "Pedagogical Language Knowledge: Preparing Mainstream Teachers for English Learners in the New Standards Era," Review of Research in Education 37, no. 1 (2013): 298–341.

2. Maria Estela Brisk, Bilingual Education: From Compensatory to Quality Schooling (Mahwah, NJ: Lawrence Earlbaum, 2006).

3. Ibid; Martin Scanlan and Francesca López, "¡Vamos! How School Leaders Promote Equity and Excellence for Bilingual Students," Educational Administration Quarterly 48, no. 4 (2012): 583–625; Martin Scanlan and Francesca López, Leadership for Culturally and Linguistically Responsive Schools (New York: Routledge/Taylor and Francis Group, 2014).

4. Nelson Flores and Jonathan Rosa, "Undoing Appropriateness: Raciolinguistic Ideologies and Language Diversity in Education," Harvard Educational Review 85, no. 2 (2015): 149–171.

5. Mariela Páez and Cristina Hunter, "Bilingualism and Language Learning for Immigrant-Origin Children and Youth," in Transitions: The Development of Children of Immigrants, ed. Carola Suárez-Orozco, Mona Abo-Zena, and Amy K. Marks (New York: New York University Press, 2015).

6. Julie Sugarman, A Matter of Design: English Learner Program Models in K–12 Education (Washington, DC: Migration Policy Institute, National Center on Immigrant Policy, 2018).

7. Colin Baker, Foundations of Bilingual Education and Bilingualism, 4th ed. (Clevedon: Multilingual Matters, 2006).

8. Elizabeth Howard et al., Guiding Principles for Dual Language Education (Washington, DC: Center for Applied Linguistics, 2018), 34.

9. Erika Feinauer and Elizabeth Howard, "Attending to the Third Goal," Journal of Immersion and Content-Based Language Education 2, no. 2 (2014): 257–72.

10. See further information at https://multilingual.madison.k12.wi.us/world-languages.

11. See further information at http://nuestromundoinc.org.

12. Elizabeth Howard, Julie Sugarman, and Donna Christian, Trends in Two-Way Immersion Education: A Review of the Research (Baltimore, MD: Center for Research on the Education of Students Placed at Risk, 2003).

13. See further data at https://dpi.wi.gov/accountability/report-cards.

14. Chimamanda Ngozi Adichie, "The Danger of a Single Story," July 2009,

TED video, 18:42, https://www.ted.com/talks/chimamanda_adichie_the_
danger_of_a_single_story.

15. National Academies of Sciences, Engineering, and Medicine, Integration of
Immigrants into American Society (Washington, DC: The National Academies Press, 2015); Ofelia Garcia, Jo Anne Kleifgen, and Lorraine Falchi,
From English Language Learners to Emergent Bilinguals (New York: Teachers College, Columbia University, Campaign for Educational Equity, 2008).

16. Paul Taylor, Mark Hugo Lopez, Jessica Martínez and Gabriel Velasco, When
Labels Don't Fit: Hispanics and Their Views of Identity (Washington, DC:
Pew Hispanic Center, 2012).

17. Nelson Flores, "A Tale of Two Visions: Hegemonic Whiteness and Bilingual
Education," Educational Policy 30, no. 1 (2016): 13–38; Zeus Leonardo, "The
Color of Supremacy: Beyond the Discourse of "White Privilege,'" Educa-
tional Philosophy and Theory 36, no. 2 (2004): 137–52.

18. Muhammad A. Khalifa, Mark Anthony Gooden, and James Earl Davis,
"Culturally Responsive School Leadership: A Synthesis of the Literature,"
Review of Educational Research 86, no. 4 (December 2016): 1275.

CHAPTER 2

1. Chris Argyris and Donald Schon, Organizational Learning: A Theory of
Action Perspective (Reading, MA: Addison-Wesley, Pub. Co., 1978).

2. See Brink's description of quality schooling for culturally and linguistically diverse populations (Maria Estela Brisk, Bilingual Education: From
Compensatory to Quality Schooling [Mahwah, NJ: Lawrence Earlbaum,
2006]); Lee and Luykx's theory of instructional congruence (Okhee Lee
and Aurolyn Luykx, "Dilemmas in Scaling Up Innovations in Elementary
Science Instruction with Nonmainstream Students," American Educational
Research Journal 42, no. 3 [2005]: 411–38); and de Jong's summary of best
practices for English-language learners (Ester J. de Jong, Foundations for
Multilingualism in Education [Philadelphia, PA: Caslon, Inc., 2011]).

3. We expand this to the broader notion of sociocultural competence. See further Elizabeth Howard et al., Guiding Principles for Dual Language Education (Washington, DC: Center for Applied Linguistics, 2018).

4. Brisk, Bilingual Education, 67.

5. Virginia Collier and Wayne Thomas, Dual Language Education for a Transformed World (Albuquerque, NM: Fuente Press, 2012).

6. Lorri Santamaria, "Culturally Responsive Differentiated Instruction: Narrowing Gaps Between Best Pedagogical Practices Benefiting All Learners," Teachers College Record 111, no. 1 (2009): 214–47; Ana Maria Villegas
and Tamara Lucas, Educating Culturally Responsive Teachers: A Coherent

Approach (Syracuse: State University of New York Press, 2002); Ana Maria Villegas and Tamara Lucas, "Preparing Culturally Responsive Teachers: Rethinking the Curriculum," Journal of Teacher Education 53, no. 1 (2002): 20–32; Ana Maria Villegas and Tamara Lucas, "The Culturally Responsive Teacher," Educational Leadership (2007): 28–33.

7. Martin Scanlan and Lauri Johnson, "Inclusive Leadership on the Social Frontiers: Family and Community Engagement," in Leadership for Increasingly Diverse Schools, ed. George Theoharis and Martin Scanlan (New York: Routledge, 2015), 162–85; Muhammad Khalifa, Mark Anthony Gooden, and James Earl Davis, "Culturally Responsive School Leadership: A Synthesis of Literature," Review of Educational Research 86, no. 4 (2016): 1272–311.

8. Django Paris, "Culturally Sustaining Pedagogy: A Needed Change in Stance, Terminology, and Practice," Educational Researcher 31, no. 3 (2012): 93–97; Django Paris and H. Samy Alim, "What Are We Seeking to Sustain Through Culturally Sustaining Pedagogy? A Loving Critique Forward," Harvard Educational Review 84, no. 1 (2014): 85–100.

9. Tamara Lucas and Ana Maria Villegas, "The Missing Piece in Teacher Education: The Preparation of Linguistically Responsive Teachers," National Society for the Study of Education 109, no. 2 (2010): 297–318; Tamara Lucas, Ana Maria Villegas, and Margaret Freedson-Gonzalez, "Linguistically Responsive Teacher Education: Preparing Classroom Teachers to Teach English Language Learners," Journal of Teacher Education 59, no. 4 (2008): 361–73.

10. Eugene García and Delis Cuellar, "Who Are These Linguistically and Culturally Diverse Students?" Teachers College Record 108, no. 11 (2006): 2220–2246.

11. Translanguaging is the theory that bilinguals (including emergent bilinguals) choose features from different languages to make meaning and communicate. This approach affirms using diverse language practices pedagogically. See further Gwyn Lewis, Bryn Jones, and Colin Baker, "Translanguaging: Developing Its Conceptualisation and Contextualisation," Educational Research and Evaluation 18, no. 7 (2012): 655–70.

12. For example, see Jana Echevarria, Deborah J. Short, and MaryEllen Vogt, Making Content Comprehensible for English Language Learners: The SIOP Model, 5th ed. (Boston: Allyn and Bacon, 2017); Pauline Gibbons, Scaffolding Language, Scaffolding Learning: Teaching Second Language Learners in the Mainstream Classroom, 2nd ed. (Portsmouth, NH: Heinemann, 2015); Diane Rodriguez, Angela Carrasquillo, and Kyung Soon Lee, The Biligual Advantage: Promoting Academic Development, Biliteracy, and Native Language in the Classroom (New York, NY: Teachers College Press, 2014).

13. Eugene García et al., "Developing Responsive Teachers: A Challenge for a Demographic Reality," Journal of Teacher Education 61, no. 1–2 (2010): 136.

14. Gloria Ladson-Billings, "Culturally Responsive Teaching: Theory and Practice," in Multicultural Education, ed. James A. Banks and Cherry A. McGee Banks, 6th ed. (Danvers, MA: John Wiley & Sons, Inc., 2007), 219–46; Francesca López, "Culturally Responsive Pedagogies in Arizona and Latino Students' Achievement," Teachers College Record 118, no. 1 (2016): 1–42; Lorri Santamaria, "Culturally Responsive Differentiated Instruction: Narrowing Gaps Between Best Pedagogical Practices Benefiting All Learners," Teachers College Record 111, no. 1 (2009): 214–47.

15. Viorica Marian, Anthony Shook, and Scott Schroeder, "Bilingual Two-Way Immersion Programs Benefit Academic Achievement," Bilingual Research Journal 36, no. 2 (2013): 167–86.

16. Lauri Johnson, "Rethinking Successful School Leadership in Challenging U.S. Schools: Culturally Responsive Practices in School-Community Relationships," International Studies in Educational Administration 35, no. 3 (2007): 49–57; John Watzke, Lasting Change in Foreign Language Education: A Historical Case for Change in National Policy (Westport, CT: Praeger Publishers, 2003).

17. Ofelia Garcia and Jo Anne Kleifgen, Educating Emergent Bilinguals: Policies, Programs, and Practices for English Learners (New York, NY: Teachers College Press, 2018).

18. Nelson Flores, "A Tale of Two Visions: Hegemonic Whiteness and Bilingual Education," Educational Policy 30, no. 1 (2016): 13–38.

19. For more on critiquing elite bilingualism, see Claudia Cervantes-Soon, "A Critical Look at Dual Language Immersion in the New Latin@ Diaspora," Bilingual Research Journal 37, no. 1 (2014): 64–82; Claudia Cervantes-Soon et al., "Combatting Inequalities in Two-Way Language Immersion Programs: Toward Critical Consciousness in Bilingual Education Spaces," Review of Research in Education 41, no. 1 (2017): 403–27; Nelson Flores, "How to Dismantle Elite Bilingualism," Education Week 38, no. 17 (2019): 14–15; Conor Williams, "The Intrusion of White Families into Bilingual Schools," The Atlantic, December 28, 2017, https://www.theatlantic.com/education/archive/2017/12/the-middle-class-takeover-of-bilingual-schools/549278/. This critique has also been made of TWI approaches. See, for instance, Guadalupe Valdes, "Dual-Language Immersion Programs: A Cautionary Note Concerning the Education of Language-Minority Students," Harvard Educational Review 67, no. 3 (1997): 391–428.

20. Haridimos Tsoukas and Christian Knudsen, eds., Oxford Handbook of Organizational Theory (New York: Oxford University Press, 2003).

21. James Spillane and Karen Seashore Louis, "School Improvement Processes and Practices: Professional Learning for Building Instructional Capacity," in The Educational Leadership Challenge: Redefining Leadership for the 21st Century, ed. Joseph Murphy, vol. 101 (Chicago: University of Chicago Press, 2002), 95.
22. Scott Cook and Dvora Yanow, "Culture and Organizational Learning," Journal of Management Inquiry 2, no. 4 (1993): 373–90; Terrance E. Deal and Kent D. Peterson, Shaping School Culture (San Francisco: Jossey-Bass, 1999).
23. Anthony Bryk, Eric Camburn, and Karen Seashore Louis, "Professional Community in Chicago Elementary Schools: Facilitating Factors and Organizational Consequences," Educational Administration Quarterly 35 (1999): 751–81.
24. Helen Marks and Karen Seashore Louis, "Teacher Empowerment and the Capacity for Organizational Learning," Educational Administration Quarterly 35 (1999): 731.
25. For more on teaching and learning environment, see Hanna Kurland and Dalia Rebecca Hasson-Gilad, "Organizational Learning and Extra Effort: The Mediating Effect of Job Satisfaction," Teaching and Teacher Education 49 (2015): 56–67; Lauren Resnick and Megan Williams Hall, "Learning Organizations for Sustainable Education Reform," Daedalus 127, no. 4 (1998): 89–118. For more on fostering relational trust among educators, see Anthony Bryk and Barbara Schneider, Trust in Schools: A Core Resource for Improvement (New York: Russell Sage, 2002). For more on promoting boundary spanning and assistance relationships, see Sanne Akkerman and Arthur Bakker, "Boundary Crossing and Boundary Objects," Review of Educational Research 81, no. 2 (2011): 132–69.
26. On general isolation, see Dan Lortie, Schoolteacher: A Sociological Study (Chicago: University of Chicago Press, 1975). On growing immigrant populations, see Rebecca Lowenhaupt and Todd D. Reeves, "Toward a Theory of School Capacity in New Immigrant Destinations: Instructional and Organizational Considerations," Leadership and Policy in Schools 14, no. 3 (2015): 308–40.
27. Linda Darling-Hammond et al., Professional Learning in the Learning Profession (Washington, DC: National Staff Development Council, 2009).
28. Alan Daly, ed., Social Network Theory (Cambridge, MA: Harvard Education Press, 2010); Chris Brown, Alan Daly, and Yi-Hwa Liou, "Improving Trust, Improving Schools: Findings from a Social Network Analysis of 43 Primary Schools in England," Journal of Professional Capital and Community 1, no. 1 (2016): 69–91.
29. Cynthia Coburn, Willow Mata, and Linda Choi, "The Embeddedness of

Teachers' Social Networks: Evidence from a Mathematics Reform," Sociology of Education 86, no. 4 (2013): 329.

30. Mel Ainscow, "Collaboration as a Strategy for Promoting Equity in Education: Possibilities and Barriers," Journal of Professional Capital and Community 1, no. 2 (2016): 169.

31. Andy Hargreaves and Michael Fullan, Professional Capital: Transforming Teaching in Every School (New York: Teachers College Press, 2012); Santiago Rincón-Gallardo and Michael Fullan, "Essential Features of Effective Networks in Education," Journal of Professional Capital and Community 1, no. 1 (2016): 5–22.

32. On foundational work on communities of practice, see Etienne Wenger, Communities of Practice: Learning, Meaning, and Identity (New York: Cambridge University Press, 1998).

33. Anthony Bryk et al., Learning to Improve: How America's Schools Can Get Better at Getting Better (Cambridge, MA: Harvard Education Press, 2015).

34. For a recent summary of research-practice partnerships, see William Penuel and Daniel Gallagher, Creating Research-Practice Partnerships in Education (Cambridge, MA: Harvard Education Press, 2017); Karen Hunter Quartz et al., "University-Partnered New School Designs: Fertile Ground for Research-Practice Partnerships," Educational Researcher 46, no. 3 (2017): 143–46. For helpful discussions of design-based research, see Terry Anderson and Julie Shattuck, "Design-Based Research: A Decade of Progress in Education Research," Educational Researcher 41, no. 1 (2012) 16–25; Susan McKenney and Thomas Reeves, "Systematic Review of Design-Based Research Progress: Is a Little Knowledge a Dangerous Thing?" Educational Researcher 42, no. 2 (2013): 97–100.

35. For instance, see Timothy Walch, Parish School: American Catholic Parochial Education from Colonial Times to the Present (New York: The Crossroad Publishing Company, 1996); Cecilia Moore, "Ethnicity and Parish Schools: African Americans," in One Hundred Years of Catholic Education, ed. John Augenstein, Christopher Kauffman, and Robert Wister (Washington, DC: National Catholic Education Association, 2003); Graham McDonough, "Cultivating Identities: The Catholic School as Diverse Ecclesial Space," Philosophical Inquiry in Education 23, no. 2 (2016): 160–77.

36. Michael Katz, Reconstructing American Education (Cambridge, MA: Harvard University Press, 1987).

37. It is beyond the scope of this brief discussion of the history of Catholic schools in the United States to dig into multiple dimensions of racial and ethnic diversity. Some important work on this that we recommend to interested readers includes Jacqueline Jordan Irvine and Michele Foster, eds.,

Growing Up African American in Catholic Schools (New York: Teachers College Press, 1996); Moore, "Ethnicity and Parish Schools"; Vernon Polite, "Getting the Job Done Well: African American Students and Catholic Schools," Journal of Negro Education 61, no. 2 (1992): 211–22; James Sanders, The Education of an Urban Minority: Catholics in Chicago, 1833–1965 (New York: Oxford University Press, 1977); Walch, Parish School.

38. Sanders, The Education of an Urban Minority, 43.

39. Joel Perlmann, Ethnic Differences: Schooling and Social Structures Among the Irish, Italians, Jews, and Blacks in an American City, 1880–1935 (Cambridge: Cambridge University Press, 1988), 70.

40. Sanders, The Education of an Urban Minority, 150

41. For more information regarding Catholic schools underserving these students, see Vivian Louie and Jennifer Holdaway, "Catholic Schools and Immigrant Students: A New Generation," Teachers College Record 111, no. 3 (2009): 783–816. For more about providing minimal support to meet their linguistic, academic, and sociocultural needs, see Martin Scanlan and Gary Zehrbach, "Improving Bilingual Service Delivery in Catholic Schools Through Two-Way Immersion," Catholic Education: A Journal of Inquiry and Practice 14, no. 1 (2010): 67–93. For more regarding the growing capacity to serve Latinx families, see Hosffman Ospino and Patricia Weitzel-O'Neill, Catholic Schools in an Increasingly Hispanic Church: A Summary Report of Findings from the National Survey of Catholic Schools Serving Hispanic Families (Chestnut Hill, MA: School of Theology and Ministry and Lynch School of Education, Roche Center for Catholic Education, Boston College, 2016), https://www.bc.edu/content/dam/files/schools/lsoe_sites/cce/pdf/STM%20Catholic%20Schools_final%20v4_opt.pdf.

42. Congregation for Catholic Education, The Catholic School (Homebush, New South Wales, Australia: St. Paul Publications, 1977).

43. Lorraine Ozar and Patricia Weitzel-O'Neill, National Catholic School Standards: Focus on Governance and Leadership (Chicago, IL: Loyola University Chicago, Center for Catholic School Effectiveness, 2012); Lorraine Ozar and Patricia Weitzel-O'Neill, "National Catholic School Standards: Focus on Governance and Leadership," Catholic Education: A Journal of Inquiry and Practice 17, no. 1 (2013): 157–62.

44. Ibid.

45. For an example of how missions shift and change, see the documentary Adelante, which recounts the story of how St. Patrick Church in Norristown, Pennsylvania, founded by Irish immigrants, is being revitalized with the influx of immigrants from Mexico (www.adelantethefilm.com). Examples of mission-focused schools are the Catholic schools sponsored by Sinsinawa

Dominicans, whose schools' missions are rooted in the five values of truth, compassion, justice, community, and partnership (https://www.sinsinawa .org/site_map/dvjune2017/sponsored-schools.html). An example of a network of Catholic schools is the Cristo Rey Network (cristoreynetwork.org).

46. Karl Weick, "Educational Organizations as Loosely Coupled Systems," Administrative Science Quarterly 21 (1976): 1–19.

47. Examples include the Cristo Rey Network at the national level and the Seton Catholic Schools at a local level (https://www.setoncatholicschools .com/).

48. Richard Murnane et al., "Who Goes to Private School?" Education Next 18, no. 4 (2018): 58–66, https://www.educationnext.org/files/ednext_xviii_4_ murnane_et_al.pdf.

49. Thomas Hunt, "The History of Catholic Schools in the United States: An Overview," in Catholic School Leadership: An Invitation to Lead, ed. Thomas Hunt, Thomas Oldenski, and Theodore Wallace (New York: Falmer Press, 2000).

50. See Murnane et al., "Who Goes to Private School?"

51. For an example of schools with a strong philanthropic base, see Stern and McCloskey's description of St. Aloysius in Harlem, New York City (Sol Stern and Patrick McCloskey, "Why Catholic Schools Matter," City Journal [Spring 2011], https://www.city-journal.org/html/why-catholic-schools-matter-13376.html). For a discussion of private schools—including Catholic schools—receiving public funds, see John Coons, "Dodging Democracy: The Educator's Flight from the Specter of Choice," American Journal of Education 111, no. 4 (2005): 596–608.

52. See www.twin-cs.org.

53. Ozar and Weitzel-O'Neill, National Catholic School Standards.

54. Ospino and Weitzel-O'Neill, Catholic Schools in an Increasingly Hispanic Church.

55. The original design team included faculty from Marquette University, the University of Connecticut, and the University of Arizona.

CHAPTER 3

1. Lee Bolman and Terrence Deal, Reframing Organizations: Artistry, Choice, and Leadership (San Francisco: Jossey-Bass, 2003), 25.

2. Ronald Heifetz and Marty Linsky, Leadership on the Line (Boston: Harvard Business Review Press, 2002), 2.

3. Ibid.

4. Ronald Heifetz, Alexander Grashow, and Marty Linsky, The Practices of Adaptive Leadership (Boston: Harvard Business Review Press, 2009), 29.

5. Ronald Heifetz, Alexander Grashow, and Marty Linsky, The Practices of Adaptive Leadership (Boston: Harvard Business Review Press, 2009), 307.

6. Nelson Flores and Jonathan Rosa, "Undoing Appropriateness: Raciolinguistic Ideologies and Language Diversity in Education," Harvard Educational Review 85, no. 2 (2015): 149–71; Gloria Ladson-Billings, "Through a Glass Darkly: The Persistence of Race in Education Research & Scholarship," Educational Researcher 41, no. 4 (May 2012): 115–20. For a description of a leader advancing critical conversations addressing prejudice and biases, see Blad's profile of Angela Ward, supervisor of race and equity in the Austin Independent School District in Austin, Texas (Evie Blad, "Confronting and Combating Bias in Schools," Education Week Leaders to Learn From, February 20, 2019, https://leaders.edweek.org/profile/angela-ward-supervisor-race-equity-programs-cultural-proficiency/).

7. Glenn Singleton, Courageous Conversations About Race: A Field Guide for Achieving Equity in Schools (Thousand Oaks: Sage Publications, 2015), 88.

8. Claudia G. Cervantes-Soon et al., "Combating Inequalities in Two-Way Language Immersion Programs: Toward Critical Consciousness in Bilingual Education Spaces," Review of Research in Education 41, no. 1 (2017): 403–27.

9. Elizabeth Howard et al., Guiding Principles for Dual Language Education (Washington, DC: Center for Applied Linguistics, 2018); Lorraine Ozar and Patricia Weitzel-O'Neill, "National Catholic School Standards: Focus on Governance and Leadership," Catholic Education: A Journal of Inquiry and Practice 17, no. 1 (2013): 157–62; National Standards and Benchmarks for Effective Catholic Elementary and Secondary Schools (Chicago: Center for Catholic School Effectiveness, School of Education, Loyola University Chicago, in partnership with Roche Center for Catholic Education, School of Education, Boston College 2012), https://www.catholicschoolstandards.org/images/docs/standards/Catholic-School-Standards-English.pdf.

10. See further the discussion of adhering to model fidelity in chapter 4 of this volume.

11. As a related note, discussions such as these reflect another key practice in the process of transformation—namely, distributing leadership. For an extensive discussion of this practice, see chapter 8 of this volume.

CHAPTER 4

1. National Academies of Sciences Engineering and Medicine, Promoting the Educational Success of Children and Youth Learning English: Promising Futures (Washington, DC: The National Academies Press, 2017).

2. See the discussion of service delivery models in chapter 1 of this volume.

3. Refer to chapter 3 of this volume for a discussion of the role of critical conversations in answering these questions.
4. Elizabeth Howard et al., Guiding Principles for Dual Language Education (Washington, DC: Center for Applied Linguistics, 2018).
5. Ibid.
6. Graciela Borsato, "Academic Achievement," in Educating English Language Learners: A Synthesis of Research Evidence, by Fred Genesee et al. (Cambridge University Press, Cambridge, 2006), 176–222; Kathryn Lindholm-Leary and Elizabeth Howard, "Language and Academic Achievement in Two-Way Immersion Programs," in Pathways to Multilingualism: Evolving Perspectives on Immersion Education, ed. Tara Williams Fortune and Diane Tedick (Bristol, UK: Multilingual Matters, 2008), 177–200.
7. Francesca López, Martin Scanlan, and Becky Gundrum, "Preparing Teachers of English Language Learners: Empirical Evidence and Policy Implications," Educational Policy Analysis Archives 21, no. 20 (2013): 1–35.
8. Elizabeth Howard and López-Velásquez, "'Put the Brakes On. If I Can't Staff the Program, We Can't Grow It': The Challenges of Recruiting and Retaining Dual Language Teachers," Dual Language Education: Teaching and Leading Through Two Languages, ed. David DeMatthews and Elena Izquierdo (New York: Springer, 2019); National Academies of Sciences Engineering and Medicine, Promising Futures.
9. Virginia Collier and Wayne Thomas, Dual Language Education for a Transformed World (Albuquerque, NM: Fuente Press, 2012), 32.
10. Elizabeth Howard, et al., Guiding Principles for Dual Language Education (Washington, DC: Center for Applied Linguistics, 2018).
11. Utah's ELs are enrolling in mostly TWI models, with 90 percent of them going into programs that match the student's home language. The data from 2016–17 showed that students designated as ELs enrolled at a higher rate in dual language immersion schools than in other schools, at 12.54 percent compared with 7.75 percent (K–12). Additionally, students designated as ELs were overrepresented in dual language immersion programs, at 8.8 percent compared with 6 percent non-EL of the entire school population (Robert Slater, Johanna Waztinger-Tharp, and Gregg Roberts, "The Impact of Dual Language Immersion on Student Achievement in Utah," 7th International Conference on Immersion & Dual Language Education, Charlotte, North Carolina, February 8, 2019).
12. "Utah Dual Language Immersion," Utah State Board of Education, http://www.utahdli.org/whyimmersion.html; "Utah Dual Language Immersion, DLI Program Fidelity Assurance Grades 1–6," http://www.utahdli.org/images/DLI-Assurances-Grades-1-6.pdf.

13. "What Are Implementation Stages," National Implementation Research Network, https://nirn.fpg.unc.edu/sites/nirn.fpg.unc.edu/files/resources/Four%20Domains%20for%20Rapid%20School%20Improvement_0.pdf, 25–28.

14. For a discussion of the history of educating linguistically minoritized students in Arizona, see Eugene García, Kerry Lawton, and Eduardo H. Diniz de Digueiredo, "The Education of English Language Learners in Arizona: A History of Underachievement," Teachers College Record 114, no. 9 (2012): 1–18.

15. Note the examples of distributed leadership, explored more in depth in chapter 8 of this volume.

16. Collier and Thomas, Dual Language.

17. Karen Beeman and Cheryl Urow, Teaching for Biliteracy: Strengthening Bridges Between Languages (Philadelphia, PA: Caslon Publishing, 2012).

18. Howard et al., Guiding Principles.

19. Leo Gómez and Richard Gómez, Gómez and Gómez DLE Model (Brownsville, TX: Dual Language Training Institute, 2017).

20. While I have focused on assuring fidelity to the TWI service delivery model, another dimension of assuring fidelity that is important in the TWIN-CS member schools is to the National Standards and Benchmarks for Effective Catholic Schools. See further discussion of this in chapter 2 of this volume. See also Lorraine Ozar and Patricia Weitzel-O'Neill, eds., National Catholic School Standards: Focus on Governance and Leadership (Chicago: Loyola University Chicago, Center for Catholic School Effectiveness, 2012).

21. International Schools/Dual Language Immersion Task Force Recommendations (Seattle: Seattle Schools, 2018). Available from https://www.seattleschools.org/UserFiles/Servers/Server_543/File/District/Departments/International%20Education/DLI_TaskForce/Intl-DLI_Task_Force_Recommendations_Part2_2018.03.21.pdf.

CHAPTER 5

1. Mary Kennedy, "How Does Professional Development Improve Teaching?" Review of Educational Research 86, no. 4 (2016): 947 (emphasis original).

2. Ibid, 974.

3. Allison Gulamhussein, Teaching the Teachers: Effective Professional Development in an Era of High Stakes Accountability (Alexandria, VA: Center for Public Education, 2013), 13. Available from http://www.centerforpubliceducation.org/system/files/Professional%20Development.pdf.

4. Ibid, 30.

5. Anthony Bryk et al., Organizing Schools for Improvement: Lessons from Chicago (Chicago: University of Chicago Press, 2010).

6. Vivienne Collinson and Tanya Fedoruk Cook, Organizational Learning:

Improving Learning, Teaching, and Leading in School Systems (Thousand Oaks, CA: Sage Publications, 2007).

7. Anthony Bryk et al., Learning to Improve: How America's Schools Can Get Better at Getting Better (Cambridge, MA: Harvard Education Press, 2015), 145. See further the discussion of the practice of distributed leadership in chapter 8 of this volume.

8. Elizabeth Howard et al., Guiding Principles for Dual Language Education (Washington, DC: Center for Applied Linguistics, 2018), 99.

9. Ibid, 101.

10. Martin Scanlan and Francesca López, Leadership for Culturally and Linguistically Responsive Schools (New York, NY: Routledge/Taylor and Francis Group, 2014).

11. This relates to the practice of adhering to model fidelity, described in chapter 4 of this volume.

12. See the general overview of the practices and organization of the network functioning in TWIN-CS described in chapter 2 of this volume.

13. Bryk et al., Learning to Improve, 148.

14. Email message to author, June 19, 2018.

15. Bryk et al., Learning to Improve, 146.

16. Ibid.

17. Howard et al., Guiding Principles.

18. Bryk et al., Learning to Improve, 153.

19. Ibid., 166.

20. Ibid., 143.

CHAPTER 6

1. Anthony S. Bryk et al., Learning to Improve: How America's Schools Can Get Better at Getting Better (Cambridge, MA: Harvard University Press, 2015); Pete Hall and Alisa Simeral, Teach, Reflect, Learn: Building Your Capacity for Success in the Classroom (Alexandria, VA: ACSD, 2015), 34–40.

2. Hall and Simeral, Teach, Reflect, Learn, 37–40.

3. For an extensive discussion about critical conversations, see chapter 3 of this volume.

4. Sandy Buczynski and C. Bobbi Hansen, "Impact of Professional Development on Teacher Practice: Uncovering Connections," Teaching and Teacher Education 26, no. 3 (2010): 599–607.

5. Bryk et al., Learning to Improve, 17; Robert B. Cooter, Jr., "Teacher Capacity Building Helps Urban Children Succeed in Reading," Reading Teacher 57, no. 2 (2003): 198–206.

6. Jamal Abedi and Patricia Gándara, "Performance of English Language Learners as a Subgroup in Large-Scale Assessment: Interaction of Research and Policy," Educational Measurement: Issues and Practice 25, no. 4 (2006): 36–46.

7. Keira D. Ballantyne, Alicia R. Sanderman, and Jack Levy, Educating English Language Learners: Building Teacher Capacity: Roundtable Report (Washington, DC: National Clearinghouse for English Language Acquisition & Language Instruction Educational Programs, 2008); Jamy Stillman, "Teacher Learning in an Era of High-Stakes Accountability: Productive Tension and Critical Professional Practice," Teachers College Record 113, no. 1 (2011): 133–180.

8. Lucinda Soltero-González, Kathy Escamilla, and Susan Hopewell, "Changing Teachers' Perceptions About the Writing Abilities of Emerging Bilingual Students: Towards a Holistic Bilingual Perspective on Writing Assessment," International Journal of Bilingual Education and Bilingualism 15, no. 1 (2012): 71–94.

9. Tamara Lucas and Jaime Grinberg, Responding to the Linguistic Reality of Mainstream Classrooms (New York: Routledge, 2008).

10. Michael AK. Halliday, "Language as Social Semiotics," Language and Literacy in Social Practice (1978): 23–43.

11. Karen Beeman and Cheryl Urow, Teaching for Biliteracy: Strengthening Bridges Between Languages (Philadelphia, PA: Caslon Publishing, 2013); Ellen Bialystok, Bilingualism in Development: Language, Literacy, and Cognition (Cambridge and New York: Cambridge University Press, 2001); Guadalupe Valdés, "The World Outside and Inside Schools: Language and Immigrant Children," Educational Researcher 27, no. 6 (1998): 4–18.

12. Luis C. Moll and Norma González, "Lessons from Research with Language-Minority Children," Journal of Reading Behavior 26, no. 4 (1994): 439–456.

13. Diane K. Brantley, Instructional Assessment of ELLs in the K–8 Classroom (Boston: Allyn and Bacon, 2007).

14. Ester J. de Jong and Candace A. Harper, "Accommodating Diversity," in Teacher Preparation for Linguistically Diverse Classrooms: A Resource for Teacher Educators," ed. Tamara Lucas (New York: Routledge, 2010), 73–90.

15. François Grosjean, Life with Two Languages: An Introduction to Bilingualism (Cambridge, MA: Harvard University Press, 1982).

16. Ruth Culham, 6+1 Traits of Writing: The Complete Guide Grades 3 and Up (New York: Scholastic Inc., 2003); Anita C. Hernández, "The Expected and Unexpected Literacy Outcomes of Bilingual Students," Bilingual Research Journal 25, no. 3 (2001): 301–326.

17. Hernández, "Literacy Outcomes of Bilingual Students," 301.

18. Ibid., 321.
19. Soltero-González et al., "Changing Teachers' Perceptions," 71.
20. Ibid.
21. Ofelia Garcia, "Education, Multilingualism and Translanguaging in the 21st Century," in Multilingual Education for Social Justice Through Multilingual Education, ed. Ajit Mohanty et al. (New Delhi: Orient Blackswan, 2009), 140–158; Nancy H. Hornberger and Holly Link, "Translanguaging in Today's Classrooms: A Biliteracy Lens," Theory into Practice 51, no. 4 (2012): 239–247; Lucinda Soltero-González, Kathy Escamilla, and Susan Hopewell, "Changing Teachers' Perceptions About the Writing Abilities of Emerging Bilingual Students: Towards a Holistic Bilingual Perspective on Writing Assessment," International Journal of Bilingual Education and Bilingualism 15, no. 1 (2012): 71–94.
22. Simultaneous bilingualism is when a person acquires two languages at the same time (e.g., when a child is raised by bilingual parents speaking more than one language in the home). See Ellen Bialystok, Gigi Luk, and Ernest Kwan, "Bilingualism, Biliteracy, and Learning to Read: Interaction Among Languages and Writing System," Scientific Studies of Reading 9, no. 1 (2005): 43–61.
23. Ellen Bialystok, Gigi Luk, and Ernest Kwan, "Bilingualism, Biliteracy, and Learning to Read: Interactions Among Languages and Writing Systems," Scientific Studies of Reading 9, no. 1 (2005): 43–61; Kathy Escamilla, "Semilingualism Applied to the Literacy Behaviors of Spanish-Speaking Emerging Bilinguals: Bi-illiteracy or Emerging Biliteracy?" Teachers College Record 108, no. 11 (2006): 2329; Karen L. Ford et al., "Diversity Among Spanish-Speaking English Language Learners: Profiles of Early Literacy Skills in Kindergarten," Reading and Writing 26, no. 6 (2013): 889–912.
24. Escamilla, "Semilingualism Applied to the Literacy Behaviors," 2329.
25. Ibid., 2329.
26. Kathy Escamilla et al., Biliteracy from the Start: Literacy Squared in Action (Philadelphia, PA: Caslon Publishing, 2014).
27. Escamilla et al., Biliteracy from the Start; María Estela Brisk, Engaging Students in Academic Literacies: Genre-Based Pedagogy for K–5 Classrooms (New York: Routledge, 2014).
28. In the context of these schools implementing the TWI model, all participating students were emerging as bilingual. This included both students whose home language was English and students whose home language was Spanish or Mandarin.
29. Garcia, "Education, Multilingualism and Translanguaging in the 21st Century"; Hornberger and Link, "Translanguaging in Today's Classrooms"; Soltero-González et al., "Changing Teachers' Perceptions"; Francois Grosjean,

"Neurolinguists, Beware! The Bilingual Is Not Two Monolinguals in One Person," Brain and Language 36 (1989): 3–15.

30. Soltero-González et al., "Changing Teachers' Perceptions," 71–94.

31. At All Souls, that included the Spanish and Mandarin program students from transitional kindergarten to second grade. At Archbishop Borders, that included students from kindergarten to fourth grade.

32. Soltero-González et al., "Changing Teachers' Perceptions," 71–94.

33. At All Souls, the first prompt was in English and the second prompt in the target language: Mandarin or Spanish. And at Archbishop Borders, in each of the TWI classrooms, half the students were given the narrative family prompt, while the other half received the narrative friend prompt. This was subsequently repeated in the second language in reverse order. All students received both prompts.

34. Brisk, Engaging Students in Academic Literacies; Nell Duke et al., Reading and Writing Genre with Purpose in a K–8 Classroom (Portsmouth, NH: Heinemann, 2012).

35. Kathy Escamilla et al., Biliteracy from the Start.

36. Pete Hall and Alisa Simeral, Teach, Reflect, Learn, 37–40.

37. These conversations have similarities with the critical conversations described in chapter 3 of this volume.

38. Duke et al., "Reading and Writing Genre."

39. Escamilla et al., Biliteracy from the Start.

40. Martin Scanlan and Francesca A. López, Leadership for Culturally and Linguistically Responsive Schools (New York: Routledge, 2014).

41. Cooter, "Teacher Capacity"; Hall and Simeral, Teach, Reflect, Learn, 37–40.

42. Django Paris and H. Samy Alim, eds., Culturally Sustaining Pedagogies: Teaching and Learning for Justice in a Changing World (Teachers College Press, 2017); Angela Valenzuela, Subtractive Schooling: US-Mexican Youth and the Politics of Caring (New York: Suny Press, 2010).

43. Luis C. Moll and Norma González, "Lessons from Research with Language-Minority Children," Journal of Reading Behavior 26, no. 4 (1994): 439–456.

44. Brisk, Engaging Students in Academic Literacies.

45. Cooter, "Teacher Capacity."

46. Bryk et al., Learning to Improve; Hall and Simeral, Teach, Reflect, Learn, 34–40.

CHAPTER 7

1. Susan Auerbach, School Leadership for Authentic Family and Community Partnerships: Research Perspectives for Transforming Practice (New York: Routledge, 2012).

2. Anne Henderson and Karen Mapp, A New Wave of Evidence: The Impact of School, Family, and Community Connections on Student Achievement (Austin, TX: Southwest Educational Development Laboratory, 2002).
3. Auerbach, School Leadership.
4. Ibid, 5.
5. Ronald Burt, Structural Holes: The Social Structure of Competition (Cambridge, MA: Harvard University Press, 1992).
6. Auerbach, School Leadership.
7. Camille Wilson Cooper, Carolyn J. Riehl, and Angela Laila Hasan, "Leading and Learning with Diverse Families in Schools: Critical Epistemology Amid Communities of Practice," Journal of School Leadership 20, no. 6 (2010): 758–788.
8. Henderson and Mapp, A New Wave of Evidence; Edward T. Hall, Beyond Culture (New York, Anchor Books, 1976).
9. Eric Johnson, "From the Classroom to the Living Room: Eroding Inequities Through Home Visits," Journal of School Leadership 24, no. 2 (2014): 357–385.
10. Carolyn Frank, Ethnographic Eyes: A Teacher's Guide to Classroom Observation (Portsmouth, NH: Heinemann, 1999); Jerry Diller and Jean Moule, Cultural Competence: A Primer for Educators (Belmont, CA: Thomson Wadsworth, 2005).
11. Auerbach, School Leadership, 32.
12. Ibid., 37.
13. Ibid., 38.
14. Martin Scanlan and Lauri Johnson, "Inclusive Leadership on the Social Frontiers: Family and Community Engagement," in Leadership for Increasingly Diverse Schools, ed. G. Theoharis and M. Scanlan (New York: Routledge, 2015).
15. Peter Miller, "Examining the Work of Boundary Spanning Leaders in Community Contexts," International Journal of Leadership in Education, 11, no. 4 (2008): 372.
16. Scanlan and Johnson, "Inclusive Leadership on the Social Frontiers," 164.
17. Kathy Au and Jana Mason, "Social Organizational Factors in Learning to Read: The Balance of Rights Hypothesis," Reading Research Quarterly 17, no. 1 (1981): 115–152; Diane August and Timothy Shanahan, Developing Literacy in Second-Language Learners: Report of the National Literacy Panel on Language-Minority Children and Youth (Mahwah, NJ: Lawrence Erlbaum Associates, 2006); James Gee, Social Linguistics and Literacies: Ideology in Discourses, 2nd ed. (New York: RoutledgeFalmer, 1996); Shirley Brice Heath, Ways With Words: Language, Life, and Work in Communities

and Classrooms (Cambridge, England: Cambridge University Press, 1983); Tamara Lucas, Ana Maria Villegas, and Margaret Freedson-Gonzalez, "Linguistically Responsive Teacher Education," Journal of Teacher Education 59, no. 4: 361–373.

18. Kathryn Bell McKenzie and James Joseph Scheurich, "Equity Traps: A Useful Construct for Preparing Principals to Lead Schools That Are Successful with Racially Diverse Students," Educational Administration Quarterly 40, no. 5 (2004): 601–631.

19. Dory Lightfoot, "Some Parents Just Don't Care: Decoding the Meanings of Parental Involvement in Urban Schools," Urban Education 39, no. 1 (2004), 91–107.

20. Auerbach, School Leadership.

21. Scanlan and Johnson, "Inclusive Leadership on the Social Frontiers," 162–185.

22. Ibid.

23. Ibid., 177.

24. Terrance L. Green, "Community-Based Equity Audits: A Practical Approach for Educational Leaders to Support Equitable Community-School Improvements," Educational Administration Quarterly 53, no. 1 (2017): 3–39.

25. Luis Moll et al., "Funds of Knowledge for Teaching: Using a Qualitative Approach to Connect Homes and Classrooms," Theory into Practice 31, no. 2 (1992): 132–142.

26. Ibid., 133.

27. Norma Gonzalez, Luis Moll, and Cathy Amanti, eds., Funds of Knowledge: Theorizing Practices in Households, Communities, and Classrooms (Mahwah, NJ: Lawrence Erlbaum Associates, 2005); Moll et al., "Funds of Knowledge for Teaching."

28. Ibid.

29. Moll et al., "Funds of Knowledge for Teaching," 132.

30. Mariela Páez, Kristen Paratore Bock, and Lianna Pizzo, "Supporting the Language and Early Literacy Skills of English Language Learners: Effective Practices and Future Directions," in Handbook of Early Literacy Research, vol. 3, ed. Susan Neuman and David Dickinson (New York: Guilford Press, 2011), 136–152; Elizabeth R. Howard et al., "Effective Vocabulary Instruction for Spanish-Speaking Students," Journal of Bilingual Education Research & Instruction 16, no. 1 (2014): 1–17.

31. Auerbach, School Leadership.

32. For further discussion about mission articulation, see chapter 2 of this volume.

33. Katie Schrodt, Jeanne Gilliam Fain, Michelle Hasty, "Culturally Relevant

Texts with Kindergartners and Their Families," The Reading Teacher 68, no. 8 (2015): 589–598, 590.

34. Ibid., 591.
35. Ibid., 591.
36. Schrodt et al., "Culturally Relevant Texts"; Geneva Gay, Culturally Responsive Teaching: Theory Research & Practice (New York: Teachers College Press, 2000).
37. Cooper et al., "Leading and Learning with Diverse Families in Schools."
38. Auerbach, School Leadership.
39. Henderson and Mapp, A New Wave of Evidence.
40. Auerbach, School Leadership.
41. Lev Vygotsky, Mind in Society: The Development of Higher Psychological Processes, ed. Michael Cole et al. (Cambridge, MA: Harvard University Press, 1978).
42. Anthony Bryk, Louis Gomez, Alicia Grunow, and Paul LeMahieu, eds., Learning to Improve: How America's Schools Can Get Better at Getting Better (Cambridge, MA: Harvard University Press, 2015).
43. Auerbach, School Leadership.
44. McKenzie and Scheurich, "Equity Traps."

CHAPTER 8

1. Gerardo R. López, María Luisa González, and Elsy Fierro, "Educational Leadership Along the U.S.-México Border: Crossing Borders/Embracing Hybridity/Building Bridges," in Leadership for Social Justice: Making Revolutions in Education, ed. Catherine Marshall and Maricela Oliva (Boston: Pearson, 2006), 64–84.
2. Django Paris, "Culturally Sustaining Pedagogy: A Needed Change in Stance, Terminology, and Practice," Educational Researcher 31, no. 3 (2012): 93–97.
3. Iliana Alanís and Mariela Rodriguez, "Sustaining a Dual Language Immersion Program: Features of Success," Journal of Latinos and Education 7, no. 4 (2008): 305–19; Mariela A. Rodriguez and Iliana Alanís, "Negotiating Linguistic and Cultural Identity: One Borderlander's Leadership Initiative," International Journal of Leadership in Education 14, no. 1 (2011): 103–117.
4. James Spillane, Richard Halverson, and John Diamond, "Investigating School Leadership Practice: A Distributed Perspective," Educational Researcher 30, no. 3 (2001): 23–28; Jay Paredes Scribner et al., "Teacher Teams and Distributed Leadership: A Study of Group Discourse and Collaboration," Educational Administration Quarterly 43, no. 1 (2007): 67–100; James Spillane and John Diamond, eds., Distributed Leadership in Practice (New York: Teachers College Press, 2007).

5. For instance, the influence of the concept of distributed leadership is reflected through several of the Professional Standards for Educational Leaders, as articulated by the National Policy Board for Educational Administration (Professional Standards for Educational Leaders 2015 [Reston, VA: National Policy Board for Educational Administration, 2015]).

6. For an example of distributed leadership practices applied to reducing educational inequities, see Jeffrey S. Brooks et al., "Distributed Leadership for Social Justice: Exploring How Influence and Equity Are Stretched over an Urban High School," Journal of School Leadership 17, no. 4 (2007): 378–408.

7. Ester J. de Jong, "Two-Way Immersion for the Next Generation: Models, Policies, and Principals," International Multilingual Research Journal 10, no. 1 (2016): 6–16; Martin Scanlan and Francesca López, "¡Vamos! How School Leaders Promote Equity and Excellence for Bilingual Students," Educational Administration Quarterly 48, no. 4 (2012): 583–625.

8. Camille Wilson Cooper, "Performing Cultural Work in Demographically Changing Schools: Implications for Expanding Transformative Leadership Frameworks," Educational Administration Quarterly 45, no. 5 (2009): 694–724.

9. Lucila E. Ek et al., "Crossing Cultural Borders: La Clase Mágica as a University-School Partnership," Journal of School Leadership 20, no. 6 (2010): 820–849.

10. Calderón Margarita and Argelia Carreón, "A Dual Language Bilingual Program: Promise, Practice, and Precautions," in Effective Programs for Latino Students, edited by Robert E. Slavin and Margarita Calderon (Mahwah, NJ: Lawrence Erlbaum Associates, Publishers, 2001), 125–170.

11. Ibid., 166.

12. Sheila M. Shannon, "The Culture of the Classroom: Socialization in an Urban Bilingual Classroom," Urban Review 27 (1995): 321–345.

13. Catherine Marshall and Maricela Oliva, Leadership for Social Justice: Making Revolutions in Education, 2nd ed. (New York: Allyn & Bacon, 2010).

14. Virginia P. Collier and Wayne P. Thomas, "The Astounding Effectiveness of Dual Language Education for All," NABE Journal of Research and Practice 2, no. 1 (2004): 1–20; Scanlan and López, "¡Vamos!"; George Theoharis and Joanne O'Toole, "Leading Inclusive ELL: Social Justice Leadership for English Language Learners," Educational Administration Quarterly 47, no. 4 (2011): 646–688.

15. Victoria Hunt, "Learning from Success Stories: Leadership Structures that Support Dual Language Programs over Time in New York City," International Journal of Bilingual Education and Bilingualism 14, no. 2 (2011): 187–206; Jeffrey S. Brooks et al., "Distributed Leadership for Social Justice: Exploring How Influence and Equity Are Stretched Over an Urban

High School," Journal of School Leadership 17, no. 4 (2007): 378–408; James P. Spillane, Richard Halverson, and John B. Diamond, "Towards a Theory of School Leadership Practice: Implications of a Distributed Perspective," Journal of Curriculum Studies 36, no. 1 (2004): 3–34.

16. Refer back to chapter 4 for a discussion of ensuring model fidelity.

17. Hanna Kurland and Dalia Rebecca Hasson-Gilad, "Organizational Learning and Extra Effort: The Mediating Effect of Job Satisfaction," Teaching and Teacher Education 49 (2015): 56–67; Anthony Bryk and Barbara Schneider, Trust in Schools: A Core Resource for Improvement (New York: Russell Sage, 2002); Eleanor Drago-Severson, "Helping Teachers Learn: Principals as Professional Development Leaders," Teachers College Record 109, no. 1 (2007): 70–125.

18. Vivian Louie and Jennifer Holdaway, "Catholic Schools and Immigrant Students: A New Generation," Teachers College Record 111, no. 3 (2009): 783–816.

19. Gerald Grace, "Renewing Spiritual Capital: An Urgent Priority for the Future of Catholic Education Internationally," International Studies in Catholic Education 2, no. 2 (2010): 117–128.

20. Claudia G. Cervantes-Soon, "A Critical Look at Dual Language Immersion in the New Latin@ Diaspora," Bilingual Research Journal 37, no. 1 (2014): 64–82.

21. Megan E. Cooley, "The Effect of the Lack of Resources in Spanish for Students in Dual Language Bilingual Education Programs" (MSEd thesis, The College at Brockport, 2014). Available from https://digitalcommons.brockport.edu/ehd_theses/383/.

22. Cataldo Raquel and Iliana Alanís, "Listening to Children and Families' Voices: How to Implement Authentic Writing Experiences" (paper presented at the annual conference of the National Association for the Education of Young Children, Atlanta, Georgia, November 15–18, 2017); Melissa Siller and Iliana Alanís, "Two Mathematical Heads Are Better Than One: The Role of 4 Year-Old Dyads Working Through a Study of Patterns," Young Children: Journal for the National Association for the Education of Young Children (forthcoming).

23. Spillane and Diamond, Distributed Leadership in Practice.

24. For further discussion of practices for family and community engagement, see chapter 7 of this volume.

CHAPTER 9

1. Etienne Wenger, Communities of Practice: Learning, Meaning, and Identity (New York: Cambridge University Press, 1998), 6.

2. Ibid., 7–8 (emphasis original).
3. For an extensive presentation of this concept, see Martin Scanlan, "A Learning Architecture: How School Leaders Can Design for Learning Social Justice," Educational Administration Quarterly 49, no. 2 (2013): 348–91.
4. Kenneth Leithwood, "Transformational Leadership: Where Does It Stand?" Education Digest 58, no. 3 (1992): 17; Kenneth Leithwood et al., How Leadership Influences Student Learning (Minneapolis, MN: Center for Applied Research and Educational Improvement, 2004); Helen Marks and Susan Printy, "Principal Leadership and School Performance: An Integration of Transformational and Instructional Leadership," Educational Administration Quarterly 39, no. 3 (2003): 370–97; Jack Mezirow, "Learning to Think Like an Adult: Core Concepts of Transformational Theory," Learning as Transformation: Critical Perspectives on a Theory in Progress, ed. Jack Mezirow et al. (San Francisco: Jossey-Bass, 2000), 3–33.
5. Nienke Moolenaar, Alan Daly, and Peter Sleege, "Occupying the Principal Position: Examining Relationships, Transformational Leadership, Social Network Position, and Innovative Climate," Educational Administration Quarterly 46, no. 5 (2010): 623–70.
6. Marks and Printy, "Principal Leadership," 394.
7. Alan Daly et al. "Why So Difficult? Exploring Negative Relationships Between Educational Leaders: The Role of Trust, Climate, and Efficacy," American Journal of Education 122, no. 1 (2015): 29.
8. Alan Daly, ed., Social Network Theory (Cambridge, MA: Harvard Education Press, 2010).
9. Degree centrality among actors includes degree, closeness, and betweenness indicators. Degree reflects whether communication was initiated by an actor (out-degree) or toward an actor (in-degree). Closeness centrality is based on the length of the average shortest path between an actor and all other actors in the network diagram. Since closeness measures relative geodesic distance to other actors, lower numbers would indicate an actor to be more central while higher values indicate the actor is more peripheral. Betweenness centrality measures the strength of an actor's ability to broker between groups in a network.
10. Borgatti and colleagues describe cohesion as how strongly the actors are connected with one another, or as a way of observing the network's well-knittedness. Key dimensions of cohesion include density, components, and fragmentation (Stephen Borgatti, Martin Everett, and Jeffrey Johnson, Analyzing Social Networks, 2nd ed. [London: SAGE Publishing, 2018]).
11. See the extensive discussion of this project in chapter 6 of this volume.
12. For a full description, see Martin Scanlan et al., "Poco a Poco: Leadership

Practices Supporting Productive Communities of Practice in Schools Serving the New Mainstream," Educational Administration Quarterly 52, no. 1 (2016): 3–44.

13. For the 2014–2015 study, see Martin Scanlan, Minsong Kim, and Larry Ludlow, "Affordances and Constraints of Communities of Practice to Promote Bilingual Schooling," Journal of Professional Capital and Community 4, no. 2 (2019): 82–106. For the 2016–2017 study, see Larry Ludlow, Matias Castro, and Martin Scanlan, "Collaboratively Transforming from Monolingual to Bilingual Service Delivery: A Social Network Analysis" (in preparation).

14. Researchers used SPSS 22, UCINET 6, and NetDraw. For a full description of this analytic approach, refer to Scanlan et al., "Affordances and Constraints."

15. Scanlan et al., "Poco a Poco," 21.

16. Ibid., 22

17. Note that these figures do not distinguish communication among teachers within a single school from communication among teachers across schools.

18. These analyses are based on betweenness centrality, which measures the strength of an actor's ability to broker between groups in a network. Betweenness centrality gives an account of the extent to which a node lies on paths between every other node. One way of thinking about this statistic is to consider that an actor is central in a network insofar as it plays the role of intermediary between the rest of the actors in the network. As Scott (2000) puts it, the betweenness centrality statistic measures the extent to which a node can play the part of a "broker" or "gatekeeper" with a potential for control over others, despite the nodal degree (John Scott, What Is Social Network Analysis? [New York: Bloomsbury Academic, 2012]).

19. Carrie Fuller, "Leading Dual Language Immersion in Catholic Elementary Schools," (PhD diss., Boston College, 2018).

20. Scanlan et al., "Poco a Poco," 31.

21. Fuller, "Leading Dual Language Immersion," 161.

22. Ibid., 202.

23. Ibid., 138.

24. Ibid., 148.

25. Ibid.

26. Scanlan et al., "Poco a Poco"; Fuller, "Leading Dual Language Immersion"; Martin Scanlan and Margarita Zisselsberger, "The Formation of Communities of Practice in a Network of Schools Serving Culturally and Linguistically Diverse Students," Journal of Education for Students Placed at Risk 20, no. 1–2 (2015): 58–78; Scanlan et al., "Affordances and Constraints."

27. Ibid.

28. National Standards and Benchmarks for Effective Catholic Schools (https://www.catholicschoolstandards.org/); Elizabeth Howard et al., Guiding Principles for Dual Language Education (Washington, DC: Center for Applied Linguistics, 2018).
29. Anthony Bryk et al., Organizing Schools for Improvement: Lessons from Chicago (Chicago: University of Chicago Press, 2010).
30. A diocese is a jurisdiction of Catholic organizations overseen by a bishop.
31. Scanlan and Zisselsberger, "The Formation of Communities of Practice."
32. Francesca López, Patrick Proctor, and Martin Scanlan, "The Use of Formative Assessment to Improve Instruction of English Learners and Evaluation of Teachers," in Evaluating Literacy Instruction: Principles and Promising Practices, ed. R. Allington and R. Gabriel (New York: Routledge, 2015), 134–50.
33. Melissa Siller and Iliana Alanís, "Two Mathematical Heads Are Better Than One: The Role of 4 Year-Old Dyads Working Through a Study of Patterns," Young Children: Journal for the National Association for the Education of Young Children (forthcoming).
34. Scanlan et al., "Poco a Poco."

CHAPTER 10

1. See chapter 2 for a discussion of asset orientations as integral to culturally and linguistically responsive schooling.
2. Francesca López, "Altering the Trajectory of the Self-Fulfilling Prophecy: Asset-Based Pedagogy and Classroom Dynamics," Journal of Teacher Education 68, no. 2 (2017): 193–212; Tamara Lucas and Ana Maria Villegas, "The Missing Piece in Teacher Education: The Preparation of Linguistically Responsive Teachers," National Society for the Study of Education 109, no. 2 (2010): 297–318; Tamara Lucas, Ana Maria Villegas, and Margaret Freedson-Gonzalez, "Linguistically Responsive Teacher Education: Preparing Classroom Teachers to Teach English Language Learners," Journal of Teacher Education 59, no. 4 (2008): 361–73.
3. Muhammad Khalifa, Culturally Responsive School Leadership (Cambridge, MA: Harvard Education Press, 2018); Muhammad Khalifa, Mark Anthony Gooden, and James Earl Davis, "Culturally Responsive School Leadership: A Synthesis of Literature," Review of Educational Research 86, no. 4 (2016): 1272–311; George Theoharis and Martin Scanlan, eds., Leadership for Increasingly Diverse Schools (New York: Routledge, 2015); Angela Valenzuela, ed., Growing Critically Conscious Teachers: A Social Justice Curriculum for Educators of Latino/a Youth (New York: Teachers College Press, 2016).
4. Andy Hargreaves and Michael Fullan, Professional Capital: Transforming Teaching in Every School (New York: Teachers College Press, 2012).

5. Tara Yosso, "Whose Culture Has Capital? A Critical Race Theory Discussion of Community Cultural Wealth," Race Ethnicity and Education 8, no. 1 (2005): 69–91.

6. Martin Scanlan and Lauri Johnson, "Inclusive Leadership on the Social Frontiers: Family and Community Engagement," in Leadership for Increasingly Diverse Schools, ed. George Theoharis and Martin Scanlan (New York: Routledge, 2015), 162–85; Nadia Ward, Michael Strambler, and Lance Linke, "Increasing Educational Attainment Among Urban Minority Youth: A Model of University, School, and Community Partnerships," The Journal of Negro Education 82, no. 3 (2013): 312–25; Khalifa, Gooden, and Davis, "Culturally Responsive School Leadership."

7. Lorri Santamaria, "Culturally Responsive Differentiated Instruction: Narrowing Gaps Between Best Pedagogical Practices Benefiting All Learners," Teachers College Record 111, no. 1 (2009): 214–47; Ana Maria Villegas and Tamara Lucas, Educating Culturally Responsive Teachers: A Coherent Approach (Syracuse: State University of New York Press, 2002); Ana Maria Villegas and Tamara Lucas, "Preparing Culturally Responsive Teachers: Rethinking the Curriculum," Journal of Teacher Education 53, no. 1 (2002): 20–32; Ana Maria Villegas and Tamara Lucas, "The Culturally Responsive Teacher," Educational Leadership (2007): 28–33.

8. López, "Altering the Trajectory," 13, 15.

9. Mónica C. Byrne-Jiménez and Irene H. Yoon, "Leadership as an Act of Love: Leading in Dangerous Times," Frontiers in Education 3 (2019): 3.

10. Ibid. See further Parker Palmer, To Know as We Are Known: Education as a Spiritual Journey (San Francisco: Harper & Row, 1983).

11. For a general discussion and application of equity audits, see George Theoharis and Martin Scanlan, eds., Leadership for Increasingly Diverse Schools (New York: Routledge, 2015). For an in-depth look at community-based equity audits, see Terrance L. Green, "Community-Based Equity Audits: A Practical Approach for Educational Leaders to Support Equitable Community-School Improvements," Educational Administration Quarterly 53, no. 1 (2017): 3–39.

12. Elizabeth Howard et al., Guiding Principles for Dual Language Education (Washington, DC: Center for Applied Linguistics, 2018).

13. Lorraine Ozar and Patricia Weitzel-O'Neill, "National Catholic School Standards: Focus on Governance and Leadership," Catholic Education: A Journal of Inquiry and Practice 17, no. 1 (2013): 157–62.

14. As shown, for instance, in the shifting communities of practice across all of TWIN-CS, from a core-and-periphery model to dispersed communities of practice; see chapter 9.

15. In the case of TWIN-CS, the centralized structure served as a catalyst of change. In other cases it is a barrier. For instance, in the opening chapter of this book, we shared an example of a transformation in the public school district of Madison, Wisconsin. It was a single school, not the central leadership, that inspired the transformation of educating ELs.

16. This is discussed further in chapter 2 of this volume. For a description of networked improvement communities, see Anthony Bryk et al., Learning to Improve: How America's Schools Can Get Better at Getting Better (Cambridge, MA: Harvard Education Press, 2015). For a recent summary of research-practice partnerships, see William Penuel and Daniel Gallagher, Creating Research-Practice Partnerships in Education (Cambridge, MA: Harvard Education Press, 2017); Karen Hunter Quartz et al., "University-Partnered New School Designs: Fertile Ground for Research-Practice Partnerships," Educational Researcher 46, no. 3 (2017): 143–46. For helpful discussions of design-based research, see Terry Anderson and Julie Shattuck, "Design-Based Research: A Decade of Progress in Education Research," Educational Researcher 41, no. 1 (2012): 16–25; Susan McKenney and Thomas Reeves, "Systematic Review of Design-Based Research Progress: Is a Little Knowledge a Dangerous Thing?" Educational Researcher 42, no. 2 (2013): 97–100.

17. Bryk et al., Learning to Improve.

18. Francesca López, Patrick Proctor, and Martin Scanlan, "The Use of Formative Assessment to Improve Instruction of English Learners and Evaluation of Teachers," in Evaluating Literacy Instruction: Principles and Promising Practices, ed. Richard L. Allington and Rachel E. Gabriel (New York: Routledge, 2015), 134–50; Martin Scanlan and Margarita Zisselsberger, "The Formation of Communities of Practice in a Network of Schools Serving Culturally and Linguistically Diverse Students," Journal of Education for Students Placed at Risk 20, no. 1–2 (2015): 58–78.

ABOUT THE EDITORS

MARTIN SCANLAN is an associate professor in educational leadership at the Lynch School of Education and Human Development at Boston College. Before becoming a faculty member in higher education, Scanlan spent a decade working in teaching and administration in urban elementary and middle schools in Washington, DC, Berkeley, California, and Madison, Wisconsin. He continues to work closely with building and district-level administrators to bridge research and practice. Scanlan's research explores how to strengthen the communities of practice in schools to promote inclusion of students across multiple dimensions of diversity. His scholarship has focused primarily on reform in special education service delivery, bilingual education, and school-community collaboration. His work can help leaders conceptualize how to structure service delivery, promote professional learning, and attain resources. He is committed to design-based research in which practitioners play a lead role in articulating the problems of practice that they seek to address, and creating collaborative research projects tackling these problems.

CRISTINA HUNTER is the associate director of research initiatives for the Roche Center for Catholic Education. She earned her doctorate in applied developmental and educational psychology from the Lynch School of Education and Human Development at Boston College in 2014. Her research has focused on the experiences of Latinx migrants in the United States with a specific emphasis on dual language development. Hunter completed a postdoctoral research fellowship on a collaborative study between Boston College and Tufts University examining character development in youth. She earned her master's degree from New York University and her bachelor of arts from Boston College.

ELIZABETH R. HOWARD is an associate professor of bilingual education in the Neag School of Education at the University of Connecticut, where she teaches graduate courses on linguistic and cultural diversity and conducts research focusing on dual language education, biliteracy development, and the preparation of teachers to work with multilingual learners. She is currently a coinvestigator of a federally funded research project exploring writing instruction and outcomes among English Learners, and has served as principal investigator of several large-scale studies of biliteracy development and dual language education. Her books include Realizing the Vision of Two-Way Immersion: Fostering Effective Programs and Classrooms and Preparing Classroom Teachers to Succeed with Second Language Learners. Previously, she worked as a senior research associate at the Center for Applied Linguistics and as a bilingual teacher in California and Costa Rica.

ABOUT THE CONTRIBUTORS

ILIANA ALANÍS is a professor in the Department of Interdisciplinary Learning and Teaching for the University of Texas at San Antonio. With over twenty years in the early childhood field, her work focuses on teaching practices in culturally and linguistically diverse early childhood contexts with an emphasis on the effect of schooling for language-minority children in Spanish/English dual language programs. She is especially interested in forms of teaching that promote native language development and its correlation to second language acquisition. Her recent research focuses on higher-order cognitive and linguistic interaction primarily found in student-student exchanges.

MARÍA CRISTINA LADAS is the Director of World Language & Immersion Programs in Cave Creek Unified School District (preK–12) in a rural, suburban area of north Phoenix. Ladas helped shape the district into a state leader, with 83 percent of all students participating in robust Spanish/French/Chinese immersion programs, FLEX and FLES models, middle school daily core language classes through Advanced Placement/International Baccalaureate levels at the high school. She received her master's degree in elementary education with bilingual/ESL endorsements from National Louis University and a principal certificate from the University of Phoenix. She began her education career as a primary bilingual education teacher and has served as grant director or external evaluator for several categories of Office of English Language Education (OELA) federal grants, and as former adjunct faculty for Arizona State University. Ladas organized a dual language/immersion network for Arizona and applied her grassroots advocacy approach to four language education bills since 2014: Arizona Seal of Biliteracy, dual language/ immersion, certification for international visiting teachers, and equal access to dual language/immersion programs for English Learners. She was also a content lead for the 2015 revision of the World and Native Languages standards at the Arizona Department of Education.

LARRY LUDLOW, PhD, is a professor and the chair of the Department of Measurement, Evaluation, Statistics, and Assessment in the Lynch School of Education and Human Development, Boston College. He teaches courses in research methods, applied statistics, and psychometric theory and practice. His research interests include longitudinal models for understanding student ratings of instruction, Rasch measurement model instrument development applications, and complexity theory applied to representing social network changes. His research collaborations include the US Department of Education, Office of Indian Education; Center for Psychiatric Rehabilitation, Boston University; St. Patrick's College, Dublin, Republic of Ireland; University of Auckland, Auckland, New Zealand; and National Research University Higher School of Economics, Moscow, Russia.

COREY MASLOWSKI became interested in immersion programming as a teenager while working at Concordia Language Villages. He has a BA in elementary education and Spanish from Concordia College, an MA in Curriculum and Instruction, and an EdD from the University of St. Thomas. He also holds principal and school district superintendent licenses. Maslowski student taught at Robbinsdale Spanish Immersion School in Minnesota, and his first teaching job was in a third-grade Spanish immersion classroom in Fairfax County, Virginia. Maslowski returned to Minnesota and began working at Park Spanish Immersion School in St. Louis Park. He taught the inaugural fourth-grade class, and he transitioned with the students to the middle school level teaching the immersion social studies classes. Maslowski worked with K–12 language teachers in St. Louis Park before becoming a school administrator in 2007. Since 2010, he has been the principal of Park Spanish Immersion Elementary School. He has also taught the world language methods course at the University of St. Thomas since 2008 and has been the mentor for Risen Christ Catholic School in Minneapolis since 2014.

KRISTIN BARSTOW MELLEY is director of professional development at Boston College's Roche Center for Catholic Education. In this role, she directs the Two-Way Immersion Network for Catholic Schools (TWIN-CS) and the Emmaus Series, a leadership development program for Catholic school administrators. She serves in a leadership capacity on national Catholic education initiatives. Before working at Boston College, Barstow Melley was the associate superintendent of schools for the Diocese of Worcester and director of research and programming for the National Catholic Center for Student Aspirations at Assumption College. She holds a master's degree in theology from Harvard University and is currently pursuing a PhD from the Lynch School of Education and Human Development at Boston College. Her current research explores collaborative learning communities and schoolwide models of Catholic education.

MATIAS PLACENCIO-CASTRO is a doctoral candidate in the Department of Measurement, Evaluation, and Statistical Analysis at the Lynch School of Education and Human Development at Boston College. Castro has a teacher certification in high school history and a master's degree in sociology from the Pontifical Catholic University of Chile. In Chile, he worked in governmental organizations such as the National Institute of Statistics and the Quality of Education Agency and as a research assistant in several government-funded projects. He has worked as a research assistant and statistical analyst for the Boston University Center for Psychiatric Rehabilitation, as a statistical intern at Boston Public Schools, and as a statistical consultant for the UNESCO Regional Bureau for Education in Latin America and the Caribbean, Santiago de Chile. His research interests include economic inequality and achievement gaps, citizenship education, and quantitative research methods, with special emphasis on psychometrics and educational measurement.

GLORIA RAMOS GONZÁLEZ is a former two-way immersion bilingual teacher and bilingual reading specialist and currently is a professional development consultant for the California Association for Bilingual Education (CABE). Before working with CABE she conducted research on the vocabulary development of English Learners (ELs) while completing her master's in language and literacy at the Harvard Graduate School of Education. Most recently, she completed her doctoral research through the University of Southern California, focusing on high-achieving dual language schools serving Latinx ELs living in high poverty.

MARIELA A. RODRÍGUEZ is an associate professor of educational leadership and policy studies at the University of Texas at San Antonio. Her research focuses on the supportive roles of school leaders in dual language programs. She currently serves on the executive committee of the University Council for Educational Administration (UCEA) as president-elect.

AMIE SARKER is an associate professor of education at the University of Dallas, where she prepares teachers for service in culturally and linguistically diverse settings, teaching courses such as literacy instruction and assessment, English as a Second Language (ESL), and linguistics. She spent several years teaching ESL and serving as a literacy strategist on a dual language campus in the Texas public school system, supporting bilingual and ESL teachers with program implementation. She completed her PhD in literacy education and linguistics at the University of North Texas, and she designed and served as program administrator for the MEd in Bilingual Education and the MEd in Reading and ESL for Dallas Baptist University. Sarker has served on the boards of two professional associations concerned with issues related to culturally and linguistically diverse (CLD) students, including TexTESOL V (Past President) and the Christian English Language Educators Association. Her research interests focus on culturally responsive instruction and literacy instruction for CLD students, including teacher self-efficacy and CLD families' "funds of knowledge" integration. She shares her work through presentations at many domestic and international research and teacher professional development conferences. Sarker has published in many journals. She is also involved in an international nonprofit that operates 28 small primer schools in rural Bangladesh (implementing bilingual education—English and Bangla). Sarker is passionate about affirming and developing the competencies of second language learners and their teachers, both in the United States and abroad.

BRIDGET YADEN is a professor of Hispanic Studies, director of the Language Resource Center, and chair of the Department of Languages and Literatures at Pacific Lutheran University in Tacoma, Washington. Her PhD is in linguistics from the University of Washington, and her research interests include dual immersion pedagogy and assessment, technology for language learning, and language teacher training. She regularly supervises preservice teachers in world languages, English language learning, and bilingual education. She also teaches preservice courses and continuing professional development workshops on second language acquisition (SLA) theories and methods with a focus on meeting the needs of culturally and linguistically diverse (CLD) students. Yaden has served as the mentor to Holy Rosary Regional School–Juan Diego Academy's Spanish-English dual immersion program since 2014. In this capacity, she has coached new teachers, provided professional development for all staff, mentored the principal, assisted in curriculum planning, and advised and assisted in assessment of student language proficiency.

MARGARITA GÓMEZ ZISSELSBERGER is an assistant professor of literacy education at Loyola University Maryland, where she teaches courses in processes and acquisition of literacy and in assessment and instruction of literacy. Her research aims to better understand how classroom contexts play a critical role for culturally and linguistically diverse learners' writing development. Margarita earned her doctoral degree in language, learning, and literacy from Boston College, and previously taught in an elementary bilingual school context in California and an inclusion classroom in New York.

INDEX